JUSTICE

according to

THE ENGLISH COMMON LAWYERS

ENGLAND: BUTTERWORTH & CO. (PUBLISHERS) LTD.
                LONDON: 88 KINGSWAY, W.C.2

AFRICA: BUTTERWORTH & CO. (AFRICA) LTD.
                DURBAN: 33/35 BEACH GROVE

AUSTRALIA: BUTTERWORTH & CO. (AUSTRALIA) LTD.
                SYDNEY: 6/8 O'CONNELL STREET
                MELBOURNE: 403 BOURKE STREET
                BRISBANE: 240 QUEEN STREET

CANADA: BUTTERWORTH & CO. (CANADA) LTD.
                TORONTO: 1367 DANFORTH AVENUE, 6

NEW ZEALAND: BUTTERWORTH & CO. (NEW ZEALAND) LTD.
                WELLINGTON: 49/51 BALLANCE STREET
                AUCKLAND: 35 HIGH STREET

U.S.A.:   BUTTERWORTH INC.
                WASHINGTON, D.C.: 7235 WISCONSIN AVENUE, 14

JUSTICE

according to

THE ENGLISH COMMON LAWYERS

by

F. E. DOWRICK, M.A.(Oxon.)

of the Inner Temple, Barrister-at-Law;
Fellow of Trinity College and Lecturer
in Law in the University of Dublin

LONDON

BUTTERWORTHS

1961

©

BUTTERWORTH & CO. (PUBLISHERS) LTD.
1961

MADE AND PRINTED IN ENGLAND AT THE THANET PRESS, MARGATE

PREFACE

This book is intended primarily for those who have been studying English law for only a year or two. Its aim is to bring into sharper focus for them the views on justice at which they must inevitably have glanced in passing while reading the law reports, statutes, text-books and legal journals. If practitioners should stumble upon this book and browse in its pages and find here propositions about justice which they have known for years to be elementary and basic, the work will have succeeded in its purpose, which is to present the notions of justice current in the English legal profession in the twentieth century. The experienced lawyer who reads further may at least be interested to follow some of the principles which he took to be axiomatic back towards their sources and forward into some of their practical applications.

The question which stimulated this work occurred to me after I had been conducting, for several years running, a lecture and seminar course on the philosophy of justice with undergraduates in their final year who had already studied several branches of the common law in some detail. They rarely displayed more than a remote interest in the ancient wisdom of Plato, Aristotle and Cicero on the problem of justice. When we took up the more modern theories I felt year after year a similar resistance, particularly to those elaborated by most continental writers; only Radbruch's relativist approach appealed regularly to some, though neo-scholastic doctrines, such as that of Maritain, would usually stir a few disciples. However, the pragmatist theories of Bentham and Pound more often touched live nerves, and Austin's positivist solution to the age-old problem never lacked supporters. At one stage I realised that by the time students began this particular course in jurisprudence they had already been indoctrinated on the subject of justice by the older common lawyers, the judges, the text-book writers and others, whose works had been their companions in their earlier years of study. Hence the question: what is the indigenous doctrine of justice among the common lawyers?

When launched on this inquiry I was tempted to investigate the opinions, not only of the English lawyers, but also those of lawyers in other common law countries as Australia, Canada, Ireland, New Zealand and the United States. But I soon found that the range of materials to be examined within the English legal system alone was almost too formidable. Besides, different notions or at least different emphases are to be expected in the various common law countries. It seemed possible that by concentrating on the English lawyers, the answers, though inevitably imprecise, might be relatively clear.

In the process of writing a book on some particular branch of the positive common law these days an author is usually following well-worn tracks and thus benefiting from the experience, including the errors, of his many predecessors. But in pursuing this jurisprudential study I have been painfully aware that I have been travelling for the most part in unexplored country, and accordingly I presume that I have made many errors, both of omission and commission, which later travellers will avoid, and which, with the help of critical readers, I might avoid in future explorations.

In composing this work I have drawn on more live human sources than I can expressly acknowledge here. Since the guiding question has been in my mind I have been noting the opinions of many English lawyers, voiced in court and in conversations in the Inner Temple and in meetings of academic lawyers in England, particularly in the Faculty of Law at Cambridge University where I was made welcome as a guest on a " sabbatical " term's leave. Reflecting on these live sources and on the range of materials written by English lawyers which I have examined, I should admit, after Montaigne, that nothing but the thread and the knots which bind them is my own. I gratefully record the help given to me by Trinity College, Dublin, Trust in 1957 to enable me to take leave to concentrate on this inquiry, and also the assistance and facilities given to me by the Librarians and staffs of the Squire Law Library, the Institute of Advanced Legal Studies and the Inner Temple. I gladly acknowledge the constructive help given to me by Professor C. J. Hamson when this work was in an amorphous state, and the criticisms of it in its penultimate state so kindly given by Professor H. L. A. Hart and Professor Dennis Lloyd. The continuous help which I have received from my wife is beyond reckoning in rubies or words. Mr. J. W. A. Thornely has saved me from many an error by his meticulous proof-reading. Mr. H. Kay Jones, personifying Butterworths, has made the last stages of the preparation of the book comparatively easy and enjoyable.

F. E. DOWRICK.

January 2nd, 1961.

CONTENTS

CHAPTER 1

INTRODUCTION

Many of the judges[1] and jurists[2] in the English legal system have avowed that its function has been the perpetual quest of justice. In an older idiom they expressed the same idea when they spoke of the common law of England as the perfection of reason.[3] In these pages an attempt is made to capture in words the idea of justice which has motivated the English common lawyers in the twentieth century.

The term "common lawyers" is used in this work generically to include those who have professed and practised common law and equity in England, and to point the contrast with "civilians", that is lawyers professing ancient or modern Roman law, and with those professing the canon law. In this enquiry into the opinions of the English common lawyers pride of place will be given to the views of the judges,[4] as in the common law system, in contrast with the civil law systems, the judges have traditionally been the principal exponents of doctrine, and even in this century with the growth of a class of academic lawyers the judges have retained their supremacy within the profession. The opinions of

---

[1]*E.g.*, Lord WRIGHT, *Legal Essays and Addresses* (1939), *passim*; Viscount HALDANE, L.C., ATKIN, L.J., Lord HEWART, L.C.J., Viscount CAVE and GREER, J., in *Memorial Volume, American Bar Association Visit to England* (1924).

[2]*E.g.*, Allen, *Law in the Making*, 6th edn. (1958), p. 283; Potter, *The Quest of Justice* (1951), *passim*; Goodhart, *Precedent in English and Continental Law* (1934), p. 32; Pollock, *Genius of the Common Law* (1912), p. 125.

[3]*E.g.*, BLACKSTONE, *Commentaries on the Laws of England* (1765), Introduction, § 3, 3rd edn. (1768), p. 70. COKE, *Institutes* (1628), I, 97 b, § 138.

[4]A table of the judges to whom reference is made in this work appears, *post*, at p. 221.

barristers, from whom the Bench has long been recruited, will be considered. But if less attention is paid to the views of counsel this is largely due to the relative dearth of recorded expressions of their opinions on the larger questions of justice. The traditional approach to specific issues in our courts has encouraged argument exclusively from statute and precedent and judicial *dicta* and discouraged argument from general principles of justice. It is recorded of one English Chief Justice[1] in the nineteenth century that he cut short argument of counsel founded on first principles by saying that the court did not want to hear what was asserted in Aristotle's *Rhetoric*, nor was he interested in principles from the *Pandects* of Justinian. Besides, it must be remembered that the barrister, in court and in chambers, is as much concerned with questions of fact and the enormous detail of evidence of fact as with questions of law. The opinions of solicitors will be given even less prominence as these practitioners, immersed in the business of mediating between the law and individual human problems, have rarely written on the subject of this enquiry. Last, but no longer least, the opinions of the relatively new class of academic lawyers will be considered. Bentham, writing about law at the end of the eighteenth century stands out as the first of these non-practising lawyers. In the nineteenth and twentieth centuries an increasingly large number of university professors and lecturers have been expounding and criticizing the common law, and they have been less inhibited than practising lawyers in the expression of views on questions of justice.

Evidence of the opinions of these lawyers on questions of justice has been gleaned from various sources. Comparatively few judges have written autobiographies or memoirs or juristic essays and of those who have done so only a very small number have gone so far as to commit themselves to a doctrine of justice, as for instance Lord WRIGHT[2] and latterly Lord DENNING,[3] and none has expounded a complete philosophy of justice. While judicial biographies are

---

[1]Lord TENTERDEN, according to Lord CAMPBELL, in *Lives of Chief Justices*, Vol. III (1857), p. 337.

[2]See *post*, pp. 150-156.

[3]See *post*, pp. 30-33, 88-93.

plentiful these usually concentrate on the dramatic details of the judge's forensic career and his famous cases at the Bar and on the Bench, ignoring the constant factors in his decisions which are our concern, though some biographies have provided pointers to these constants. Most of the judges have been content to make their contribution to English law specifically in their judgments, so that the law reports constitute the principal source of material indicating their notions of justice. The academic lawyers, on the other hand, have been less reluctant to commit themselves to general doctrine, and their essays on jurisprudence may exhibit directly their views on justice, while their treatises and articles on specific legal topics disclose, sometimes unwittingly, the authors' criteria for law. A particularly rich source of material for this enquiry is the many reports of a variety of law reform commissions and committees which have been issued intermittently since the 1820's.[1] In the nineteenth century these commissions were composed of judges and senior members of the Bar. In the twentieth century these law reform committees have been composed mainly of judges and senior counsel but with a leavening of academic lawyers and solicitors. As their reasons for disapproving of the existing law and for recommending some other rule of law amount to admissions of their views on injustice and justice, extensive use will be made of this material. Exceptionally resort has been made to Hansard to establish the opinions of some leading counsel or Lord Chancellor on a question of law reform. The *general* law-making opinion in England in the nineteenth and twentieth centuries has been analysed by Dicey[2] and in a recent

---

[1]*E.g.*, Real Property Commission, Reports 1-4, 1829-1833; First Common Law Commission, Reports 1-6, 1829-1834; Second Common Law Commission, Reports 1-3, 1851-1860; Judicature Commission, First Report, 1869; Law Revision Committee, Reports 1-8, 1934-1939; Law Reform Committee, Reports 1-8, 1953-1958. However, no use has been made of the many reports of Royal Commissions and Departmental Committees which have recommended changes in the law as these have been composed of laymen as well as lawyers.

[2]*Law and Public Opinion in England*, 1st edn. (1905), 2nd edn. (1914).

symposium:[1] but no attempt is made here to consider the
opinions of persons other than lawyers.

As we have chosen to restrict this enquiry to the views of
the English lawyers it will be hardly surprising if the answers
reveal a professional and a national bias. The professional
lawyer is inclined to give prominence in his views on justice
to such factors as courts, procedures, disputes between
specific persons and rules for deciding such disputes, whereas
the philosopher reflecting on the subject would be more disposed to emphasise general axioms for the structure of
society. The lawyers are first and foremost men of affairs.
Maitland wrote of the earlier members of the Inns of Court
that they were " worldly men, not men of the sterile caste . . .;
they [were] in their way learned, cultivated men, linguists,
logicians, tenacious disputants, true lovers of the nice case
and the moot point . . . the great mediators between life and
logic, a reasoning, reasonable element in the English
nation ".[2] At the end of the eighteenth century a Chief
Justice, speaking of the earlier English jurists, insisted that
they were not " men writing from their closets without any
knowledge of the affairs of life, but persons mixing with the
mass of society, and capable of receiving practical experience
of the soundness of the maxims they inculcate ".[3] And down
to the present day the typical common lawyer remains one
who couples a knowledge of legal doctrine with an abnormally
wide experience of the hurly-burly of life. He is a master of
the practical, his touchstone is the practicable, he is forever
invoking " experience ", he relies continuously on " common sense ". In contrast to the traditional philosopher the
common lawyer eschews abstractions and axioms in the air.
His contempt of pure theory is expressed in his adage: " an
ounce of practice is worth a ton of theory ". One Chief Justice
in the early nineteenth century would often say that he did
not sit in the Court of King's Bench as pedagogue to hear
first principles argued, and would demand—and here he

---

[1] *Law and Opinion in England in the Twentieth Century* (1959), ed.
Ginsberg.
[2] Selden Society, Vol. 17. *Y.B.* 1 & 2 *Edw. III*, at p. lxxxi.
[3] *R.* v. *Waddington* (1800), 1 East 143, at p. 157, *per* KENYON,
C.J.

spoke for generations of judges of the common law before and
since—" what are the issues? "[1] Even the academic lawyers
have mostly eschewed the theoretical *à priori* approach to
legal problems.[2] The common law discipline rather requires
its practitioners to rely on particular rulings on conflicts
between particular humans and to distrust general axioms of
supposedly universal application. It is not only as a convenient economy of wording that common lawyers refer to
rules of law by reference to the names of the parties, *e.g.*,
" the rule in *Rylands* v. *Fletcher* " or " the doctrine of *Walsh*
v. *Lonsdale* ". In contrast to the old Roman system of *res-
ponsa prudentium* the common law judges decide only questions which have actually arisen in the realm of fact and they
refuse to utter judgments on purely hypothetical questions.[3]
It is perhaps significant that though many of our most distinguished judges were trained in our older universities in
classics, before taking up the study of law, they have hardly
ever in later life upon the Bench expressly relied on the
general axioms of justice propounded by Plato, Aristotle or
Cicero. In contrast to these philosophers the common lawyer
will stoutly maintain that he does not understand justice in
the abstract. Lord WRIGHT, who has gone much further than
most of our judges towards articulating a complete philosophy of justice, himself admitted a reluctance to deal with
too general notions: " There is indeed no such thing as
abstract justice. It is an ideal which can be realised only in
the concrete, and within such limits as the practical conduct

---

[1] Lord ELLENBOROUGH, C.J., according to Lord CAMPBELL, *Lives of
Chief Justices*, Vol. III (1857), p. 227.

[2] *E.g.*, Maitland's stringent criticism of Herbert Spencer's principle
of equal liberty, which Spencer postulated as a first principle for an
ideal system of law; Maitland demonstrated that this principle was
itself a completely impracticable formula: *Collected Papers* (1911),
Vol. I, pp. 267-303. Likewise Dr. Glanville Williams has dismissed
Salmond's theory of justice as an unworkable monistic system of
ethics: Salmond, *Jurisprudence*, 10th edn. (1947), p. 525.

[3] *E.g.*, in 1928 several of the English judges protested vigorously
and successfully against a clause in the Rating and Valuation Bill
which proposed to authorise Ministers to submit doubtful questions
to the High Court before a specific dispute had in fact arisen: see
Lord HEWART, *The New Despotism* (1929), pp. 119-139.

of disputes in courts of law permits."[1] And the modern judge who has made the most extensive use of the concept of justice *ex cathedra*, Lord DENNING, has confessed to his own " deep-seated distrust of abstract philosophy, a failing shared by many of (his) fellow-countrymen ".[2] The common lawyer, in the modern idiom, speaks of keeping his feet on the ground; he is fearful of losing his way in the mists of abstractions. Philosophy and metaphysics are words which, if used by him at all, are used pejoratively; epistemology is lumped by him with such subjects as cosmology and, say, entomology as unnecessary to his professional equipment. In this attitude the common lawyer differs markedly from the traditional civil lawyer[3] but does not differ so much from the ordinary Englishman. For this preference for specific solutions to actual problems is but one facet of the empirical and pragmatic cast of mind and the passion for the language of facts which, if not peculiar to Englishmen, is particularly highly developed and common among them. Yet, in spite of all this professed aversion to philosophy it will be demonstrated in these pages that some of the English judges consciously, and others unconsciously, have been great mediators between moral philosophy and every-day life.

The layman glancing at the literature of English law over the last century might well wonder whether the modern

---

[1]*Legal Essays and Addresses* (1939), p. 392.

[2]Introduction to Friedmann, *Law and Social Change in Contemporary Britain* (1951).

[3]Lord MACMILLAN has underlined this difference between English and Scots lawyers: " The Scottish nation has always been credited with a special aptitude for philosophy and a special devotion to logical principles. . . . The English lawyer's logic was always subordinated to rules which had been gradually and empirically developed from the cases. . . . The contrast between the English and the Scottish lawyer is a contrast between the logical and the empirical schools of thought.": quoted by Holdsworth in *Essays in Law and History* (1946), ed. Goodhart and Hanbury, p. 136. Salmond explained thus the remarkable indifference of the common lawyers to the modern continental legal philosophy. " Most of this literature is remote from the main current of English thought. It is for the most part so devoted to metaphysics . . . it condescends so little to the facts of the concrete legal system, as to have little direct bearing on the task and problems to which the traditional jurisprudence of England has been devoted ": *Jurisprudence*, 7th edn. (1924), p. 14.

English lawyer had not dispensed with the concept of justice and now relied exclusively on the established system of courts and the huge corpus of statutes and rules of the mature common law and equity. For instance, if he probes into the many volumes of the authoritative work which purports to state the modern English law, *Halsbury's Laws of England*,[1] he will be surprised to find that it contains no volume, nor even one title on " Justice ". If he should turn to the classic work on English legal history, Holdsworth's *History of English Law*,[2] in the index volume he will find among several thousand headings only a solitary reference to " justice, delay of ". The layman still incredulous that this concept is apparently ignored in these leading works, might turn more expectantly to the leading journals in which the law is not only expounded but also criticised, such as the Law Quarterly Review (1885-current), the Cambridge Law Journal (1923-current) and the Modern Law Review (1937-current), but there too he will search the indexes in vain for a main heading " Justice " and he will find very few articles which include this word in their titles. He will not have to read far in the modern literature of English law before he meets the ironical reference of a distinguished Lord Justice of Appeal to " that vague jurisprudence which is sometimes attractively styled ' justice as between man and man '."[3] The type of treatise on particular branches of the positive law which begins with a general chapter on justice and then descends to a detailed exposition of justice in that branch of law is to be found on the bookshelf of the continental civil lawyer but not on that of the modern common lawyer. One has to go back to the eighteenth century and earlier for treatises on the common law with prolegomena on justice.[4] Nowadays it is only in

---

[1]Second edn., ed. HAILSHAM (1931-1942), 37 volumes; 3rd edn., ed. SIMONDS (1952-current).

[2]Holdsworth, *History of English Law* (1903-1952), 13 vols.

[3]*Baylis* v. *Bishop of London*, [1913] 1 Ch. 127, at p. 140, *per* HAMILTON, L.J. (later Lord SUMNER). But this observation, torn out of its context, misrepresents Lord SUMNER's views on justice: see *Sinclair* v. *Brougham*, [1914] A.C. 398 and *post*, pp. 84 and 96.

[4]*E.g.*, BLACKSTONE, *Commentaries* (1765), Introduction, Section II; BRACTON, *De Legibus et Consuetudinibus Angliae* (*circa* 1256), ed. Woodbine (1915-1942), Vol. II, pp. 22-23.

avowedly jurisprudential works written for the English lawyer or for the student of modern English law that one finds
any direct discussion of the problem of the nature of justice;
and the problem has only been at all fully discussed in this
branch of legal literature since the Second World War.[1] But
the layman who concluded on such evidence that the modern
common lawyer had dispensed with the concept of justice
would be deceived by words. All he would have discovered
is that one abstract noun " justice " and its derivatives are
avoided or used most sparingly in the modern literature of
English law: the concept of justice might nevertheless be
fundamental and ubiquitous in these volumes.

Still, there has flourished in the English Inns of Court and
Universities a school of thought which has endeavoured to
reduce the concept of justice to a rôle subordinate to the concept of law. Baron PARKE, one of the most experienced of
the nineteenth century judges,[2] epitomised this school of
thought a hundred years ago when he advised the supreme
tribunal in the English legal system that: " It is the province
of the judge to expound the law only; the written from the
statutes; the unwritten or common law from the decisions of
our predecessors and of our existing courts, from text-writers
of acknowledged authority and upon principles to be clearly
deduced from them by sound reason and just inference; not
to speculate upon what is the best, in his opinion, for the

---

[1]Allen, *Aspects of Justice* (1958); Potter, *The Quest of Justice* (1951);
Lloyd, *Introduction to Jurisprudence* (1959), Chaps. 3 and 5; Dias and
Hughes, *Jurisprudence* (1957), Chaps. 13 and 16; Stone, *Province and
Function of Law* (1947), Chaps. 8-16 and 20-27; Friedmann, *Legal
Theory*, 1st edn. (1944), 4th edn. (1960), Chaps. 5-18, 24-26, 29, 30;
Paton, *Text-book of Jurisprudence*, 1st edn. (1946), 2nd edn. (1951),
Book II.
Contrast the relatively slight discussion of the subject in the
following works: Keeton, *Elementary Principles of Jurisprudence*,
1st edn. (1930), pp. 10 and 33; Salmond, *Jurisprudence*, 1st edn.
(1902), 7th edn. (1924), Sections 16 and 19; Pollock, *First Book of
Jurisprudence*, 1st edn. (1896), 6th edn. (1929), Chap. 2; Holland,
Jurisprudence, 1st edn. (1880), 13th edn. (1924), Chap. 6; Markby,
Elements of Law, 1st edn. (1871), 6th edn. (1905), Chap. 1.
It is significant that neither Goodhart's *Essays in Jurisprudence and
the Common Law* (1931) nor Pollock's *Essays in Jurisprudence and
Ethics* (1882) contains one essay which is directed exclusively to a
discussion of the problem of the nature of justice.
[2]See *post*, p. 181.

advantage of the community ".[1] Some members of the House of Lords in this century have vigorously endorsed this view.[2] Austin, in his lectures in London nearly a century and a half ago, likewise taught that the concept of justice, so far as it concerns the lawyer, is but the proper application of the given law to the particular case: justice is conformity to law.[3] Around Austin's teaching there developed in the later nineteenth and early twentieth centuries in the English universities and in the courts a formidable school of thought which dismissed the discussion of ethical or ideal versions of justice from the province of jurisprudence. This positivist school and their legal version of justice will be fully examined in a later chapter.[4] Here it is only pertinent to point out that this school of thought, though it relegated the concept of justice for some lawyers, could not eliminate it for all lawyers.

The truth of the matter is that the English lawyer even in the twentieth century cannot dispense with the concept of justice. This positivist version of the law as the measure of justice is not itself sufficient for him. For, once a lawyer, whether in an academy or in his Inn of Court or in the courts themselves, begins to criticise any particular law as " unfair " or " undesirable " or " objectionable ", he is invoking consciously or otherwise some criterion for law, that is, some notion of justice other than legal justice. While it is especially the business of the academic lawyer to criticise, nevertheless judges and counsel occasionally feel themselves driven to express criticisms of the positive law. Pre-eminently the many judges and counsel who have in the last one hundred and thirty years served on commissions and committees for law reform have been compelled to adopt some extra-legal criteria for assessing the particular laws under review.

Moreover, this notion of legal justice is inadequate for the

---

[1]*Egerton* v. *Earl Brownlow* (1853), 4 H.L.Cas. 1, at p. 123; cf. *Mirehouse* v. *Rennell* (1832), 8 Bing. 490, at pp. 515-516.

[2]*E.g.*, Lord HALSBURY, L.C. in *Janson* v. *Driefontein Consolidated Mines, Ltd.*, [1902] A.C. 484, at p. 496; and Lord SIMONDS in *Jacobs* v. *L.C.C.*, [1950] 1 All E.R. 737, at p. 743; [1950] A.C. 361, at p. 373: see *post*, pp. 184-194.

[3]See *post*, pp. 176-179.

[4]See *post*, Chap. 8.

judge in the performance of his duties in court and consequently for the lawyer whose function it is to advise on the probable outcome of litigation. In the first place, the duty of the common law judge is not simply to administer the given law, the statute or the precedent ruling. The judges in the superior courts and no less magistrates in the local courts are by their judicial oath under the constitutional duty " to do right to all manner of people after the laws and usages of this realm, without fear or favour, affection or ill-will ".[1] Thus while the judges are bound to act " after the laws . . . of the realm " they are not under oath simply to act " after the laws " but " to do right . . . to people . . . after the laws ". Unless the first phrase of the oath is to be dismissed as a tautology then a concept of " right ", that is, an ethical version of justice is a necessary concept for the judge. In the second place, the assumption that there is to hand a statute or precedent which provides a law applicable to every case does not correspond with experience. Judges do find from time to time that they are faced with an issue for the resolution of which Parliament has made no provision and which has never been resolved by any court. In such cases of first impression the judge is bound " to do right ": *ex hypothesi* he cannot do so " after the laws of the realm ": he must resort to an ethical notion of justice. Third, the judge not infrequently has to deal with a case on which there are precedent rulings, but contradictory precedents of equal authority: he must choose between them, and his choice is likely to be guided by some extra-legal consideration. Fourth, the judge may be faced with a precedent decision on similar facts which he must follow, but whose *ratio decidendi* is not clear: the judge must ascertain for himself which of several possible *rationes* he will attribute to the precedent court: again, he has to make a choice, and the notion of legal justice will not suffice. Fifth, even when a statute is relevant to an issue before a court its application is far from being an automatic process. For instance, the wording may be vague or ambiguous. Then the judicial function is to interpret the statute. Several interpretations may be tenable. The practice is for

---

[1] Promissory Oaths Act, 1868, s. 4.

the court to call in aid the various maxims of statutory interpretation. But the interpretation ultimately adopted often depends on the judge's choice of maxims of interpretation, a choice in which there is concealed a value-judgment. Sixth, while statutes are of absolute obligation in the English legal system, a precedent ruling is not binding on a higher court. So, it is not infrequently open to the Court of Appeal or the House of Lords to decide a case otherwise than according to the precedent ruling. While it is obvious that when such a higher court overrules a previous case the later court is invoking some notion of justice other than legal justice, it is not so obvious that when they follow the previous case they may do so for similar reasons. Seventh, both magistrates and judges in the superior courts are frequently driven to invoke considerations other than the positive law by the law itself. For example, numerous statutes[1] require a judge to act " justly ", such as the Judicature Act, 1925, s. 45 (1): " The High Court may grant a mandamus or an injunction or appoint a receiver . . . in all cases in which it appears to the court to be just or convenient to do so ". Equally, the common law itself, in various of its branches, prescribes only a general rule involving an indeterminate standard such as what the court deems "reasonable" or "fair" or even "just".[2] Eighth, the outcome of some cases will depend on whether the judge relies on one category of legal doctrine rather than another, say on contract rather than tort, or equity rather than quasi-contract; the judge may be inclined to choose one category rather than another by some extra-legal consideration. Ninth, statutes and common law mostly leave the quantum of punishment in a criminal case within broad limits to the discretion of the judge, so that in the determination of this matter the judge must invoke other notions than the law. Tenth, the award of costs in a civil case is not determined by mandatory rules of law but rests with the discretion of the judge in each case.

Thus, the purely legal version of justice is inadequate even for the judge on the Bench. One of the greatest of the

---

[1] See *post*, p. 85.
[2] See *post*, pp. 84-85.

nineteenth century English judges, Chief Baron POLLOCK, after twenty-two years' experience as the principal judge in the Court of Exchequer, conceded this in a letter in 1868 to his grandson, the future jurist Frederick Pollock;[1] " The common law of England is really nothing more than ' summa ratio ', the highest good sense. Even PARKE, Lord WENSLEY-DALE (the greatest legal pedant that I believe ever existed) did not always follow even the House of Lords; he did not overrule (oh no!) but he did not act upon cases which were nonsense. . . . Juries, having the power to believe or disbelieve the evidence, have really the decisions in their own hands, but the court has the power to set aside the verdict and grant a new trial, which they profess not to do where substantial justice has been done." In this century Lord WRIGHT,[2] after more than twenty years' experience on the Bench in the High Court, in the Court of Appeal and as a Lord of Appeal in Ordinary, asserted that he was not afraid of being accused of sloppiness of thought when he said that the guiding principle of a judge in deciding cases was to do justice: that is, justice according to law, but still justice.[3] " I am most firmly convinced by all my experience and study of and reflection upon law, that its primary purpose is the quest of justice ".[4] Of cases of first impression when the judge must legislate he wrote: " I repeat that the law must be regarded as a living organism: its rules are subsidiary to justice and must, so far as precedent and logic permit, be moulded so as to conform with justice ".[5] And of the case which is covered by precedent authority he explained, that while the English judge would invariably consider the relevant authority, yet " in the end he may find that justice requires some modification of the rules apparently settled by the cases ".[6] Again, a contemporary judge whose predilection is to administer justice strictly according to law, Viscount

---

[1]Lord HANWORTH, *Lord Chief Baron Pollock, A Memoir* (1929), p. 198.
[2]See *post*, pp. 150-156.
[3]*Legal Essays and Addresses* (1939), p. 344.
[4]*Interpretations of Modern Legal Philosophies* (1947), ed. Sayre, p. 794.
[5]*Legal Essays and Addresses*, p. 344.
[6]*Ibid.*, p. 341.

SIMONDS,[1] was recently driven to admit that " in the end and in the absence of authority binding this House, the question is simply: What does justice demand in such a case as this?"[2]

Any suspicion that the English common lawyers unanimously hold and for centuries have held to one clearly formulated doctrine of justice, and that therein lies their strength, is soon dispelled. A closer examination of the opinions of individual lawyers soon reveals that no one doctrine is shared by all, but that there is and long has been a wide range of opinions at large within the profession.

It is not proposed to examine every shade of opinion on justice to which English lawyers have subscribed. At the one extreme, we can say nothing further of the opinion of the few who share with Plato the view that justice is a transcendental and ineffable idea. At the other extreme we can ignore the superficial use of the terms " justice " and " injustice " made by some lawyers to indicate their transitory approval or disapproval of the matter in question. Some notions which may have been important in the profession once, but which are nowadays neglected will not be elaborated. Among these are the axioms of distributive justice which were to the forefront in ancient classical legal philosophy; that justice is the set and constant purpose which renders to every man his due[3] and the allied principle which prescribes equal treatment for equals and unequal treatment for those who are unequal.[4] Though these axioms may have commanded the allegiance of the common lawyers in the Middle Ages[5] and though they

---

[1]See *post*, pp. 192-194, 214.

[2]*National Bank of Greece and Athens, S.A.* v. *Metliss*, [1957] 3 All E.R. 608, at p. 612; [1958] A.C. 509, at p. 525.

[3]" *Justitia est constans et perpetua voluntas jus suum cuique tribuendi* "—Justinian, *Institutes*, Book I, Tit. 1. " *Honeste vivere, alterum non laedere, suum cuique tribuere* "—Ulpian, *Digest*, Book I, i, 10. These maxims derive ultimately from Aristotle, *Nicomachean Ethics* and *Politics*: see Barker, *Politics of Aristotle* (1946), Book III, Chaps. IX-XIII and Appendix II; Del Vecchio, *Justice*, English ed. (1952), ed. Campbell, § 6.

[4]Aristotle, *op. cit.*

[5]*E.g.*, BRACTON, *De Legibus et Consuetudinibus Angliae* (*circa* 1256), ed. Woodbine (1915-1942), Vol. II, p. 23.

occur in some modern works of English jurisprudence,[1] and
though they are very occasionally invoked by modern lawyers in support of some other notions,[2] they play little part
in the modern English lawyers' thinking. The typical common lawyer, if he considers these axioms at all, is quick to
discern that they afford him no complete guide to the solution of any dispute. They presuppose an extremely detailed
system of ethical or legal rules defining what is due to individuals, and which individuals are equals. While on the
continent such axioms are still respected as purely formal
theories of justice the common lawyer rejects them as
supreme examples of axioms in the air. Further, notions of
justice which are peculiar to individual lawyers, however
distinguished, will not be discussed. For instance, Vinogradoff's theory of justice as a system of delimitation of
individual wills[3] which may fit into the tradition of German
legal philosophy, is not representative of any school of legal
thought in modern England.

Discounting the above opinions there remains a cluster of
notions of justice within the ethos of the English legal profession in the twentieth century. Several notions can be discerned, but the difficulty of separating them without distorting
them is considerable. Nevertheless in the following pages,
in an attempt to analyse and to expound clearly subject-
matter which is essentially amorphous and indistinct, it is
proposed to examine some seven notions in separate chapters.

In each chapter a notion of justice will be considered in
four sections.

§A. The particular notion will first of all be presented as far
as possible in the words of some distinguished judge or jurist.
In nearly every case these *dicta* taken alone do not represent
the whole of the doctrine of justice to which the lawyer in
question subscribed. But at least they express a facet of his
more complex philosophy, and, what is important for our
purpose, they express one of the notions of justice which we
are endeavouring to isolate in a preliminary analysis.

[1]Salmond, *Jurisprudence*, 7th edn. (1924), § 19, 11th edn. (1957),
§ 21; Friedmann, *Legal Theory*, 4th edn. (1960), p. 145.
[2]See *post*, p. 189.
[3]Vinogradoff, *Common Sense in Law* (1913), Chaps. 2 and 3.

§B. As ideas are rarely static this selected version will itself be the development of some earlier thought and may itself have been modified subsequently. So the developments of the notion will be sketched in in bold strokes in a rough chronological account of other common lawyers who have subscribed to it. Of course in the history of ideas it is rarely possible to fix a point in time at which it can be said with confidence that a certain idea was first conceived by a particular man; in the history of the idea of justice this difficulty is acute. The notions on the subject which were current in the embryonic legal profession in England in the twelfth century were not all native conceptions but were largely part of the stock of ideas common to the educated classes of Christendom[1] and the ancestry of this stock of ideas can be traced back through Roman and Greek philosophy into the history of the ancient Indo-European peoples.[2] It is proposed therefore to adopt arbitrarily as a *terminus a quo* the middle of the twelfth century, a period when a class of professional judges officiating in the King's central and itinerary courts is clearly recognizable and the law common to the English counties was beginning to be collected and consolidated by these judges. Still it must be emphasised that it is not intended to offer estimates of the complex of notions prevailing among the common lawyers in the Middle Ages or in any subsequent century except the twentieth. Resort to legal history is made in this second section in each chapter only to trace the roots and to explain more fully that particular notion of justice which has some currency amongst members of the English legal profession in the twentieth century. The main emphasis will be on twentieth century lawyers' use of the notion, examples of which will accordingly be given at some length.

§C. A notion of justice if held by a number of judges or parliamentary legislators is fertile in producing or modifying institutions and laws. Accordingly in the third section of each chapter it is proposed to exhibit a few of the historical precipitates within the English legal system of the notion in

---

[1]See Carlyle, R. W. and A. J., *A History of Mediaeval Political Theory in the West* (1903-1936), especially Vols. V and VI.

[2]See Maine, *Early Law and Custom* (1883), Chap. VI.

question. In doing so oversimplification is inevitable as any one complete doctrine of positive law is the product of a variety of notions operating contemporaneously or over a period of time. Examples have been chosen of doctrines in which the particular notion under review has been the main if not the only inspiration. The reader who can cap the illustrations given with others from different branches of the positive law will have taken the point of this section.

§D. In the final section in each chapter some criticisms of the notion in question, as voiced by the English lawyers themselves, will be given. It is only proposed to set out the lawyers' own criticisms of each other's opinions; no systematic subjective critique is offered.

The critical reader of the following pages will quickly appreciate that while some of the notions treated separately are in the main distinct from one another, the treatment of others under separate rubrics is manifestly artificial, as no sharp dividing line can properly be drawn between them. In the concluding chapter an attempt is made to remove this artificiality by synthesising, so far as the subject-matter permits, the notions examined separately in the intervening chapters.

CHAPTER 2

JUSTICE AS JUDICATURE

§A

An elementary but persistent notion held by English lawyers is that justice involves not doctrine so much as practical process. They have seen it to consist in proceedings in tribunals, before a judge or a judge and jury, in which persons are tried for alleged wrongs with the sequel of punishment or reparation. Justice thus conceived is no more than adjudication, arbitration, the judicial settlement of public disorders and private disputes. As such it is the relatively civilised alternative to leaving disorders to multiply and private wrongs to be redressed by violent self-help. Justice in this sense is hardly an ethical value, but is rather a mechanism of government directed to realising the political value of social order. On this view " justice " is synonymous with " judicature ".

Such a notion was clearly expressed as far back as the thirteenth century in the works of the English judge and jurist HENRY DE BRACTON. In *De Legibus et Consuetudinibus Angliae*,[1] BRACTON rehearses the power of the Crown as follows:

> " And it is to be known that the lord king himself . . . has all rights in his hand . . . which pertain to the government of the realm. He has likewise justice and judgment which are of jurisdiction (*Habet etiam iustitiam et iudicium quae sunt iurisdictionis*). . . . Those things which are of jurisdiction and of peace, and those things which are annexed to justice and to peace, pertain to nobody so much as to the Crown. . . . For the Crown is to do justice and judgment (*facere iustitiam et iudicium*) and to maintain peace."[2]

---

[1]Composed *circa* 1256. Citations are from the edition by G. E. Woodbine (1915-1942) in four volumes.
[2]*Op. cit.*, Vol. II, pp. 166-167.

Later he examines more closely this royal power of justice:
      " Who in the first place and principally may and ought
to judge? And it is to be known that the King himself and
no-one else, if he alone can suffice to do it, since he is bound
by virtue of his oath to do it. For the King ought at his
coronation . . . to promise three things. . . . First, that he
will enjoin and as far as his power lies take care, that a true
peace shall be maintained. . . . Secondly, that he will inter-
dict all rapacities. . . . Thirdly, that in all judgments he
will enjoin equity and mercy . . . so that all persons may
enjoy a firm peace through his justice (*per iustitiam
suam*)."[1]
BRACTON'S own comment on this oath is particularly
significant:
      " For this purpose the king has been created and elected,
that he should do justice to all persons (*ut iustitiam faciat
universis*) . . . and that he should of himself decide his own
judgments, and maintain and defend what he has justly
judged, for if there was no-one to do justice peace would
be easily exterminated. . . ."[2]
Of course, BRACTON added, from first-hand experience,
that for practical purposes in exercising this power of justice
for the whole kingdom the King could not himself " determine all causes " but must delegate the power to " justices
(*iustitiarii*), sheriffs, and other bailiffs and ministers ".[3]

These excerpts from BRACTON's treatise at least illustrate
the notion of justice as mere judicature. Far from epitomising
BRACTON's whole concept of justice, they only express one
facet of the complex doctrine to which he as cleric and as
lawyer subscribed.[4] Nor is it suggested that BRACTON was
adumbrating a novel or particularly English theory: similar
theories were to be found in the texts of other mediaeval
writers in other parts of Christendom.[5] Nor do BRACTON's

---

[1] *Op. cit.*, Vol. II, p. 304.
[2] *Op. cit.*, p. 305.
[3] *Op. cit.*, p. 306.
[4] See *ante*, p. 13, and *post*, pp. 33, 53, 78, 179.
[5] See R. W. and A. J. Carlyle, *History of Mediaeval Political Theory
in the West*, Vol. III, 2nd edn. (1928), Part II, Chaps. 2 and 8; O.
Gierke, *Political Theories of the Middle Age*, ed. Maitland (1900), p. 34
and n. 125. " There has been a time in the history of every state when
the administration of justice consisted in nothing more than invita-
tions to people to forgo the settlement of disputes by fighting, and to
have them dealt with by arbitration ": Eastwood and Keeton,
Austinian Theories of Law (1929), p. 28.

dicta, which insist that justice is a royal power, accurately describe the legal system of his day: for while the Curia Regis and the itinerant judges dealt with much litigation, still litigation was largely conducted in the seignorial and communal courts, which did not as a matter of history derive their judicial powers from the Crown.[1] But what is significant for our purpose is that in these passages BRACTON was urging a theory which expressed the contemporary royal policy, a policy to which great impetus had been given in the preceding century by Henry II, and which was pursued by most of his successors, and which eventually became a part of the dogma of the royal judges and the class of professional lawyers which developed around the courts, the common lawyers.

§B

This notion of justice as at the very least a process of adjudication was evidently commonplace for the mediaeval English lawyers. The author[2] of the very first treatise on the common law of England, which appeared in the twelfth century, *De Legibus et Consuetudinibus Regni Angliae*[3] harboured such a notion. The long title of the book described GLANVILL as holding the helm of justice (*iustitiae gubernacula tenente*); the prologue credits the King with various powers, notably the power of justice, and by such remedial justice deciding disputes and putting an end to litigation.[4] In the fourteen parts which follow the author developed this notion in severely practical terms by exhibiting and commenting on the various procedures in the royal courts. BRACTON, in the following century, in the passages cited above, only brought the notion into sharper focus. Several of the great statutes

---

[1]Plucknett, *Concise History of the Common Law*, 5th edn. (1956), pp. 80-81; Pollock and Maitland, *History of English Law*, 2nd edn. (1898), Vol. I, pp. 528-529.
[2]*Either* RANULF DE GLANVILL, for the last ten years of the reign of Henry II his Chief Justiciar, and thus the principal judge in the realm after the King, *or* HUBERT WALTER who became Chief Justiciar under Richard I.
[3]*Circa* 1187; ed. Woodbine (1932).
[4]*Op. cit.*, pp. 23-24.

of the twelfth and thirteenth centuries, products of the King's Council in which the lawyers still played a prominent rôle, assume this simplest notion of justice.[1] The Assize of Clarendon, 1166, which established the machinery for the investigation of crimes throughout the country and for charging those suspected, recites that the new procedure is " for the maintenance of peace and justice ". Chapter 5 provides that of those who have been captured " none shall have court or justice or chattels (*nullus habeat curiam vel justitiam nec cattala*) except the King in his court before his justices ". One of the provisions of Magna Carta involves the same notion. John had abused his power, *inter alia*, by charging exorbitant fees for special writs and had accepted monies to stop or delay proceedings in his court. But by Chapter 40 of the Charter of 1215[2] the King solemnly undertook that " to no-one would he sell, refuse or delay right or justice (*nulli vendemus nulli negabimus aut differemus rectum vel justitiam*) ".[3] The justice which the King in effect guaranteed is access to his tribunals and unimpeded proceedings in those tribunals. Again, in the Statute of Marlborough, 1267, the noun " *justitia* " recurs with the same connotation. There it was recounted that in the recent troubled times many men " refused to be justified by the King and his court . . ." but " by themselves took great revenges and distresses . . ."; whence it was prescribed " that all persons, as well of high as of low estate, shall have and receive justice in the King's court (*justiciam habeant et recipiant in Curia Domini Regis*); and that none henceforth shall take any revenges or distresses of his own pleasure ".

In the eighteenth century, BLACKSTONE, the first Professor of English Law at an English university, himself a Judge of

---

[1]See J. H. Baxter and C. Johnson, *Mediaeval Latin Word List* (1934): " *justitia* " = " right or jurisdiction, *cira* 1070, 1461 A.D."

[2]Re-enacted as c. 29 in the fourth Charter, 9 Hen. 3, 1225.

[3]Later commentators, notably COKE, credited the legislators of 1215 with a more highly developed theory of justice: see *post*, p. 34. But this seems to be an anachronism. In the historical context of 1215 the King evidently was undertaking to rectify the recent abuses, by guaranteeing access to his courts and full trial: see McKechnie, *Magna Carta*, 2nd edn. (1914), pp. 395-398; Stubbs, *Constitutional History*, 5th edn. (1891), §§ 155 and 295; Holdsworth, *History of English Law*, Vol. I, 55-58.

the Court of Common Pleas, and a model of orthodoxy, employed it prominently in his *Commentaries*. Reviewing the law of the various prerogatives of the King, he described the prerogative of justice as follows: " Another capacity in which the King is considered in domestic affairs is as the fountain of justice and the general conservator of the kingdom. By the fountain of justice the law does not mean the author or original, but only the distributor. Justice is not derived from the King as from his free gift; but he is the steward of the public to dispense it to whom it is due. He is not the spring, but the reservoir; from whence right and equity are conducted by a thousand channels, to every individual. The original power of judicature, by the fundamental principles of society, is lodged in the society at large: but as it would be impracticable to render complete justice to every individual, by the people in their collective capacity, therefore every nation has committed that power to certain select magistrates, who with more ease and expedition can hear and determine complaints; and in England this authority has immemorially been exercised by the King or his substitutes. He therefore has alone the right of erecting courts of judicature: for, though the constitution of the kingdom has entrusted him with the whole executive power of the laws, it is impossible, as well as improper, that he should personally carry into execution this great and extensive trust: it is consequently necessary, that courts should be erected, to assist him in executing this power, and equally necessary that, if erected, they should be erected by his authority. And hence it is that all the jurisdictions of courts are either mediately or immediately derived from the Crown, their proceedings run generally in the King's name, they pass under his seal and are executed by his officers."[1] BLACKSTONE and BRACTON assume different political theories: BLACKSTONE assumes the power of justice is vested in the people and by a social contract delegated to the King, where BRACTON had attributed the power of justice to the King by virtue of his kingship: but they express a common notion of justice, as the judicial settlement of disputes in royal courts.

---

[1]*Commentaries on the Laws of England*, 1st edn. (1765); 3rd edn. (1768), Book I, Chap. 7, pp. 266-267.

In the modern era the English lawyers who would admit to being satisfied with this elementary notion of justice *simpliciter* are indeed rare.[1] This is not to say that they have dispensed with it, but rather that they have developed more complex notions which assume the original one. But still this original notion remains in their basic technical vocabulary.

So it is still asserted by judges and professors of law that the Crown has " the prerogative of justice ",[2] or that the Crown is the " fountain of justice ".[3] Thus adjudication before the principal courts of the land is spoken of as " royal justice ", whereas adjudication by provincial courts is referred to as " local justice ", the modern practice of adjudication in tribunals within government departments as " administrative justice ", and that within professional or trade organisations or clubs as " domestic justice ".

An injured or outraged person who seeks his remedy by court process is still said to " seek justice ". His opponent who comes voluntarily to trial or is arrested and dragged there is still said by the lawyers to be " brought to justice "; but if he flees rather than face trial he is dubbed a " fugitive from justice ", or if he can otherwise evade trial he " defeats justice ", or if he eventually gives himself up to stand trial he " surrenders to justice ". A cause which the court is competent to hear and determine is, technically, " justiciable ". An aggrieved individual who seeks in vain a remedy in courts is said to suffer " a denial of justice " and the legal system is said to produce a " failure of justice ". For instance, in a leading case, in which the plaintiff sought a remedy in England for acts alleged to have been done by the defendants in African territories which then lacked a complete legal system, FRY, L.J. said: " In a case like the present, where, according to the allegations of the plaintiffs, there are no

---

[1] Sir William Markby, a colonial judge turned jurist, in his influential treatise on jurisprudence, *Elements of Law*, 1st edn. (1871), 6th edn. (1905), discussed various doctrines of justice: but he came down most firmly in favour of the severely practical and limited view that justice is in essence a court process whereby disputes are authoritatively settled: *ibid.*, pp. 30-35 and 111-112.

[2] *Hull* v. *M'Kenna*, [1926] I.R. 402, at p. 404, *per* Viscount HALDANE in the Privy Council.

[3] Wade, *Constitutional Law*, 6th edn. (1960), p. 13.

courts of adequate jurisdiction in the *locus rei sitae*, it is obvious that to repel the jurisdiction is to produce a total failure of justice. If neither Africa nor England affords a forum the plaintiff is remediless."[1]

The court in question may be described without rhetoric, as " the seat of justice ".[2] Delays in the court proceedings are " delays in justice ". As for the climax of the whole proceedings, the judging of the issue by judge or by judge and jury, this is the essence of the notion of justice under consideration: and the lawyers are still in the habit of speaking of the judge or jury performing this essential process as " doing " or " distributing " or " dispensing justice ".[3] If the proceedings are short and minimal they are described as " summary justice "; but if all the legal mechanisms of full trial are utilised " full justice " is supposed to be done; if all the aspects of the dispute can be settled by the court " complete justice " is said to be done.

Even the legal proceedings after trial, the execution or enforcement of the judgment of a competent court, are spoken of as part of the " machinery of justice "; thus " justice is carried out " when a person convicted of a crime is punished, or the property of a judgment debtor is seized and sold.

To describe the whole range of these proceedings, the stock phrase used by the lawyers is " the administration of justice ". So, for example, Lord Chief Justice ALVERSTONE, addressing King Edward VII, at the opening of the Old Bailey new buildings in 1907, used the term " justice " as BRACTON might have used it in addressing Henry III in the thirteenth century: " I am permitted, on behalf of the judges who administer justice in this place in your name . . . to convey to Your Majesty a humble expression of our loyal devotion. . . . We to whom Your Majesty entrusts from time

---

[1]*Companhia de Moçambique* v. *British South Africa Co.*, [1892] 2 Q.B. 358, at p. 413.

[2]*Ambard* v. *A.-G. for Trinidad and Tobago*, [1936] 1 All E.R. 704, at p. 708; [1936] A.C. 322, at p. 335, *per* Lord ATKIN.

[3]Of course these terms can be and frequently are used by modern lawyers with a much more extensive meaning, as shown in the following chapters. Here it is only sought to fix their minimal meaning.

to time the administration of justice here, keep steadily before us this thought—that from Your Majesty . . . is derived our jurisdiction: that we act for you and that we act in your name; and this thought ought to make us . . . determined . . . that we may not be unworthy instruments in the exercise of the greatest of the prerogatives of Your Majesty—justice and mercy."[1]

A clear illustration of the use of the term " justice " in this elementary and minimal sense, connoting mere judicature, in the technical vocabulary of the modern common lawyer is to be found in a recent case, *St. John Shipping Corporation* v. *J. Rank, Ltd.*[2] DEVLIN, J., in the course of a long judgment cast doubt on the wisdom of the policy of nullifying a commercial contract whenever one party to it has incidentally committed a statutory offence: " It may be questionable also whether public policy is well served by driving from the seat of judgment everyone who has been guilty of a minor transgression. Commercial men who have unwittingly offended against one of a multiplicity of regulations may nevertheless feel that they have not thereby forfeited all right to justice, and may go elsewhere for it if courts of law will not give it to them. In the last resort they will, if necessary, set up their own machinery for dealing with their own disputes . . ."

§C

This ancient theory of justice, adopted as royal policy and implemented by royal judges, has in the long run yielded some of the basic institutions in the English legal system, and traces of its influence are discernible in some branches of the substantive law.

The foundation of the legal system, the cluster of royal courts which developed in mediaeval England and lasted into the second half of the nineteenth century, is the complex of institutions which has given life and force to this notion of justice. In the twelfth century the royal power of justice might be exercised by the King himself in his Court (*Curia*

---

[1]*Recollections of Bar and Bench* (1914), pp. 267-268.
[2][1956] 3 All E.R. 683, at p. 691; [1957] 1 Q.B. 267, at pp. 288-289.

Regis) or Council. But the Council would then meet to perform various governmental functions—legislative and de-
liberative as well as judicial; only when performing the latter
would it have been described as a " court of justice ". With
the increasing complexity of the business of government, and
with the royal policy of extending the judicial power of the
Crown to cover all disputes and all disorders in the whole
kingdom—" bringing justice to the King's court " as Maitland describes the process[1]—the King and his Council were
compelled to delegate this power of justice to individual
itinerant judges and to benches of judges, and later to the
Chancellor. Hence evolved the Assize Courts, the superior
courts of common law—Exchequer, Common Pleas and
King's Bench—and eventually the Court of Chancery, to
mention only the great and enduring tribunals which evolved
to administer justice in the King's name. Each of these tribunals has traditionally been called a court of justice. Even
in the nineteenth and twentieth centuries this ancient notion
of justice as mere judicature manifests itself in the new
system of courts, established under the Judicature Act of
1873. Admittedly the Judicature Commissioners, in their
First Report in 1869[2] which finally proposed the consolidation of all the old superior courts of common law and equity
into one great court, prudently avoided the ambiguous term
" justice " for the most part, preferring the term " judicature "; but occasionally they used these terms interchange-
ably. In the result the Act of 1873 established one Supreme
Court of Judicature—" for the better administration of
justice in England ", and one of its permanent components,
" Her Majesty's High Court of Justice ", perpetuates the
traditional title.[3] A series of amendments to these Acts, dealing with such matters as the constitution of the Supreme
Court, its jurisdiction, modes of adjudication and the enforcement of judgments, have been enacted from 1920-1960,
under the appropriate rubric—Administration of Justice
Acts.

---

[1]*Constitutional History of England* (1908), p. 111.
[2]Parlt. Papers, XXV, 1 *et seq.*
[3]Supreme Court of Judicature Act, 1873, s. 4; now replaced by the
Supreme Court of Judicature (Consolidation) Act, 1925, s. 1.

The very titles of most of the judges in England stem from this notion of justice as judicature. In the twelfth century the royal power of justice was exercised on behalf of the King by his chief minister. In GLANVILL'S day the office of that minister is already entitled *Justiciarius Capitalis*;[1] in the vernacular the chief minister became the Chief Justiciar. When that office and title lapsed in the mid-thirteenth century there had evolved a more clear-cut system of royal courts, and two of them, Common Pleas and King's Bench, each had its own Chief Justice.[2] As even in the twelfth century the King and Chief Justiciar could not adjudicate on all the disputes and disorders of the Kingdom, there were associated with them for the business of judicature other officers, then called, after their function, " *Justitiae* " or " *Justitiarii* ", and those who travelled around representing the King in the counties, " *Justitiae Errantes* ".[3] Certainly in the thirteenth century the King's judges are officially styled " Justices learned in the law ".[4] The anthropomorphic title " Mr. Justice " has remained in use for most of the puisne judges in the superior courts of common law in England down to the twentieth century.[5] Again, the same influence gave rise to the title of the provincial judges. In the early fourteenth century royal officers were appointed in the shires to assist the sheriff in the executive function of keeping the peace and arresting persons accused of felonies; as such they were known as Keepers of the Peace. But after they had been authorised by statute in 1360[6] actually to hear and determine

---

[1]Stubbs, *Constitutional History*, 5th edn. (1891), § 120; *De Legibus et Consuetudinibus Regni Angliae* (*circa* 1187), ed. Woodbine, 1932, prologue.

[2]Maitland, *Constitutional History of England* (1908), p. 133.

[3]Stubbs, *op. cit.*, § 127; Holdsworth, *History of English Law*, Vol. I, p. 38; Magna Carta, 1215, as confirmed in 1225, 9 Hen. 3, c. 12, provided that actions of Novel Disseisin were to be heard in the shires and that the King or the Chief Justice (*capitalis Justiciarius noster*) shall send Justices (*Justiciarios*) into the counties: difficult questions were to be referred to the Justices of the Bench (*Justiciarios nostros de Banco*) for determination.

[4]Pollock and Maitland, *History of English Law*, 2nd edn. (1898), Vol. I, p. 170.

[5]The Judicature Act, 1925, s. 2 (4) maintains the usage.

[6]34 Edw. 3, c. 1.

at the King's suit all manner of felonies and trespasses done in their counties, they were soon credited with the title corresponding to their new function, Justices of the Peace.[1] It is typical of the common lawyers of England, with their aversion from abstractions and their passion for facts, that they should personify the notion of the royal power of justice in the various traditional judicial titles.

Vestiges of the influence of this ancient notion of justice are to be found in the substantive law.

So, for example, it is an axiom of the unwritten constitution of the United Kingdom in the mid-twentieth century— that the Crown is the fountain of justice[2]—though the axiom is mainly of historical significance.

Again, as justice in this most elementary sense is authoritative adjudication over private disputes, so the interference by an outsider in the disputes and litigations of two others is an abuse of justice. Such officious intermeddling by strangers in the disputes of others has long been proscribed by common law and by statutes, and branded as the wrong of maintenance (or as champerty if the stranger is to take a share of the winnings). These wrongs are both crimes and torts, and agreements which involve such conduct are not enforceable as contracts.[3] To constitute these wrongs there must be " something against good policy and justice, something tending to promote unnecessary litigation . . ."[4]

A final illustration of the effect of this notion of justice on the positive law may be found in the modern law of contracts. It is now an established principle that any agreement having a tendency to affect the administration of justice is illegal and void.[5] Accordingly, " the court will not allow as legal any agreement which has the effect of withdrawing from the

---

[1]Maitland, *Constitutional History of England*, p. 206; Plucknett, *Concise History of the Common Law*, 5th edn., pp. 167-168.

[2]See Wade, *Constitutional Law*, 6th edn. (1960), pp. 13 and 300-312.

[3]See Winfield, *Present Law of Abuse of Legal Procedure* (1921), Chaps. 1-3.

[4]*Fischer* v. *Kamala Naicker* (1860), 8 Moo. Ind. App. 170, at p. 187.

[5]See Cheshire and Fifoot, *Law of Contract*, 5th edn. (1960), pp. 282-283.

ordinary course of justice a prosecution, when it is for an act which is an injury to the public ".[1]

§D

Though moral philosophers seeking the universal and eternal nature of justice might well overlook this notion of justice as involving judicature, the pre-eminently practical common lawyers of England insist that justice at the lowest reckoning involves a regular process of adjudication before the established courts of the land. It is not only a matter of self-interest, in that the lawyers have a professional and financial interest in regular litigation, but that the practising lawyer, judge, counsel or solicitor, and even the academic lawyer, is not infrequently reminded starkly, by some case involving the collision of human beings, that without these mechanisms for the settlement of disputes and the trial and punishment of disorders, his complex, civilised and relatively orderly society of several score million people living in one small island would erupt into chaos. The lawyer sees occasionally the truth of the axiom, which is constantly before the mind of the political scientist,[2] that order in a society is an indispensable condition of civilisation.

While no common lawyer today would deny that justice involves the process of judicature, he would be a strange lawyer who would go to the extreme of seriously maintaining that justice was done in modern England simply by regular trials in the Royal courts, irrespective of the way the trials were conducted or the doctrines which formed the bases of

---

[1]*Windhill Local Board of Health* v. *Vint* (1890), 45 Ch. D. 351, at p. 363, *per* COTTON, L.J.

[2]" The history of mediaeval society constantly impresses upon us the conviction that the real difference between a barbarous and a civilised political system lies in the fact that the latter has an almost automatically working administration and judicial machinery, while the former is dependent upon the chance presence of some exceptionally competent and clear-sighted individual ruler. . . . It has taken centuries to work out an adequate instrument." R. W. and A. J. Carlyle, *History of Mediaeval Political Theory in the West*, Vol. III, 2nd edn. (1928), p. 31.

the judgments. Indeed it is a commonplace amongst the English lawyers of today to speak derisively of a trial, in which the judge has been unfettered by rules of procedure and without doctrine to guide him in reaching his decision, as " palm-tree justice ".[1] Pollock has dismissed mere judicature —" the eastern king sitting in the gate "[2]—as tolerable only in a small and relatively uncivilised community.[3]

Rather, the English lawyer would maintain that justice is only adequately done when the trial of disputes or disorders is conducted within certain canons of fairness, and when the judge decides the case according to moral principles or takes into account the human interests at stake, or applies established laws. But this is to anticipate the other notions of justice which, superimposed upon this basic notion of judicature, go to make up the common lawyers' complex working doctrine of justice—notions which are examined in turn in the following chapters.

---

[1] Presumably the allusion is to the ancient Jewish judge, Deborah, of whom it is recorded that she dwelt under a palm-tree near Mount Ephraim " and the children of Israel came up to her for judgment". *Judges*, iv, 4, 5. See Maine, *Early Law and Custom* (1883), Chap. VI, " The King and Early Civil Justice."

[2] *Cf*. Browning, *Pippa Passes*:
> " A King lived long ago,
> In the morning of the world,
>
> .   .   .   .
>
> Among the rocks his city was:
> Before his palace, in the sun,
> He sat to see his people pass,
> And judge them every one
> From its threshold of smooth stone.
> They haled him many a valley thief."

[3] *First Book of Jurisprudence*, 6th edn. (1929), p. 42.

CHAPTER 3

JUSTICE AS FAIR TRIAL

§A

An extension of the version of justice as judicature is the notion that justice involves a system of fair trials. No doubt the notion of a fair trial originated in the demands of parties to court proceedings that the process of adjudication should be fair to them, and the notion has been nourished by the developing public opinion on what is and is not fair, so that this notion is closely related to the notion we shall be considering later under the rubric, moral justice.[1] Besides, as disputes are not likely to be settled once and for all by court proceedings unless the parties are satisfied with the manner of adjudication, it was in keeping with the royal policy of maintaining order in the kingdom that trials in the royal courts should be conducted in accordance with the popular sense of fairness. But the notion that a trial should be fair has been adopted by the English lawyers themselves and elaborated by them into a series of canons of what constitutes a fair trial, and these have become an essential part of their concept of justice.

Although the common lawyers, particularly the English judges, have for centuries been evolving empirically the canons of fair trial there is still even in the twentieth century no definitive version of them.

Lord DENNING recently formulated some of them in a series of lectures published under the rubric *The Road to Justice*.[2] He maintained that the principles which go to make a fair trial are as follows:

---

[1] See *post*, Chap. 5.
[2] (1955), pp. 1-44.

(i) " The judges should be absolutely independent of the Government."

It is of the essence of fair trial that the judge should be dependent on no man who can by any possibility become a party to a proceeding before him, so that he can adjudicate evenly between the parties—whether these are private citizens or whether a private citizen is opposed to a government official or to the government itself. And in jury trials the absolute independence of the jury is no less important than the independence of the judge.

(ii) " The judge must have no interest himself in any matter that he has to try. He must be impartial. No person can be a judge in his own cause."

(iii) " The judge, before he comes to a decision against a party, must hear and consider all that he has to say. No-one ought to be condemned unheard . . . the only fair way of reaching a correct decision on any dispute is for the judge to hear all that is to be said on each side and then come to his conclusion."

(iv) " The judge must act only on the evidence and arguments properly before him and not on any information which he receives from the outside."

(v) " The judge must give his reasons for his decision."

(vi) " A judge should in his own character be beyond reproach, or at any rate should have so disciplined himself that he is not himself a breaker of the law."

(vii) " Each side should state its case as strongly as it can . . . [since] truth is best discovered by powerful statements on both sides of the question."[1]

The search for the truth of the matter before the court is of the essence of a fair trial but counsel must contain themselves within bounds : accordingly they " must never distort or suppress the truth ", and in criminal cases counsel for the prosecution should act " not as an advocate to condemn the accused, but as a minister of justice to see that he is fairly treated ".

This statement of the principles which go to make a fair trial does not claim to be exhaustive. Lord Chief Justice HEWART in 1929 in his extra-judicial essays, *The New*

---

[1]Lord DENNING is quoting Lord ELDON, L.C., in *Ex Parte Lloyd* (1822), Montague's Reports, p. 70, n.

Despotism[1] agreed with most of the above canons and emphasised several others, *viz.*:

    (viii) The parties are to be treated as equals before the court.

    (ix) A case should be heard in public.

    (x) The judge should be identified and be personally responsible for his decision.

    (xi) To ensure the regular application of the above canons in courts of first instance the parties should have a right of appeal to a higher judicial tribunal on questions of procedure.

A further vital element in a fair trial is that the judge should decide the case not by caprice but in accordance with some rules or doctrine. But when one begins to consider which rules or doctrines should guide the judge to his decision —pre-existing laws established by authorities, moral doctrine or rules devised to achieve human happiness or satisfy current interests—one invokes other notions of justice which we shall examine under separate rubrics in later chapters. Lord DENNING has himself made extensive use of moral doctrine in adjudication[2] and is by no means orthodox among the common law judges of his generation in this respect. But he speaks with the authentic voice of the common lawyer when he stresses the paramount importance of fair trial:

> " When you set out on this road (to justice) you must remember that there are two great objects to be achieved: one is to see that the laws are just; the other that they are justly administered. Both are important; but of the two, the more important is that the law should be justly administered. It is no use having just laws if they are administered unfairly by bad judges or corrupt lawyers. A country can put up with laws that are harsh or unjust so long as they are administered by just judges . . . but a country cannot long tolerate a legal system which does not give a fair trial."[3]

§B

This contemporary version of justice as fair trial is the

---

[1] (1929), pp. 9-164.
[2] See *post*, pp. 88-93.
[3] *The Road to Justice*, pp. 6-7.

culmination of a long development within the English legal system.

The mediaeval jurists entertained an inchoate theory of a just trial. The author of " GLANVILL "[1] in the reign of Henry II, in his elaborate prologue, conceived that no trial in the King's court could be presumed to deviate from the path of justice or truth, that in that tribunal a poor man could face up to a powerful adversary, and that there no man would be driven away as a result of the judge's partiality to friends. In the next century BRACTON,[2] postulated the qualities of a judge as the delegate of the King in his power of justice; that he be not only wise and God-fearing, but that he use truth, that he accept parties equally and impartially—" you shall hear the lowly equally as the great, and neither shall you respect the person of any one ",—that he accept no gifts nor be biassed by ties of blood, and that he conduct diligent examinations to search out everything. And FORTESCUE, a former Chief Justice, writing in exile in the middle of the fifteenth century,[3] praising the English legal system, extolled the jury as an instrument for impartial adjudication and for ascertaining the truth of questions in dispute. In those centuries these were statements of ideals, counsels of perfection, to which the English kings, their justices and juries by no means invariably conformed. But it is germane to our inquiry that these ideals were mooted within the legal profession even in the mediaeval period.

In these fragments from the work of the mediaeval jurists several of the modern canons of fair trial which we have enumerated earlier can be discerned, *viz.* those of equality, impartiality and incorruptibility. Conspicuously absent is the first, namely the principle that the judges should be absolutely independent. As the judges originally were and in constitutional theory remained the delegates of the King himself, and as they could be and occasionally were dismissed

---

[1] *De Legibus et Consuetudinibus Regni Angliae* (*circa* 1187); ed. Woodbine (1932), pp. 23-24.

[2] *De Legibus et Consuetudinibus Angliae* (*circa* 1256), ed. Woodbine, Vol. II, pp. 302 and 306.

[3] *De Laudibus Legum Anglie* (*circa* 1470: printed 1546): ed. Chrimes (1942), Chaps. XXVI and XXX.

at the King's displeasure, it is hardly surprising that the principle was not urged within the legal profession in the first centuries of the common law. Nevertheless the principle was asserted most vigorously in the seventeenth century by Sir EDWARD COKE, both as judge and as jurist. As Chief Justice of the Court of King's Bench in the *Case of Commendams*[1], he denied that the King was entitled to stay proceedings and thus delay justice in his courts, only to be dismissed for his uncongenial opinions by James I. Later, in his *Second Institute*[2] he reaffirmed the principle that judicature must proceed notwithstanding any royal order, even one made under the Great Seal, to the contrary, calling in aid Magna Carta as his authority.[3] But within a century the heterodox opinion of COKE became the orthodox opinion of the lawyers and in effect an article of the English constitution. BLACKSTONE, in the middle of the eighteenth century, in his *Commentaries*, is able to speak dogmatically of the independence of the judges, then firmly secured by statutes,[4] and to record that the King —George III—has been pleased to declare " that he looked upon the independence and uprightness of the judges as essential to the impartial administration of justice . . ."[5]

In the early nineteenth century most of the canons of fair trial enumerated earlier were accepted as " good sense " or " sound policy " if not as " the elementary dictates of justice " by the bulk of the members of the English Inns of Court. For instance, Lord CAMPBELL, reflecting on the lives of the Chief Justices of England[6] used as his criteria of the just judge, *inter alia*, that he be incorruptible and impartial. Lord CAMPBELL was able to maintain that by the nineteenth century incorruptibility was common to all English judges,[7]

---

[1](1617) Hob. 140; *sub nom. Colt and Glover* v. *Bishop of Coventry and Lichfield.*

[2](1642), Chap. 29; (1792 edn.), p. 55.

[3]Cap. 40 of the Charter of 1215; c. 29 of the Charter of 9 Hen. 3. *Nulli vendemus nulli negabimus aut differemus rectum vel justitiam.* See *ante*, p. 20.

[4]Act of Settlement, 12 & 13 Will. 3, c. 2; 1 Geo. 3, c. 23; see *post*, p. 40.

[5]*Commentaries*, 3rd edn. (1768), Book I, p. 268, citing the preamble to 1 Geo. 3, c. 23.

[6]*Lives of the Chief Justices*, 3 vols. (1849-1857).

[7]*Op. cit.*, Vol. III, p. 154.

but that some of them still erred with respect to his second criterion, in the sense that they showed partiality to particular counsel. The gap between precept and practice in the matter of fair trial, which had been so wide at various earlier periods in English history, had narrowed by Lord CAMPBELL'S day, and the extensive legislation which reformed procedure in the nineteenth century reduced it still further. The notion of fair trial, powerfully boosted by the Benthamite doctrine of utility,[1] provided the dynamic in the Reports of the several Common Law Commissions, 1829-1834 and 1851-1860, which recommended these extensive changes in the procedural law. These Commissioners, all senior practising lawyers, included several judges: PARKE, ALDERSON, POLLOCK, WILLES, and COCKBURN. They condemned the law which sanctioned the arrest and imprisonment until trial of a person for an alleged debt on the grounds (a) that when the parties eventually came to trail they would not meet on equal terms, and (b) that " by an inversion of the ordinary course of justice " the creditor is made judge in his own cause, with a power of committing to prison anyone he alleges is his debtor.[2] They approved of some and condemned other rules governing the issue of process and the exchange of pleadings between the parties to a civil action on the ground that fairness required that the parties should each have notice of the allegations made against him by the other and have time to prepare his answer, and thus obviate surprise.[3] When they turned their criticism to the law of evidence it is clear that their basic criterion was that the court should be enabled to arrive at the truth of the facts in the case; thus they approved of the new rule[4] which provided that persons who were parties to a suit were competent as witnesses; and they recommended

---

[1] See *post*, Chap. 6.

[2] First Common Law Commission, 4th Report, Parlt. Papers, 1831-1832, Vol. XXV, p. 27.

[3] First Common Law Commission, 1st Report, Parlt. Papers, 1829, Vol. IX, p. 70; and 3rd Report, Parlt. Papers, 1831, Vol. X, p. 375; Second Common Law Commission, 1st Report, Parlt. Papers, 1851, Vol. XXII, pp. 575-577.

[4] Under the Evidence Act, 1851.

that even spouses should be competent and compellable for and against one another.[1]

The various canons of fair trial enumerated at the beginning of this chapter have become principal articles in the judges' professional creed in modern England. It is a commonplace nowadays in judicial biography to find it recorded that the judge was an ardent exponent of or a scrupulous observer of these principles in the conduct of trials.[2] When the maxim *ruat coelum fiat justitia* is invoked in judicial biography or autobiography, the term *justitia* is used more often than not with precisely this connotation. Lord Justice BOWEN spoke for the modern generation of English judges when he said: " These are not days . . . in which any English judge will fail to assert his right to rise in the proud consciousness that justice is administered in the realms of Her Majesty the Queen, immaculate, unspotted and unsuspected. There is no human being whose smile or frown, there is no Government, Tory or Liberal, whose favour or disfavour can start the pulse of an English judge upon the Bench, or move by one hair's breadth the even equipoise of the scales of justice ".[3] And this is not to be dismissed as empty rhetoric. No charge that a judge in the superior courts in England has deviated from the canons of independence, impartiality or incorruptibility has ever been pressed in Parliament or outside it in the twentieth century.[4]

Though incorruptible the judges are not infallible and the

---

[1]Second Common Law Commission, 2nd Report, Parlt. Papers, 1852-1853, Vol. XL, pp. 713-716.

[2]*E.g.*, Atlay, *The Victorian Chancellors*, 2 vols. (1906-1908), *passim:* Lord HANWORTH, *Lord Chief Baron Pollock, A Memoir* (1929), p. 110.

[3]Cunningham, *Lord Bowen* (1897), p. 175.

[4]A motion for an address to remove McCARDIE, J. from the Bench was put down in the House of Commons in 1924, after *O'Dwyer* v. *Nair* (unreported) in which the judge criticised *adversely* a Cabinet Minister. The motion petered out, and later McCARDIE wrote: " Judges seek no popularity. They will not yield to the passing winds of popular excitement." D.N.B. (1931-1940). The last judge to be charged with corruption was Lord WESTBURY, L.C. in 1865. The House of Commons adjudged him guilty only of laxity and want of caution in the matter of a minor appointment to an *administrative* office. Nevertheless Lord WESTBURY resigned to vindicate the principle that a judge should not only be incorruptible but that no suspicion of corruption should linger around him.

minor deviations from other canons of fairness in trial which inevitably occur are likely to be rectified on appeal to a higher court. So, for instance, recently in *Bartley* v. *Bartley*[1] the judgment of a county court judge, who evidently jumped to a conclusion before he had heard all the evidence and argument on behalf of the plaintiff and discouraged the presentation of the plaintiff's case, was set aside by the Court of Appeal and a retrial of the case by another judge was ordered. Again, in *Jones* v. *National Coal Board*[2] in 1957, a new trial was ordered by the Court of Appeal when it found that in the court of first instance the judge had interfered too frequently in the course of argument by counsel on both sides and had arrogated to himself the function of examining the witnesses. DENNING, L.J., speaking for the whole court, re-affirmed the principles of fair trial.[3] " In the system of trial which we have evolved in this country, the judge is to hear and determine the issues raised by the parties, not to conduct an investigation or examination on behalf of society at large. . . . Truth is best discovered by powerful statements on both sides of the question. Justice is best done by a judge who holds the balance between the contending parties without himself taking part in their disputations . . . (else) he descends into the arena and is liable to have his vision clouded by the dust of the conflict . . .[4] It is for the advocate to state his case as fairly and strongly as he can, without undue interruption, lest the sequence of his argument be lost. . . . The judge's part in all this is to hearken to the evidence . . . and to make up his mind where the truth lies. . . . There is one thing to which everyone in this country is entitled, and that is a fair trial at which he can put his case properly before the judge." Most recently, in *R.* v. *McKenna*[5] the Court of Criminal Appeal had occasion to vindicate the principle that in trial by jury the jury should be absolutely independent and able to deliberate in complete freedom. On trial at

---

[1](1956), *Times*, November 15.
[2][1957] 2 All E.R. 155; [1957] 2 Q.B. 55.
[3][1957] 2 Q.B., at pp. 63-67.
[4]Quoting Lord GREENE, M.R., in *Yuill* v. *Yuill*, [1945] 1 All E.R. 183, at p. 188; [1945] P. 15, at p. 20.
[5][1960] 1 All E R. 326; [1960] 1 Q.B. 411.

Assize the jury had been threatened by the presiding judge
in mid-afternoon that they would all be locked up all night
if they did not reach a verdict within ten minutes. Under the
pressure of this ultimatum the jury did find the accused
guilty within several minutes. Quashing the convictions, the
Court of Criminal Appeal insisted that the principle at stake
was more important that the case itself. These cases demonstrate that in the detached atmosphere of appellate courts
the modern English judges are vigilant in maintaining the
canons of fair trial.

It is not only the judges who cherish this notion of fair
trial. The English Bar is equally vigilant that trials should be
conducted according to these canons of fairness. Several of
the latter, particularly (vi) and (vii), *supra*, modified only to
emphasise the rôle of the advocate, are incorporated in the
strict code of professional etiquette of the Bar[1] and jealously
guarded by the General Council of the Bar and by the
Benchers of the Inns of Court.[2]

Nowadays the English lawyer is prepared to treat these
canons, which have been evolved empirically within his own
system, as if they were of universal validity, and accordingly
to use them as criteria for evaluating the performance of
tribunals elsewhere. So, between the World Wars the Lord
Chief Justice of England, Lord HEWART, led the body of
professional opinion which challenged the wisdom of the
practice, then on the increase, of the Government arrogating
to its own departments the exclusive power of adjudicating
on certain kinds of disputes arising between individuals and
those departments.[3] The argument is fully developed in his
essays on *The New Despotism* (1929). It is summed up in
delightful irony in an extra-judicial speech: " The inhabitants

---

[1]See J. E. Singleton, K.C. *Conduct at the Bar* (1933); and *Beevis
v. Dawson*, [1956] 3 All E.R. 837, at p. 839; [1957] 1 Q.B. 195, at
p. 201, *per* SINGLETON, L.J.

[2]*E.g.*, *Re Marrinan* (1957), *Times*, July 3.

[3]*E.g.*, the Town Planning Act, 1925, s. 7 (3), " If any question
arises whether any building or work contravenes a town planning
scheme . . . that question shall be referred to the Minister, and shall,
unless the parties otherwise agree, be determined by the Minister as
arbitrator, and the decision of the Minister shall be final and conclusive ".

of these islands are within measurable distance of an El
Dorado where there will be no judges at all. In those Isles of
the Blest . . . all controversial questions will be decided in
the third floor back of some one or other Government Department; the decision so reached will not be open to
appeal . . . by any means whatsoever; no party or other
person interested will be permitted to appear or offer any
evidence; the whole law will have been codified in a single
interminable statute . . . no lawyers will be tolerated except
a group of advisers, departmentally appointed; any questions
likely to excite difference of opinion will be submitted to
those advisers beforehand on hypothetical facts and behind
the back of the parties; and the Lord Chancellor himself will
have been exchanged for a Minister of Administration for
whose office any knowledge of law, however slight, will be a
statutory disqualification. Meanwhile, and until that happy
day arrives, our fellow countrymen seem somehow to think
not too unkindly of judicial decisions given in open court
upon real cases by perfectly independent and impartial
judges, who are individually responsible and who have heard
both sides."[1] Further, since the Second World War, an influential association of English lawyers,[2] who have adopted
for themselves the title " Justice ", and whose object is " to
uphold the principles of justice and the right to a fair trial ",
have been using the above canons of fair trial as their criteria
in criticising certain political trials in Eastern Europe and
elsewhere,[3] as well as in proposing reforms within the English
legal system.[4]

§C

Historical precipitates of these canons of fair trial are to

---

[1]*Essays and Observations* (1930), pp. 122-123.

[2]The association was formed *ad hoc* in December, 1956, when
members of the Inns of Court Conservative and Unionist Society, of
the Society of Labour Lawyers and of the Association of Liberal
Lawyers, met to try to secure fair trials for those accused of treason
in Hungary and in South Africa. By June, 1960 it had some 800
lawyers as members, mostly barristers and solicitors but also 74
academic lawyers and 16 judges.

[3]See " Justice ", Annual Reports, June 1958-current.

[4]See *Contempt of Court*, a Report by " Justice " (1959); *Preliminary
Investigations of Criminal Offences*, a Report by " Justice ' '(1960).

be found in several branches of the positive law of England. They have been the guiding principles in the development of many of the modern rules of civil and criminal procedure and of the laws of evidence. Their influence on the lawyers who proposed some of the procedural reforms has already been mentioned;[1] their influence—when boosted by principles of utility—on the system of civil procedure will be considered in some detail in a later chapter.[2] Here it is only proposed to give examples of some doctrines within the provinces of constitutional and administrative law and conflict of laws which are demonstrably the products of this notion of justice as fair trial.

The principle of the independence of the judges has become one of the articles of the uncodified constitution of Great Britain. Originally a provision of the Act of Settlement, 1700, it is now re-enacted in the Supreme Court of Judicature (Consolidation) Act, 1925,[3] that all judges of the High Court and the Court of Appeal shall hold their offices during good behaviour, subject only to a power of removal on an address presented to the Queen by both Houses of Parliament. Besides, the principles of impartiality and the equality of the parties are embodied in the traditional oath, which is now written into a statute[4]: every judge must swear " to do right to all manner of people . . . without fear or favour, affection or ill-will."

The judges in the superior courts in England have not been content to ensure that justice is done, in the sense of conducting fair trials, in their own courts. Exercising a supervisory jurisdiction, derived from the prerogative power of the Crown to do justice throughout the realm, they have insisted that trials in all other tribunals in the kingdom (whether courts of summary jurisdiction, or domestic tribunals within certain trades or professions or within the universities, or administrative tribunals set up as part of the modern machinery

---

[1]*Ante*, pp. 35-36.

[2]*Post*, Chap. 6.

[3]Section 12 (1); *cf.* Appellate Jurisdiction Act, 1876, s. 6, for a similar provision governing Lords of Appeal in Ordinary. Only the Lord Chancellor is outside the protection of these Acts; he is liable to resign or to be dismissed with the Government of the day.

[4]Promissory Oaths Act, 1868, s. 4.

of government) should be conducted according to " the principles of natural justice ". The highest judicial authorities[1] now agree that there are two main principles in this context: the first, that the judges must deal with the question referred to them without bias;[2] and the second, that they must give to each of the parties the opportunity of adequately expressing his case.[3] The use of the term " natural justice " to refer to these principles, though now hallowed by usage, is misleading. Its use has been challenged even in the House of Lords, where Lord SHAW once described it as " a high-sounding expression ", " harmless if it means that a result or process should be just " but otherwise " confusing " or " vacuous ".[4] Certainly it was a strange title for the English

---

[1]*General Medical Council* v. *Spackman*, [1943] 2 All E.R. 337, at p. 340; [1943] A.C. 627, at p. 636, *per* Viscount SIMON, L.C., and at p. 644, *per* Lord WRIGHT; *Local Government Board* v. *Arlidge*, [1915] A.C. 120, at p. 132, *per* Viscount HALDANE, L.C.; *Board of Education* v. *Rice*, [1911] A.C. 179, at p. 182, *per* Lord LOREBURN, L.C.; *Spackman* v. *Plumstead District Board of Works* (1885), 10 App. Cas. 229, at p. 240, *per* Earl of SELBORNE, L.C.

[2]*E.g.*, in *Dimes* v. *Grand Junction Canal Proprietors* (1852), 3 H.L.Cas. 759, the House of Lords set aside a decree made by a Lord Chancellor in a case in which he had some pecuniary interest in a company which was a party to the proceedings. Lord CAMPBELL emphasised that all inferior tribunals should not only take care that in their decrees they were not influenced by personal interest, but should take care to avoid the appearance of labouring under such an interest (*ibid.*, at pp. 793-794). In *R.* v. *Sussex Justices, Ex parte McCarthy*, [1923] All E.R. Rep. 233; [1924] 1 K.B. 256, the King's Bench Division quashed a conviction on the ground that the magistrates retired to deliberate upon their decision with a clerk who as a solicitor was interested in the subject-matter of the case. Lord HEWART, C.J. said: " . . . it is of fundamental importance that justice should not only be done, but should manifestly and un-doubtedly be seen to be done " (*ibid.*, at pp. 234 and 259 respectively).

[3]*E.g.*, In *R.* v. *University of Cambridge* (*Dr. Bentley's Case*) (1723), 1 Stra. 557 the Court of King's Bench restored to Bentley his degree of Doctor of Divinity, which had been improperly suspended by the court of the Vice-Chancellor of Cambridge in a proceeding in which Bentley was not given an opportunity to defend himself. In *Stafford* v. *Minister of Health*, [1946] K.B. 621, an order for the compulsory purchase of land was declared invalid in the High Court as the Minister, acting *quâ* judge, had not given the landowner an adequate opportunity to make a detailed reply to the case presented to the Minister by his opponent, the local authority.

[4]In *Local Government Board* v. *Arlidge*, [1915] A.C. 120, at p. 138.

judges to invoke in the nineteenth century when they otherwise eschewed the doctrine of natural justice proper;[1] for it
was not asserted by them that these principles are universal
and eternal, the dictates of reason or expressions of divine
will, nor have the great exponents of natural law to whom the
English lawyers have paid some attention, as Aquinas, St.
Germain or Locke,[2] included these principles in their
schemes.[3] The use of this exalted title for these principles is a
good example of what Pound has called the ethically idealised
law of the time and place,[4] for these principles are two of the
leading canons of fair trial then realised in judicial practice
in the superior English courts—the familiar canons of
impartiality and *audi alteram partem*.

A similar development is to be observed within the
doctrine of conflict of laws. It is an established axiom in that
branch of English law " that a foreign judgment which contravenes the principles of natural justice cannot be enforced
in England ".[5] According to the stream of decided cases on
this matter " the principles of natural justice " in point resolve into two: the first, that the foreign court should have
given notice to the litigant that they were about to proceed
to determine the case and that he should be afforded an
opportunity of substantially presenting his case before the
court;[6] and the second, that the judge in the foreign court
should not himself have any interest in the proceedings.[7]

---

[1]See *post*, Chap. 4.

[2]Locke actually argued the contrary, *viz.* that the law of nature
authorises men to be judges and executioners in defence of their own
natural rights: *Second Treatise on Government* (1690), §§ 7, 8 and 13.

[3]But Hobbes included as precepts of natural law (1) " that no
man is a fit arbitrator in his own cause " and (2) " that no man is to
be a judge that has in him a natural cause of partiality ": *Leviathan*
(1651), Chap. 15. The pedigree of these canons of " natural justice "
is traced in de Smith, *Judicial Review of Administrative Action* (1959),
at pp. 102-103 and 137-140.

[4]Roscoe Pound, *Law and Morals*, 2nd edn. (1926), p. 88.

[5]Dicey, *Conflict of Laws*, 6th edn. (1949), rule 79; *cf.* 7th edn. (1958),
pp. 1010-1012. *Cf.* Cheshire, *Private International Law*, 5th edn.
(1957), p. 642.

[6]*Jacobson* v. *Frachon* (1927), 44 T.L.R. 103, at p. 105, *per* ATKIN,
L.J.; *Fisher* v. *Lane* (1772), 3 Wils. 297; *Buchanan* v. *Rucker* (1808),
1 Camp. 63, 180; *Bruce* v. *Wait* (1840), 1 Man. & G. 1; *Rudd* v.
Rudd, [1923] All E.R. Rep. 637; [1924] P. 72.

[7]*Price* v. *Dewhurst* (1837), 8 Sim. 279.

Again the misleading technical title of " natural justice " was attached to these principles by the judges in the middle of the nineteenth century.[1] In the earlier cases the judges were content to condemn foreign judgments on the above grounds as " contrary to all notions of justice ",[2] or as " contrary to the first principles of justice ".[3] The principles of justice in point were the two familiar canons, *audi alteram partem*, and impartiality, which the English judges had come to regard as essential to a fair trial.

§D

Adverse criticism of these canons of fair trial has not fallen from the common lawyers themselves[4] at least since the controversy over procedural law in the first half of the nineteenth century. No judge, counsel, solicitor or academic lawyer in the twentieth century in England would deny that justice involves at the very least that trials of civil disputes and criminal charges should be conducted fairly. At the same time there is room for disagreement amongst the lawyers as to the definition, the scope and the priority *inter se* of the canons of fair trial. For instance, should the canon which

---

[1]*Vallee* v. *Dumergue* (1849), 4 Exch. 290. The title survived the well-merited onslaught of BLACKBURN, J., in *Schibsby* v. *Westenholz* (1870), L.R. 6 Q.B. 155, at p. 160, that it was no more than " declamation ".

[2]*Price* v. *Dewhurst, supra*, at p. 308.

[3]*Fisher* v. *Lane, supra*, at p. 303.

[4]Very exceptionally a lawyer's voice is still raised challenging the justice of the proceedings in the modern English courts. For instance, C. P. Harvey, Q.C., in *The Advocate's Devil* (1958) has condemned as unjust *inter alia*, (i) the judge who jumps to his conclusions before he has heard all the evidence, (ii) the counsel whose cross-examination descends into browbeating of witnesses to a degree unnecessary for eliciting the truth of relevant matters, and the judge who permits this practice, and (iii) the procedure which licenses a powerful advocate to overwhelm or outmanoeuvre his opponent by sheer technical skill. But it is to be observed that these criticisms assume as the criteria of justice that the judge before he comes to a decision should hear and consider all that the parties have to say, and that the court is concerned only with the search for the truth of the matter in issue, and that *each* side should state its case strongly, without distorting the truth—the very canons of fair trial.

requires trials to be conducted in public be implemented in preliminary hearings in criminal trials, when publication of the evidence for the prosecution in newspapers is likely to prejudice the jury at full trial, and thus violate the canon that they as judges should consider only the evidence adduced at that trial?[1]

To the layman some features of the system of trials in England have seemed to be eminently unfair, and his doubts have been echoed within the legal profession.[2] So it is maintained that it is improper that an experienced advocate should use his acquired skill to the full to defend a man in whose innocence he does not believe. Similarly it is contended that it is grossly unfair for counsel to take every possible technical point within the procedural law to secure victory for his client, irrespective of his opinion of the merits of his client's case. As often as advanced these arguments have been met by the typical common lawyer with the answer credited to Dr. Johnson: " The justice or the injustice of the cause is to be decided by the judge. Consider, Sir, what is the purpose of the courts of justice. It is that every man shall have his cause fairly tried by men appointed to try causes. A lawyer . . . is not to usurp the functions of the jury or judge, and determine what shall be the effect of evidence, what shall be the result of legal argument. . . . A lawyer is to do for his client all that his client might fairly do for himself, if he could."[3]

Most common lawyers, while affirming that justice involves the notion of fair trial, would concede that a system of judicature in which trials are regularly conducted in accordance with the various canons of fairness is not the whole of their doctrine of justice. Adjudication should not only be fair, it

---

[1]E.g., in R. v. Adams (1957), Times, April 9, DEVLIN, J., speaking with the approval of Lord GODDARD, C.J., censured the Eastbourne magistrates for refusing the application of the defence that some of the sensational evidence in an accusation of murder should be heard in camera. See Report of the Tucker Committee on Proceedings before Examining Magistrates (1958), Cmnd. 479.

[2]Harvey, The Advocate's Devil, supra.

[3]Quoted by Lord BIRKETT in " Advocacy " (1954): an address published by the Holdsworth Club of the University of Birmingham, at p. 7; cf. Joshua Williams in Letters to John Bull, Esq., on Lawyers and Law Reform (1857), pp. 24-25.

should be made by judges or juries directing their judgment in accordance with some ascertainable general rules. As to which rules should be the basis of judgment, whether rules of natural law or moral doctrine or established rules of law, there is a variety of opinions. So notions such as natural justice or moral justice or legal justice are linked with the notion of fair trial in many a lawyer's complete working philosophy of justice. These notions will be considered separately in the succeeding chapters. Nevertheless, the typical modern English lawyer, if driven to choose between the notions of fair trial and one of these further notions, is emphatic that the former is indispensable.[1]

---

[1] *E.g.*, Lord HANWORTH, *Lord Chief Baron Pollock, A Memoir* (1929), p. 141; *Esso Petroleum Co., Ltd.* v. *Southport Corporation*, [1955] 3 All E.R. 864; [1956] A.C. 218.

CHAPTER 4

NATURAL JUSTICE

§A

In England, as in other civilised countries, some men have conceived of justice as an absolute value. Of those who have subscribed to such a sublime concept some reach out to it as an idea representing the ideal order in human relations, but an ineffable idea resisting men's efforts to fix it within the limited resources of language. Others, and these have constituted a major school of thought, contend that the idea though absolute is approximately reducible to propositions, and that broadly speaking justice is a state of human affairs in which men in their private lives and their social lives conform to a series of ascertainable precepts and principles which are universal, eternal and immutable—precepts and principles which in English have been traditionally called natural law.[1]

---

[1] In English the precepts and principles have long been labelled natural *law*. The corresponding titles in other languages—φυσικὸν δίκαιον, *jus naturale, droit naturel, Naturrecht*—are less misleading than the English title, for they are patently ambiguous, and may be immediately understood as referring to an ethical as well as to a legal doctrine. The English title is less obviously ambiguous and the English reader must constantly remind himself that the doctrine referred to is primarily *ethical*. An exponent of natural justice, urging that XY is a precept of natural law is not saying that XY is a rule recognised in a specific community as binding and administered in the courts of that community and enforced by its executive; rather he is saying that XY is a precept which ought to be so implemented in that and in every other community. In English the term natural *right* would have more aptly described the doctrine in question. In 1895 in 11 L.Q.R. pp. 121, *et seq*. Salmond belatedly pleaded for the use of the term " Natural Right " with this connotation. But the term " natural law " has passed into the English language (probably from the Scholastic use of the terms *lex naturalis* and *lex naturae*) and is now inveterate, however misleading.

Our concern is with the English lawyers who have subscribed to this transcendental theory of natural justice.

Though natural justice is a concept which has been expounded by philosophers, theologians and jurists over at least the last two thousand years, and its exponents have regarded it as an absolute value, still it must be conceded that historically it has admitted of several interpretations.[1] The many who have professed a belief in natural justice have differed both as to the means of ascertaining its precepts and as to the contents of the precepts thus ascertained. However, not all the versions of natural justice concern us, as the common lawyers of England have remained indifferent to many of them. For instance, the theory of natural justice (φυσικὸν δίκαιον) indicated by Aristotle[2] and developed by the Stoic philosophers in Greece and at Rome and expressed so vividly by Cicero,[3] has evidently made little impression on English lawyers, even on those reared on *literae humaniores*. The early Christian theory[4] of natural law as the eternal law of God, revealed to man in the gospels and by the prophets has had a more noticeable influence. The later mediaeval theory,[5] propounded by the scholastic philosophers, which blends Christian doctrine with Aristotelian moral philosophy, has been the most prominent within the English legal profession. And the English lawyers have not been entirely indifferent to, though they have stoutly resisted complete conversion to, the rationalist theories of natural justice advanced by their native philosophers Hobbes[6] and Locke[7]

---

[1]The world's literature on this subject is immense. In English the student will find synopses in Friedmann, *Legal Theory*, 4th edn. (1960), Chaps. 5-12, and in Lloyd, *Introduction to Jurisprudence* (1959), Chap. 3, a fuller discussion in D'Entrèves, *Natural Law* (1951) and a comparatively full bibliography in Del Vecchio, *Justice*, English edn., ed. Campbell (1952).

[2]*Nicomachean Ethics*, Book V, Chap. VII, §§ 1-5; *Rhetoric*, Book I, Chap. XIII, § 2.

[3]*De Re Publica*, Book III; *De Legibus*, Book I.

[4]St. Augustine, *De Civitate Dei*; St. Isidore, *Etymologies*; Gratian, *Decretum*.

[5]See *post*, pp. 49-53.

[6]*Elements of Law, Natural and Politic* (completed 1640, published circa 1650), Chaps. 14-18; *Leviathan* (1651), Chaps. 14-15.

[7]*Essays on the Law of Nature* (completed circa 1660, published 1954, ed. von Leyden); *Treatises of Civil Government* (1690), §§ 6-24.

in the seventeenth century. Besides the notion which links the law of nature with the *jus gentium*[1]—the positive law common to various states—has been invoked very occasionally by the English judge and jurist.[2] The philosophy of natural justice which has flourished on the European continent since Kant, and which has produced significant juridical versions of natural law in the works of German, French and Italian jurists, has made very little impression on the practitioners or even on the professors of English law, and accordingly falls outside the scope of this enquiry.

To examine in any detail even the few versions of natural justice which have had some currency within the English legal profession would involve extensive wandering through the mazes of metaphysics and passing and repassing along some of the tracks. Some of the precepts in, say, the early Christian doctrine are to be found in the Scholastic doctrine as well as in the rationalist schemes of natural law set out by Hobbes and Locke.[3] But the schemes of precepts offered by the various exponents of natural law are far from identical: some of the precepts laid down by St. Germain's Doctor are not to be found in Aquinas' scheme or that of Hooker, and the schemes postulated by Hobbes and Locke do not tally *inter se*[4] or with those given by the theologians. It is proposed only to isolate the theological doctrine of natural justice, which has in the long run proved to be the most influential amongst the English lawyers, and to set out some of the precepts which are common to several of the theological schemes.

---

[1] Gaius, *Institutes*, Book I, 1; Justinian, *Digest* I, i, 1, and *Institutes* I, ii, 1.

[2] *E.g.*, *Carrier's Case* (1473), Y.B. 13 Ed. IV, reported in S.S. Vol. 64, p. 30.

[3] *E.g.*, the precept " do to other men all that you would have them do to you ", which is given in St. Matthew, vii, 12 (Knox), and in St. Luke, vi, 31, appears in St. Germain's *Dialogues* (1532) I, Chap. 2 as one of the primary precepts urged by his Doctor of Divinity, and the negative form of it, " do not that to another which thou wouldst not have done to thyself ", is treated by Hobbes in *Leviathan* (1651) ed. Oakeshott (1946) Chap. 15, p. 103, as epitomising his many laws of nature.

[4] *E.g.*, in *Leviathan* Hobbes postulated some eighteen laws of nature, most of which have no counterpart in the scheme of natural rights laid down by Locke in *Treatises of Civil Government*.

The theory of natural justice which the English lawyer St. Germain[1] in the early sixteenth century attributed to his Doctor of Divinity in his *Dialogues*,[2] may be taken as a typical formulation of the theological concept of natural justice. It substantially corresponds with the classical Catholic doctrine formulated by Aquinas in the thirteenth century[3] and has many features in common with that expounded to Englishmen by the Protestant Anglican theologian, Hooker, in the late sixteenth century.[4]

The basic assumptions in this doctrine are that God exists and that immanent in all creation is God's eternal law. St. Germain's Doctor defines the eternal law as

" the reason of the wisdom of God, moving all things by wisdom made to a good end."[5]

The eternal law is not wholly known to men. It is known in part through revelation, as recorded in the New and Old Testaments, that part being called the law of God or positive divine law; and it is known further through reason, that part being called the law of nature or the law of reason.[6] So, natural law is unequivocally established on a divine basis. Since it is part of God's will or plan for mankind natural law is neither parochial or temporary. According to the Doctor of Divinity

" This law ought to be kept as well among Jews and Gentiles, as among Christian men . . . it is never changeable by no diversity of place, ne time."[7]

---

[1] 1460-1540; Barrister of the Inner Temple.

[2] *Two Dialogues Between a Doctor of Divinity and a Student in the Laws of England.* (1st Dialogue published in Latin *circa* 1523; 2nd Dialogue published in English 1530; revised edition of both published in English in 1532.) Citations are from the reprint of 1709.

[3] *Summa Theologica* (*circa* 1270). Vinogradoff, in " Reason and Conscience in 16th Century Jurisprudence ", 24 L.Q.R. 373-384, shows how closely St. Germain's exposition corresponded to the Scholastic pattern laid down by Aquinas, though St. Germain actually drew directly on the works of John Gerson (*circa* 1364-1429) rather than on Aquinas.

[4] *Of the Laws of Ecclesiastical Polity* (1593-1597).

[5] St. Germain, *op. cit.*, I, Chap. 1; *cf.* Aquinas, *op. cit.*, I-II, 93; and Hooker, *op. cit.*, I, Chap. III.

[6] St. Germain, *op. cit.*, I, Chap. 1; *cf.* Aquinas, *op. cit.*, I-II, 91, 2; Hooker, *op. cit.*, I, Chap. III.

[7] St. Germain, *op. cit.*, I, Chap. 2.

According to these theologians the knowledge of this law is acquired by the exercise of human reason. As the Doctor expressed it: this part of the will of God is known to his creatures reasonable " by the light of natural understanding, or by the light of natural reason ".[1] This natural reason he explains more fully as a human power which responds to the highest faculty of man's soul which inclines him to seek good and abhor evil: the power which implements that inclination by actually distinguishing between good and evil, between good and better, between true and false.[2] Thus, the reason which these theologians rely on is not simply that mental power of perceiving the relations between propositions but also the mental power of appreciating the truth of certain propositions immediately, *i.e.* intuitively.

Accordingly, reason is said to give men knowledge of the following primary or truly fundamental precepts:

I " Good is to be loved and evil is to be fled."[3]

II " Do to another that thou wouldst another should do to thee."[4]

III " Do nothing against truth."[5]

IV " A man must live peacefully with others."[6]

V Men should live in society.[7]

VI Actions by which human life is to be preserved are to be pursued.[8]

VII Male and female should join together and children be educated.[9]

Besides, their reason dictated to these theologians various secondary precepts, deducible from one or more of the pri-

---

[1] St. Germain, *op. cit.*, I, Chap. 1.

[2] St. Germain, *op. cit.*, I, Chaps. 13 and 14; Hooker, *op. cit.*, I, Chap. VIII; Copleston, *Aquinas* (1955), p. 213.

[3] St. Germain, *op. cit.*, I, Chap. 2; Aquinas, *op. cit.*, I-II, 94, 2; Hooker, *op. cit.*, I, Chap. VIII, 5.

[4] St. Germain, *op. cit.*, I, Chap. 2; Hooker, *op. cit.*, I, Chap. VIII, 5.

[5] St. Germain, *op. cit.*, I, Chap. 2; Aquinas, *op. cit.*, I-II, 94, 2.

[6] St. Germain, *op. cit.*, I, Chap. 2; Aquinas, *op. cit.*, I-II, 94, 2.

[7] Aquinas, *op. cit.*, I-II, 94, 2.

[8] Aquinas, *op. cit.*, I-II, 94, 2.

[9] Aquinas, *op. cit.*, I-II, 94, 2; Hooker, *op. cit.*, V, Chap. LXXIII.

mary precepts. For example, from the primary precept concerning marriage [VII, *supra*] the theologians deduced several general canons for marriage such as:

(a) that matrimony be limited to the union of one man with one woman[1];

(b) that matrimony be altogether indissoluble.[2]

These theologians were far from maintaining that these precepts were exhaustive of the principles of justice. In the first place, overlapping but reaching beyond such principles ascertained by reason remained the positive divine law, given to man by God through Christ as recorded in the New Testament and through the old prophets as recorded in the Old Testament, a perennial source of principles for the regulation of human affairs. In the second place, they acknowledged that reason operating in the conscience of men would dictate a myriad of more particular principles and rules in particular circumstances.

Nor were such precepts as those set out above regarded as definitive of the principles of justice. In the mediaeval world and in the sixteenth century there was no doctrine of papal or doctorial infallibility. To the theologians who formulated them, even to Aquinas, they were at best approximate expressions of fragments of a sublime concept, the eternal law of God.

These precepts of the positive divine law and the natural law, though they were urged as relevant to a wide range of human relations, were not regarded as prescribing rules for every social problem. The theologians admitted that there remained a considerable range of social problems to which these precepts offer no solution, questions the solution of which are morally indifferent. In dealing with the latter type of question they were prepared to admit that the criterion of justice was to be sought elsewhere than in the natural law.

This doctrine was advanced not only as part of a system of theology but also as part of an ethical system. But ethical principles apply not only to the private life of individuals but also to their social life. Therefore the doctrine was offered to

---

[1]Aquinas, *Summa Contra Gentiles*, III, 124; Copleston, *Aquinas* (1955), p. 218.

[2]Aquinas, *op. cit.*, III, 123; Hooker, *op. cit.*, V, Chap. LXXIII.

those who control public affairs, statesmen, legislators and lawyers. For them the doctrine could serve three main purposes:

(α) The precepts of natural law could be invoked to provide major premisses for legislation.

(β) Besides, these precepts could be used as the criteria for simply evaluating positive laws, without reference to the validity or obligation of the laws in question. Thus an established law in a given community could be adjudged just if it is consistent with these precepts, or unjust if it is contrary to them.

(γ) Further, they might be used not only as criteria of the justice but also of the validity or obligation of positive laws. Thus a law in a given community which is contrary to a precept of natural law could be adjudged not only unjust but also invalid and not binding on the members of the community.

St. Germain's Doctor of Divinity was prepared to affirm the last-mentioned, revolutionary function of natural law. Considering the fundamental question of the obligation of the unjust law, he answered peremptorily:

" Against this law [natural law] prescription, statute nor custom may not prevail, and if any be brought in against it, they be not prescriptions, statutes nor customs, but things void and against justice . . ."[1]

He was no doubt relying on the pronouncement of Aquinas that

" every human law has the nature of law in so far as it is derived from the law of nature. If in any case it is incompatible with the natural law, it will not be law, but a perversion of law."[2]

But he overlooked the important qualification added by the angelic Doctor which tempers the revolutionary character of the answer,

" that unjust laws do not bind in conscience unless observance of them is required to avoid scandal or public disturbance for which cause a man should even yield his right."[3]

The judicious Hooker gives an even less revolutionary

---

[1] St. Germain, *op. cit.*, I, Chap. 2.
[2] Aquinas, *Summa Theologica*, I-II, 95, 2.
[3] Aquinas, *op. cit.*, I-II, 96, 4.

answer. Laws, he says, which are apparently good are things
copied out of the very tables of eternal law. Laws not
apparently good should nevertheless be treated with respect,
lest unknown to us they are after all in accordance with
the eternal law. " Surely there must be very manifest
iniquity in laws, against which we shall be able to justify
our contumelious invectives." Rather, positive laws must be
obeyed unless it can be demonstrated convincingly that the
laws of reason or of God enjoin the contrary. " Because
except our own private and but probable resolutions be by
the law of public determinations over-ruled, we take away
all possibility of sociable life in the world."[1]

§B

Doctrines of natural justice were more prominent in
English legal thinking in the earlier centuries of the common
law than they have been in the nineteenth and twentieth
centuries.

The theological doctrine of natural justice, outlined above,
was an integral part of Christian dogma in Western Europe
in the later Middle Ages, and the English lawyers were
Christians. Indeed in the first phase of the history of the
common law, in the twelfth and thirteenth centuries, most
of the royal judges were clerics.[2] Later, when the professional
lawyers were being schooled in their Inns, so one of them tells
us,[3] they occupied themselves with holy scripture as well as
legal science. The old Inns of Court have been described as
" the university and church militant of the common law ",[4]
in which the law of nature or reason was taught and disputed
along with the law of the land. In the thirteenth century,
BRACTON, who was prelate as well as judge and jurist, opened
his great legal treatise[5] with the firm acknowledgement of

---

[1]Hooker, *op. cit.*, I, Chap. XVI.
[2]Pollock & Maitland, *History of English Law*, I, 132-133.
[3]FORTESCUE, *De Laudibus Legum Anglie* (written *circa* 1470;
printed 1546: ed. Chrimes (1942), Chap. XLIX.
[4]O'Sullivan, *Inheritance of the Common Law* (1950), p. 16.
[5]*De Legibus et Consuetudinibus Angliae* (*circa* 1256), ed. Woodbine,
Vol. II, pp. 22-23.

God as the author of justice and with statements of several of the primary precepts which we have listed earlier as the criteria of natural justice. In the fifteenth century FORTESCUE, after nearly twenty years as Chief Justice of the King's Bench (1442-1461), writing in exile on English law, taught his young prince that the law of nature, alias divine law, as revealed in the Old and New Testaments, was one of the main sources of English law.[1] A contemporary judge, YELVERTON, could argue in the Court of King's Bench that they ought in a novel case to resort to the law of nature, which is the ground of all laws.[2] Indeed, the old serjeants-at-law, from among whom most of the judges were recruited from the early fourteenth century onwards, were sworn in to give counsel according to law " that is to say, the law of God, the law of reason and the law of the land ".[3] To our modern eyes the significant factor is that the mediaeval lawyer did not distinguish as sharply as we do between religion, ethics and positive law.

St. Germain's *Dialogues Between a Doctor of Divinity and a Student in the Laws of England* epitomise two of the main streams of legal thought in the sixteenth century. As we have seen, the Doctor expounded the theological doctrine of natural justice, emphasising the rôle of conscience in the decision of concrete cases according to the law of God and the law of nature. St. Germain's Doctor was but expressing the fundamental notions which had been guiding the ecclesiastical Chancellors in the relatively new Court of Chancery and which were to guide lay Chancellors and Chancery lawyers in the succeeding generations.[4] Plowden, " perhaps the most learned lawyer in a century of learned lawyers ",[5] stands out as one committed to this scholastic doctrine of natural justice,[6] and Sir THOMAS MORE, Lord Chancellor from 1529-1532, as a martyr to it.[7] St. Germain's Student, in reply

---

[1] *De Laudibus Legum Anglie*, Chaps. I-XVI.

[2] Y.B. 8 Edw. IV (1469) Mich. Term, pl. 9; *cf.* Y.B. 4 Hen. VII (1489) Hil. Term, pl. 8.

[3] O'Sullivan, *Under God and the Law* (1949), xvii.

[4] See Holdsworth, *History of English Law* Vol. V, pp. 266-269.

[5] Holdsworth, *op. cit.*, Vol. V, p. 372.

[6] See *Edmund Plowden* (1518-1585) *A Reading*, O'Sullivan (1952).

[7] See *The King's Good Servant* (1948), papers read to Thomas More Society of London.

to the Doctor's argument, conceded that the first two of the six grounds of the law of England were the law of reason and the law of God.[1] Only he emphasised the different terminology in the common lawyers' vocabulary: " It is not used among them that be learned in the laws of England to reason what thing is commanded or prohibited by the law of nature, and what not, but all the reasoning in that behalf is under this manner. As when any thing is grounded upon the law of nature, they say, that reason will that such a thing be done: and if it be prohibited by the law of nature, they say it is against reason." The Student does not define his essential term " reason ", but the central meaning in the context is evidently " self-evident moral propositions ". The Student goes on to lay down the primary precepts of the law of reason, under such titles as murder, perjury, deceit and breaking the peace, which in substance correspond with those laid down by the Doctor, and to give instances of secondary precepts under their traditional legal titles as prohibitions on disseisins, trespasses and theft. He explains that such reasoning from primary to secondary precepts is not much used by the common lawyer, whose arguments are mostly directed to the technicalities of the secondary precepts, the primary precepts being assumed as matters of common and elementary knowledge. The Student is far from paying mere lip-service to these laws of reason and of God, for when he proceeds to set out the other four grounds of the law of England—general customs, maxims, particular customs and statutes, in that order—he is careful to affirm that these four are only valid if they offend neither the law of God nor the law of reason[2] and throughout the dialogue he tests particular laws against the dictates of conscience informed by these fundamental precepts. Plainly the Student uses these precepts as the principal criteria of justice. If the Doctor spoke for the Chancery lawyers of the day, the Student spoke with the authentic voice of the typical member of the Inns of Court and the common law Bench.[3] It is

---

[1]*Doctor and Student*, I, Chaps. 5 and 6.
[2]*Op. cit.*, I, Chaps. 6-11.
[3]Pollock, " History of the Law of Nature " in *Essays in the Law* (1922), pp. 57-58.

obvious that there is much in common between the theories of justice advanced by the Doctor and the Student: they are complementary rather than contradictory. But there is a difference in emphasis if not in essence: where the Doctor emphasises the will of God, the Student relies on the dictates of common reason: we may say the one expounds natural justice, the other moral justice;[1] and we cannot but observe how the one notion shades into the other.

After the Reformation in England the judges continued, on occasions, to invoke the natural law or law of reason, but the tide of natural law was running out. In 1608, according to COKE, in the great legal debate in the Court of King's Bench and in the Exchequer Chamber in *Calvin's Case*[2] not only counsel but the judges unhesitatingly based one of their main arguments on the law of nature. This "law" they regarded as part of God's eternal law, immutable, infused into the heart of man, antecedent to all municipal law, eventually a ground of all municipal law and therefore part of the law of England.[3] Chief Justice COKE himself resorted to the concept of natural justice to buttress an argument in his judgment in *Dr. Bonham's Case*[4]: "For when an Act of Parliament is against common right and reason . . . the common law will controul it, and adjudge such Act to be void"[5]— a highly controversial proposition in his own day and since.[6] Another Chief Justice, HOBART, accepted this contention and its natural law basis only a few years later.[7] And under the Commonwealth, KEBLE, J., did once say indignantly in a treason trial: "There is no law in England but is as really and truly the law of God as any Scripture phrase. . . . For there are very many consequences reasoned out of the texts of Scripture: so is the law of England the very consequence of the decalogue itself; and whatsoever is not consonant to Scripture in the law of England is not the law of England."[8]

---

[1]See *post*, Chap. 5.

[2](1608), 7 Co. Rep. 1a.

[3]*Ibid.*, 12b.

[4](1610), 8 Co. Rep. 114.

[5]*Ibid.*, at 118a.

[6]See Plucknett, " Bonham's Case and Judicial Review " 40 H.L.R. 30-70 (1926).

[7]*Day* v. *Savadge* (1614), Hob. 85, at p. 87.

[8]*R.* v. *Love* (1651), 5 State Tr. 43, at pp. 171-172.

But these are exceptional *dicta* in this century and political motives can be detected behind most of them. The doctrine of natural justice is receding into the background of orthodox legal philosophy.

It is true that in the late eighteenth century BLACKSTONE in the introductory part of his *Commentaries on the Laws of England*, addressed to students at Oxford but destined to reach generations of common lawyers, expounded the doctrine of the law of nature in terms to which a disciple of Aquinas could hardly take exception: " Man as a creature must necessarily be subject to the laws of his creator. . . . This will of his maker is called the law of nature. . . . God laid down certain immutable laws of human nature . . . and gave him the faculty of reason to discover the purport of those laws . . . laws founded in those relations of justice, that existed antecedent to any positive precept . . . the eternal, immutable laws of good and evil."[1] BLACKSTONE gives as instances the three great classical precepts: live honestly; hurt nobody; render to every one his due. Besides, as man's reason is but an imperfect means of ascertaining the divine will, divine interposition has given us the divine or revealed law. " Upon these two foundations, the law of nature and the law of revelation, depend all human laws ", though, BLACK-STONE adds, these two leave many points open for settlement by human laws. Thus BLACKSTONE reproduces the traditional theological doctrine of natural justice, presumably to *justify* the positive law of England—or large sections of it—to a Christian audience, and possibly to offer a basis for future legislation. He does not attempt to prove historically that the law of England derived from these doctrines.

On the fundamental question, whether the positive law which offends natural law is binding, BLACKSTONE in his In-troduction reproduced the theologians' answer: " This law of nature, being co-eval with mankind and dictated by God himself is of course superior in obligation to any other. It is binding . . . in all countries, at all times; no human laws are of any validity if contrary to this. . . ."[2] To be consistent

---

[1]*Commentaries* (1765), 3rd edn. (1768), Introduction, § 2, pp. 39-43.
[2]*Ibid.*, p. 41.

BLACKSTONE must go on to maintain that customs, precedent
decisions and Acts of Parliament which offend natural law or
divine law are not binding on the English judges. But he was
only prepared to take a few steps along this road to revolu-
tion. He laid it down that a custom which offended the law
of nature or Divine law would not be recognised by the judges
as part of the law of England.[1] With regard to precedent
decisions of courts, BLACKSTONE taught that the general rule
that they be followed admitted of an exception " where the
former determination is most evidently contrary to reason;
much more if it be contrary to the divine law. . . ."[2] But
when he came to consider directly the obligation of statute-
law BLACKSTONE abandoned the theologians' answer altogether. After stressing that wherever possible the judges
should endeavour to interpret an Act of Parliament in conformity with reason, he admitted finally that " if the parliament will positively enact a thing to be done which is
unreasonable, I know of no power that can control it . . . for
that were to set the judicial power above that of the legislature, which would be subversive of all government ".[3]

BLACKSTONE's final answer to the problem of the obligation
of the unjust statute was undoubtedly representative of the
opinion of all English lawyers in his day. Since the Revolu-
tion of 1688 it was hardly possible for a lawyer to challenge
the axiom of the legislative supremacy of Parliament in the
English constitution.[4] Indeed, it had been a tacit principle of
the constitution, since the Reformation, if not before, that
an Act of Parliament was absolutely binding in the English
legal system. In the passages cited above from *R. v. Love* in
1651, KEBLE, J., was indulging in rhetoric, not pronouncing
any specific Act of Parliament to be invalid. And in *Bonham's
Case* (1610), while COKE said that an Act of Parliament

---

[1]*Ibid.*, § 3, pp. 69-70, 77.
[2]*Ibid.*, p. 70.
[3]*Ibid.*, p. 91.
[4]Holdsworth, *History of English Law*, Vol. IV, p. 186. The *dicta*
to the contrary attributed to HOLT, C.J., in *City of London* v. *Wood*
(1701), 12 Mod. Rep. 669, at pp. 687-688, may have been the gloss of
the reporter: other *dicta* in the same report also attributed to HOLT
are contradictory. At all events HOLT did not pronounce the statute
in question to be void.

which was against common right and reason would be void, he refrained from pronouncing the legislation in question[1] to be devoid of legal effect.[2] It is true that in the throes of the Reformation a former Lord Chancellor, Sir THOMAS MORE, did pronounce that an Act of Parliament directly repugnant to the laws of God and his Holy Church and against the law of reason was not binding on him,[3] but he did so, not from the Woolsack but as a prisoner after conviction for treason. Indeed it is extremely doubtful whether any English lawyer before BLACKSTONE ever actually acted on the axiom of the theologians, that a statute which was unjust by the criteria of natural law was devoid of obligation.[4] Certainly since BLACKSTONE no English lawyer has seriously maintained that the obligation of Acts of Parliament may be qualified by the doctrine of natural justice. When last counsel attempted to question the validity of even a private Act in the courts in 1871, WILLES, J., rejected emphatically the possibility of judicial review of parliamentary legislation: " I would observe, as to these Acts of Parliament, that they are the law of this land; and we do not sit here as a court of appeal from Parliament."[5]

After BLACKSTONE not only did the lawyers cease to invoke natural justice as a doctrine capable of qualifying the obligation of positive law; they ceased to invoke it to justify the positive law or as a source of inspiration for the reform of the law. At the beginning of the nineteenth century natural law thinking was at its lowest ebb. A solitary English treatise on natural law[6] aroused little interest. The effect of the

---

[1]The Charter of the College of Physicians, as confirmed by 14 Hen. 3, c. 5.

[2]Plucknett has shown that of the older cases which COKE cited in support of his *dictum* none precisely supports it: 40 H.L.R. 30-70.

[3]See *Under God and the Law*, ed. O'Sullivan (1949), xx.

[4]" There is not, so far as I am aware, a single example in our books of the courts rejecting the plain and express provisions of a statute on the ground that it was contrary to any ethical principle ": Allen, *Law in the Making*, 6th edn. (1958) at p. 435.

[5]*Lee* v. *Bude and Torrington Junction Rly. Co., Ex parte Stevens, Ex parte Fisher* (1871), L.R. 6 C.P. 576, at p. 582.

[6]Thomas, *Treatise on Universal Jurisprudence* (1828). Lorimer's *Institutes of Law, A Treatise on the Principles of Jurisprudence as determined by Nature* (1872), had little popularity south of the Scottish border. See Pollock's comments, *post*, p. 71.

various assaults on the efficacy of reason and consequently
on the theory of natural law delivered by Hume, Bentham
and Austin[1] was virtually to obliterate the notion[2] from the
common lawyers' thinking during the nineteenth and well
into the twentieth century.

The maxim *naturam expelles furca, tamen usque recurret*,
which seems to be disproved by the condition of English
thought in the nineteenth century, is vindicated again by
developments in the twentieth. Again some English lawyers
are reaching out to an absolute doctrine of justice and dis-
cerning the criteria in the form of cognizable, eternal, immutable and universal principles, revealed to men through
Christianity supplemented by human intelligence. The
cataclysms of two world wars may be responsible for this
re-orientation.

Sir HENRY SLESSER, a Lord Justice of Appeal from 1929
to 1940, has in recent years declared himself an apostle of the
theological version of natural justice. In various theological
and political essays he has re-examined some fundamental
religious problems and has found Aquinas' answers still un-
surpassed.[3] In essays on the judicial office,[4] written after his
retirement from the Court of Appeal, he reveals his sensitivity
to the claims of legal justice, moral justice, and social justice,
but he gives priority to the claims of natural justice. Looking
back on judicial practice, he described how some judges still
have recourse sometimes to the transcendental method:
" The true principal transcendent notions which have in
greater or less degree influenced the judiciary for the most
part have been Christianity and the natural law. . . . The
judges, being for the most part Christians, and England still

---

[1] See *post*, pp. 70-71.

[2] But not the terminology. The term " natural justice " is still used
to justify items of judicial legislation, though the judge does not
profess to rely on reason or any of the primary precepts or on
revelation; *e.g.*, in *Valentini* v. *Canali* (1889), 24 Q.B.D. 166, and in
the many cases in which the judges have asserted control over
inferior tribunals: see *ante*, pp. 41-42.

[3] *The Judicial Office and Other Matters* (1943); *Order and Disorder:
A Study of Mediaeval Principles* (1945).

[4] *The Judicial Office*, pp. 106-149. *Cf.* " The Art of Judgment ",
Haldane Memorial Lecture, 1950; *The Administration of the Law*
(1949), Chap. IV.

presumably a Christian country, it is suggested that appeal to the Christian standard as ultimate, even if only sub-conscious, is far more insistent among judges than many modern writers on jurisprudence would have us believe."[1] At least his own judgment in the Court of Appeal in *Re Carroll (No. 2)*[2] is very much in point. The court was faced with rival claims to the custody of an illegitimate child made by its mother, a Roman Catholic, and by Protestant foster-parents. The question of law before the court was whether the older equitable principle that a parent has a right to control the religious education of a young child had been abrogated by modern statutes concerning the custody of infants. The judgment of SLESSER, L.J.,[3] turns on the doctrine of guardianship by nature and nurture, " based upon the doctrine of natural justice as derived from antiquity ". He finds authority for this not only in the relatively modern Chancery cases and in the Year Books of the mediaeval common lawyers, but in the canon law and in the opinion of Aquinas, *viz.*, " It is against natural justice if a child before coming to the use of reason were to be taken away from its parents' custody, or anything done to it against its parents' wish ",[4] an opinion derived from one of the primary precepts of natural law which we have set out earlier in this chapter.[5] In the result he decided that the modern statutes did not abrogate this older principle of equity which safeguarded a natural law. Again, in *Fender* v. *Mildmay*,[6] in the Court of Appeal SLESSER, L.J., held that a promise to marry, made by a married man after a decree nisi of divorce had been pronounced against him, but before the decree absolute, was not enforceable as a contract. In doing so he professed to follow the ruling of the Court of Appeal in an analogous but by no means identical case, *Wilson* v. *Carnley*[7]. It is evident from his judgment[8] that he chose to follow the last-mentioned

---

[1] *The Judicial Office*, p. 129.
[2] [1930] All E.R. Rep. 192; [1931] 1 K.B. 317.
[3] [1931] 1 K.B. 317, at pp. 348-364.
[4] *Summa Theologica*, I-II, Q. 10, Art. 12; also III, Q. 68, Art. 10: cited in [1931] 1 K.B. at p. 354.
[5] *Ante*, p. 50, canon VII.
[6] [1936] 1 K.B. 111.
[7] [1908] 1 K.B. 729.   [8] [1936] 1 K.B. 111, at pp. 121-127.

case (whereas one colleague in the Court of Appeal and three
of the judges in the House of Lords[1] chose to distinguish it)
to implement as far as possible without contradicting Acts
of Parliament the secondary precept of natural law—that
marriage is the union of one man with one woman to the
exclusion of all others.[2]

Looking forward into the second half of the twentieth
century, Sir HENRY SLESSER commends to the English
lawyers " the possibility of a jurisprudence based positively
on the Christian religion, in the hope that the principle of
transcendent reference to natural law and Christian doctrine
may once more come into its own in the judicial process.[3] On
the crucial question of the obligation or validity of a law,
condemned by these ultimate criteria as unjust, his solution
is clear: it is not for the judge to deny the validity of an
" evil law " but to resign.[4]

The most vigorous exponent of the theory of natural
justice within the English profession in the middle of the
twentieth century is Richard O'Sullivan, Q.C.[5] Having himself reconciled a devotion to the common law with a deep
allegiance to the Roman Catholic faith, including the theological doctrine of natural justice, he has offered his synthesis
to a troubled generation in a series of papers and lectures.[6]
The natural law which he urges as the measure of justice is
the blend of Christian and classical precepts for social life
which was achieved in the scholastic philosophy of Aquinas.[7]
O'Sullivan uses the doctrine of natural justice for the most

---

[1][1938] 1 A.C. 1; see *post*, pp. 153-155 and 212-213.
[2]See *ante* p. 51.
[3]*The Judicial Office*, pp. 147-149.
[4]*Ibid.*, p. 149.
[5]Called to the Bar, Middle Temple 1914; Q.C. 1934; Lecturer at
University College, London, 1946-1957.
[6]" A Scale of Values in the Common Law ", 1 M.L.R. 27 (1937);
" The Bond of Freedom ", 6 M.L.R. 177 (1943); " Natural Law and
the Common Law ", 31 Tr. of Grotius Society 117 (1945); *Christian
Philosophy in the Common Law* (1947); " Changing Tides in English
Law and History "—introductory paper in *The King's Good Servant*
(1948); " The Christian Spirit of the Common Law "—introductory
paper in *Under God and the Law* (1949); *The Inheritance of the Common
Law* (1950); *Edmund Plowden: A Reading* (1952).
[7]*E.g.*, *The Inheritance of the Common Law*, pp. 96-113.

part to *justify* the common law of England; the largest part of his writing being devoted to an endeavour to show historically that the bulk of the mediaeval common law is the product of Christian and rational principles. On occasions he has employed it as a live criterion for the solution of current legal problems, *i.e.* as a guide for legislation.[1] More often it is used as the canon of criticism of some parliamentary legislation; such as those Acts legitimising the dissolution of marriage which appear to derogate from the relevant precepts of the theological doctrine. On the fundamental question of the validity of the unjust law, *e.g.*, the Matrimonial Causes Act, 1857, O'Sullivan, though a great admirer of Sir THOMAS MORE, is not disposed to give, in the twentieth century, MORE's revolutionary answer. On this issue he is evidently at one with the mass of common lawyers and Socrates: while they may condemn some laws as unjust and press for their reform they would not deny that they remained valid and binding on subjects.

While these two modern common lawyers have gone so far as to admit natural justice to the forefront of their legal philosophies, others, though they have not granted to it such prominence, have invoked the notion from time to time. Several judges even in the House of Lords have relied on precepts of Christianity or on natural law precepts as the major premises, articulate or inarticulate, of their judgments.[2] One county court judge[3] has freely invoked New Testament precepts both in the performance of his judicial function and in proposing law reforms. Lord DENNING, who has been an outstanding exponent of moral justice in the years since the Second World War[4] has reached out to natural

---

[1]*E.g.*, Whether a workman who claims compensation under the Workmen's Compensation Acts should lose his old common law remedy: " The Bond of Freedom " 6 M.L.R. 177, at p. 182.

[2]*E.g.*, Lord FINLAY, L.C. in *Bowman* v. *Secular Society, Ltd.*, [1917] A.C. 406, at p. 428; Lord ATKIN in *Donoghue (or McAlister)* v. *Stevenson*, [1932] All E.R. Rep. 1, at p. 11; [1932] A.C. 562, at p. 580; Lord RUSSELL and Lord ROCHE in *Fender* v. *Mildmay*, [1937] 3 All E.R. 402, at pp. 416-422 and 434-437; [1938] A.C. 1, at pp. 26-35 and 51-56.

[3]Sir Edward PARRY, Judge of the County Court, Manchester, 1894-1911 and Lambeth, 1911-1927: *The Gospel and the Law* (1928).

[4]See *post*, pp. 88-93.

justice as the ultimate idea of justice.[1] Professor Potter in
effect argued for the theological doctrine of natural justice in
his lectures at London University in 1951.[2] The Lord
Chancellor, Viscount KILMUIR, found the occasion in 1957[3]
to remind the English as well as the American common
lawyers of the timeless concepts of natural law. More recently
an academic lawyer has dared to plead with the profession
for the renewed study of natural law in university law
courses.[4] Moreover practising barristers who are sympathetic
to this notion have organised themselves into societies named
after Thomas MORE and Edmund Plowden.[5]

If O'Sullivan is over sanguine in perceiving a change in the
tide of opinion in the common law and in maintaining that
it is flowing again in the direction of natural justice,[6] at least
it is observable that a current of opinion is running in that
direction.

§C

Large claims have been made as to the extent to which the
doctrines of natural justice have actually influenced the positive law of England. For instance, it has been claimed that
the theological doctrine of natural justice was the principal
agent in the evolution of the common law down to the
Reformation.[7] Agreed, if one juxtaposes some precept of
Christianity or natural law with certain branches of positive

---

[1] *The Changing Law* (1953), lecture 5.

[2] *The Quest of Justice* (1951).

[3] American Bar Association Journal, 1957, pp. 887-888.

[4] Chloros, " What is Natural Law?" in 21 M.L.R. (1958), p. 609.

[5] The Thomas More Society of London in 1960 has had some 60
lawyers as members, including 7 judges. The Edmund Plowden
Society in 1959 had a membership of some 40 lawyers, mostly junior
barristers.

[6] " Changing Tides in English Law and History ", in *The King's
Good Servant* (1948).

[7] " The common law owes its first principles and its whole philosophy
to the canonists and the theologians of the creative centuries that
gave us also the old universities and the cathedrals. . . . ": O'Sullivan,
Under God and the Law, xii; *cf.* " Natural Law and the Common
Law ", 31 Tr. of Grotius Society; *cf.* also Lord DENNING in *The
Changing Law* (1953), Lecture 5.

law, *e.g.*, " that a man must live peaceably with others " with
large tracts of the law of crimes and the law of torts which
proscribe the use of force, the latter look as if they were an
elaboration of the former in such detail and with such
practical sanctions as to make them effective *via* litigation in
the complex realm of fact. But to assert that the former
actually inspired the latter is to make a most sweeping claim
about a massive historical process. It is remarkable that the
historians of the common law[1] have not substantiated such
large claims. They have not found it necessary to explain at
every turn the origins and early development of the law in
England in terms of the precepts of the decalogue or of the
New Testament or natural law. While their relative silence on
this truly fundamental question does not prove that these
precepts were without influence in the formation of English
law, it does indicate that the influence of such precepts is
exceedingly difficult to establish.

It is more plausible to claim that the theory of natural
justice has influenced if not inspired various particular
doctrines of common law, doctrines in which the terminology
of natural justice still appears as terms of art. Pollock in his
essay on the " History of the Law of Nature "[2] has drawn
attention to a number of particular doctrines of positive law
which seem to bear the imprint of the doctrine of natural
justice; *viz.*:

(*a*) the law of quasi-contracts;

(*b*) the flexible principles within the law of contracts and
torts which involve the concept of " the reasonable man ";

---

[1] In the 13 volumes of his *History of English Law* (1903-1952)
Holdsworth only rarely refers to natural law, and then mostly in
connection with the Chancellors' administration of Equity, and the
later political theory of natural rights. In Vol. II, Appendix II, he
directly considers the law of nature and the common law, and notes
that the work done elsewhere by the law of nature was done here by
" reason ", and that appeals to reason are often but appeals to
expediency. Pollock and Maitland, in their *History of English Law
Before the Time of Edward I*, 2nd edn. (1898), 2 vols., recognised the
contribution of the clerical judges in systematising the customary law,
(Vol. I, pp. 132-135), but they expounded the origins of the substantive law with the merest passing reference to natural law.

[2] *Essays in the Law* (1922), pp. 31-79.

(c) the rules of " natural justice " used by the High Court in controlling the exercise of judicial and quasi-judicial powers by inferior tribunals;

(d) the principles of " natural justice " which our Courts insist must be observed by a foreign court before they will recognise its judgment;

(e) the doctrine of conflict of laws in general;

(f) the maxim that a custom cannot be good if it is contrary to reason.

Again it is difficult to accept the conclusion that even these particular branches of the positive law were directly inspired by the precepts of natural law or Christianity, without much more evidence. It is easier to establish that most of these judge-made laws have been inspired by less exalted notions of justice and by more practical considerations operating in the minds of the judges. So, it is more apparent from the law reports that the first two of these doctrines, the law of quasi-contract and the laws involving " the reasonable man " have been influenced more directly by the notion of moral justice.[1] The rules of " natural justice " employed by the High Court when it supervises the exercise of judicial and quasi-judicial power by administrative tribunals and when it decides whether to recognise or enforce foreign judgments are not demonstrably deductions actually made by the judges in the last two hundred years from the precepts of the natural law or the Old and New Testaments, but are more obviously the historical deposits of those considerations which go to make the common lawyers' notion of fair trial.[2] The many principles of the modern doctrine of conflict of laws are not demonstrably deductions actually made by the judges in the last two centuries from such exalted precepts but stem from a variety of considerations which are related to the several notions of justice examined in this work, *viz.*, moral justice *simpliciter*, utility, social justice, fair trial and even judicature. Only the sixth item set out by Pollock, the maxim that a custom to be valid must not be unreasonable, can be

---

[1] See *post*, pp. 95-101.
[2] See *ante*, pp. 41-42.

traced directly to its source in the doctrine of natural justice.[1] But so far as the maxim has any operation in the modern law, the standard of reasonableness is not the precepts of divine or natural law, but the judges' estimate of what is fair and right between the parties in the circumstances of the case,[2] *i.e.* the criterion has become that of moral justice.[3]

Surprisingly, Pollock did not cite the one important branch of the positive law of England which most clearly has been inspired by the theological doctrines of natural law— the laws of marriage and ancillary doctrines. Marriage, as a concept of the law of England, has been authoritatively defined as " the voluntary union for life of one man and one woman to the exclusion of all others "[4]—a concept which is congenial to and indeed closely linked with the primary and secondary precepts of natural law concerning marriage which we noted earlier.[5] The concept can be traced through the work of such divines as Hooker and Aquinas to the very early Christian doctrine and the New Testament.[6] It is the resultant of the continuous invocation of this religious doctrine in the ecclesiastical and lay courts in mediaeval and modern England. Of the two secondary precepts of natural law concerning marriage, which we noted earlier[7] the first—the rule of monogamy—has throughout our history been a rule of the

---

[1]The maxim appears in Gratian's *Decretum* (*circa* 1140), in Aquinas, *Summa Theologica* (*circa* 1270), I-II, 97, 3, and is iterated and reiterated in the 16th century in St. Germain's *Doctor and Student* (1532) I, Chaps. 2, 4, 6, 7 and 10. It was evidently adopted by the common law judges in the late 15th and 16th centuries: Plucknett, *Concise History of the Common Law*, 5th edn. (1956), pp. 307-314; *Case of Tanistry* (1608), Dav. Ir. 28; COKE, *Institutes*, I (1628), 62 a, § 80; Comyn's *Digest*, 5th edn. (1822), title " Copyhold " (S), Custom ss. 3-18.

[2]*Robinson* v. *Mollett* (1875), L.R. 7 H.L. 802, at p. 810, *per* BLACKBURN J., and at pp. 817 and 818, *per* BRETT, J.; *Produce Brokers Co., Ltd.* v. *Olympia Oil and Cake Co., Ltd.*, [1916] 2 K.B. 296, at p. 298, *per* HORRIDGE, J., and at p. 301, *per* ROWLATT, J.; Allen, *Law in the Making*, 6th edn. (1958), pp. 136-143.

[3]See *post*, Chap. 5.

[4]*Hyde* v. *Hyde and Woodmansee* (1866), L.R. 1 P. & D. 130, at p. 133, *per* Lord PENZANCE.

[5]See *ante*, pp. 50-51.

[6]See *Beamish* v. *Beamish* (1859-1861), 9 H.L.Cas. 274, at pp. 284-334, *per* WILLES, J.; O'Sullivan, *Inheritance of the Common Law* (1950), Lecture 2.

[7]See *ante*, p. 51.

positive law, and the second—the principle of indissolubility —was a fundamental principle of English law, until exceptions were created as from the late seventeenth century by private Acts and since the middle of the nineteenth century by public Acts of Parliament, and, subject to these wide statutory exceptions, nevertheless remains a leading principle of our matrimonial law. These precepts were translated into positive law primarily by the ecclesiastical lawyers who had exclusive jurisdiction over matrimonial cases in the courts Christian in the Middle Ages and down to the middle of the nineteenth century. But even before these principles were absorbed into the common law (*i.e.* before the matrimonial jurisdiction of the courts Christian was transferred to the lay court by the Matrimonial Causes Act, 1857), the common lawyers had had to consider incidentally questions of marriage in the course of trying other issues, *e.g.* the title of one who claims land as an heir, and had likewise assumed as unchallengeable premises the theological precepts of natural law on monogamy and indissolubility.[1] Ancillary doctrines, such as the matrimonial wrong of adultery, the crime of bigamy, and the rights of parents to the custody of their children and to determine their children's education,[2] these too are related historically to the precepts of natural law which we have instanced, in that these precepts in the minds of ecclesiastical and lay judges and members of Parliament have led to the formation of the detailed legal doctrines.

If it is difficult to accept the very general claim that the common law owes its first principles to the doctrines of natural justice, it is more difficult to accept the very limited conclusion that apart from such narrow sectors of the law as those relating to custom and matrimony the law of England is unrelated to Christian and natural law precepts. The fact is that most common lawyers in England before and since the Reformation have been Christians and endowed with the faculty which the theologians and the rationalist philo-

[1]See *R.* v. *Millis* (1843-4), 10 Cl. & Fin. 534, at pp. 653-689, *per* TINDAL, C.J.; and *Beamish* v. *Beamish* (1859-61), 9 H.L.Cas. 274, at pp. 284-334; and Holdsworth, *History of English Law*, Vol. I, pp. 621-624.
[2]See Re *Agar-Ellis, Agar-Ellis* v. *Lascelles* (1883), 24 Ch. D. 317; *Re Carroll (No. 2)*, [1930] All E.R. Rep. 192; [1931] 1 K.B. 317.

sophers called reason. Unless we are to believe that these
judges and counsel have been schizophrenics to a man we
must allow that these precepts have influenced their professional thinking and hence the law itself. The antinomy is
resolved if we admit that the influence of these Christian and
natural law precepts, while deep and continuous, has not been
direct or articulate; then it is conceivable that these truly
fundamental principles have been the inarticulate major
premises in legal thinking, and have inspired at a more
articulate level the notions which we are considering separately in this work, under the titles " moral justice ", " fair
trial ", " utility " and even " social justice ".

§D

It is undeniable that most common lawyers in the nineteenth and twentieth centuries have rejected the doctrines of
natural justice as part of their conscious legal philosophy.
But it does not follow that these lawyers have rejected the
Christian doctrine which is interwoven with the theological
version of natural justice. On the contrary it appears that
most of the judges who have been on the Bench in England
in these centuries have been no less sincere Christians than
their predecessors who acknowledged the supremacy of
natural justice. The point of reconciliation is that the lawyers
have become increasingly aware that their professional
functions for the most part begin when the Christian precepts have been disregarded by laymen. Solicitors may find
occasion to remind clients of their duties as Christians, but
the services of counsel and judges are sought only after
parties have disregarded the fundamental Christian precepts
of love, of forgiveness and of compromise before suit. These
precepts are understood by the English lawyers of today to
be directed rather to the conscience of individuals than to the
public activities of counsel and judges and legislators.

The notion of natural justice faded from the minds of most
English lawyers in the nineteenth century with the increasing
scepticism as to the efficacy of reason. In both the theological
version of natural justice which we have considered at some

length and in the version expounded by the rationalist philosophers of the seventeenth and eighteenth centuries it was fundamental that human reason could discover the universal, eternal and immutable precepts of the natural law.[1] Hume shook this foundation in the middle of the eighteenth century[2] when he demonstrated that " the ultimate ends of human actions can never, in any case, be accounted for by *reason*, but recommend themselves entirely to the sentiments and affections of mankind, without any dependence on the intellectual faculties ".[3] Without subscribing to current philosophical argument it must have occurred to many a common lawyer to doubt the efficacy of reason in establishing universal and invariable precepts for all systems of law when he observed that the " reason " of the theologians such as Aquinas and Hooker led them to propound schemes of natural laws which were not identical, and that the " reason " of Hobbes and Locke led them to propound schemes which differed *inter se*, as well as differing from those of the theologians. Bentham, writing for legislators in the late eighteenth century, carried Hume's attack on reason and the natural law into the sphere of the lawyer. Advocating positively the axiom of utility as the criterion of justice, Bentham attacked the theory of justice as conformity with precepts of natural law as but one version of the principle of sympathy and antipathy, which resolved into no more than the exercise of caprice on the part of each expositor.[4] The greatest defect of the theory, in his reckoning, was that it provided no one objective standard of value for laws—a defect on to which many English lawyers, particularly those who are partisans

---

[1]Locke, in his Oxford days, in *Essays on the Law of Nature* (written *circa* 1660: published only in 1954, ed. von Leyden), Essay II, had observed acutely that reason builds on basic knowledge but does not supply it. But in his later more famous political treatise he ignored this insight and asserted dogmatically as rational principles a scheme of precepts of Natural Law: *Two Treatises of Civil Government* (1690).

[2]*Treatise of Human Nature* (1738); *Enquiry Concerning the Principles of Morals* (1751).

[3]*Enquiry Concerning the Principles of Morals*, Appendix I, § V.

[4]*Principles of Morals and Legislation* (1789), Chap. II, §§ 11-18; *Theory of Legislation*, ed. Ogden (1931), pp. 6-10, 82-87.

of legal justice[1] have since fastened. In the nineteenth century John Austin, speaking primarily to the lawyers, continued the attack on the notion of natural law on this point. While he taught that divine law is the supreme criterion of justice he rejected natural law as the index of divine law since it was said to depend on practical reason, or more properly on sentiments, and it was notorious that the moral sentiments of different men differed infinitely.[2]

A deep-rooted objection of the common lawyer to these precepts of natural law as the criteria of justice stems from his distrust of propositions conceived *in vacuo, sub specie aeternitatis*, even though so conceived by the finest intelligences. The cast of mind which is most characteristic of the English Bar and Bench rejects the *à priori* approach to practical questions and relies on the indigenous empirical method, working from concrete human situations. In the 1880's Pollock expressed this reaction vividly in his criticism of a treatise on natural justice by a Scots jurist:[3] " My own view (and, I think, the view of most English students) is a totally different one. I think it is a mistake to preface the study of legal conceptions by an exposition of transcendental ethics. . . . It may be the radical perverseness of English habits of thinking, but in my eyes much of the work done by Professor Lorimer . . . either arrives by high-flying and circuitous roads at obvious general conclusions, or arrives at more precise ones by a slenderly disguised appeal to the principle of . . . ' expediency '."[4]

Finally, the English lawyer who is confronted by the precepts of natural law and asked to accept them as the very first principles for his system of law and its administration balks at them on account of their extreme generality. To him they are too wide and too vague to be useful in practice. The precepts advanced by St. Germain, which we noticed earlier, which enjoin on men to love good, to do nothing against truth and to live peacefully, provide no practical guide to the

---

[1]See *post*, Chap. 8.
[2]*Province of Jurisprudence Determined* (1832), ed. Hart (1954), pp. 34-37 and 87-99.
[3]Lorimer, *Institutes of Law* (1872); 2nd edn. (1880).
[4]*Essays in Jurisprudence and Ethics* (1882), pp. 22-28.

lawyer who is confronted with a specific problem arising from, say, a conveyance of land, or the interpretation of a commercial contract, or a workman's claim to compensation, or a claim for damages arising out of a collision between two motor cars. Likewise, to the judge who has the opportunity of legislating in the course of judgment and to the members of the parliamentary legislature, in the vast majority of cases these precepts afford no reliable assistance in the formulation of specific laws. They are to the lawyer, in Maitland's phrase, " unmanageable formulae ".[1] By themselves they dictate no workable rules of law: only if other principles, drawn from experience or from other theories of justice are added can such precepts be translated into laws sufficiently detailed to cover the manifold activities of a community of millions and sufficiently precise to be administered regularly in a system of law-courts.

---

[1] *Collected Papers*, I, p. 303.

CHAPTER 5

MORAL JUSTICE

§A

To most laymen and philosophers questions of justice are essentially ethical questions, involving the values right and wrong. Ethical versions of justice have certainly played a major rôle in the traditional philosophy of the common lawyers. We have already considered the notion of fair trial which involves moral opinion. The doctrine of natural justice examined in the last chapter and the doctrine of utility which is to be examined in the next are, notwithstanding their different contents, essentially ethical versions of justice. But both are absolute doctrines, postulating universal and eternal principles. English lawyers have long subscribed to a less exalted and more variable ethical version of justice, in which the essential standards are those of current moral opinion in the country. Such versions may be labelled moral justice, to distinguish them as far as possible from natural justice and individual utility and social justice. This distinction cannot be pressed too far, as the following discussion of moral justice will reveal, for the notions of moral justice and natural justice in particular are complementary.

English lawyers often invoke moral justice by referring to a decision or a situation or a rule of law as " just and right ". But a variety of other terms are used by lawyers with the same or approximately the same connotation; such as—that XY is " fair ", " proper ", " reasonable ", or " sound "; " just and reasonable " is common; or that XY is in accordance with " common sense " (a favourite term), " good sense ", " decency ", " humanity ". The phrase " natural justice " is also used on occasions without implying any absolute precepts of natural law but rather to refer to this more everyday notion of moral justice. Even the terms " equitable " and " in equity " and " *ex aequo et bono* " fall from lawyers with this moral connotation and without any necessary reference to the practices of courts of Chancery. The common lawyer is prone to talk about the " merits " of a case, a term which involves the morality of the subject under discussion. In practice the above terms are used in their negative forms even more frequently: the justice or rightness or reasonableness of a thing is more likely to be passed over in silence than its injustice, wrongness or un-reasonableness. But the invocation of a standard of moral justice in a legal context is not always heralded by any such terminology; as often as not it is concealed in a judgment or an argument or in some cryptic choice of alternative authorities or interpretations.

Sir Frederick Pollock[1] has expounded most lucidly in several of his works[2] the notion of moral justice which is traditional in the English legal profession. In an early work, *Essays in Jurisprudence and Ethics,* his principal concern in the field of ethics was with " moral rules proceeding from the invisible and informal judgment-seat of righteous men "[3] rather than with the speculative or ideal versions of moral philosophers or theologians, though he regards these as ele-ments in the formation of " common sense ". He wrote of the term " just " in legal contexts as retaining its ethical signi-ficance, since in " the development of law . . . appeal is

---

[1]1845-1937. Called to the Bar 1871; Professor of Jurisprudence at University College, London 1882-1883; Corpus Christi Professor of Jurisprudence in the University of Oxford 1883-1893; Editor of the Law Reports 1895-1935; Editor of the Law Quarterly Review 1885-1919.

[2]*Essays in Jurisprudence and Ethics* (1882), Chaps. X and XI; *First Book of Jurisprudence* (1st edn., 1896; 6th edn., 1929), Chap. 2.

These *dicta* on moral justice cited in the text only represent one facet of Pollock's own philosophy of justice. He was predominantly concerned with " justice according to law "; see *First Book of Jurisprudence,* Chap. 2; *Oxford Lectures* (1890), p. 7. While he criticised severely the notion of natural justice as a live concept for lawyers in his early essays, *e.g.,* in *Essays in Jurisprudence and Ethics,* pp. 18-28, he treated this notion much more sympathetically in his later work, *e.g.,* in *Essays in the Law* (1922), Chaps. II and III.

[3]*Essays in Jurisprudence and Ethics,* at p. 297.

constantly made to ethical reason and the moral judgment of the community ".[1] The canon he relies upon is the moral opinion of the more righteous members of the community:

> " The moral ideal present to lawyers and judges, if it does not always come up to the highest that has been conceived, will at least be, generally speaking, above the common average of practice; it will represent the standard of the best sort of citizens."[2]

In his most mature essay on the judicial process, after nearly sixty years' experience in the legal profession, he expressed the notion under examination most vividly. To the question —what is to guide a court in developing law?—he replied:

> " the usual and accepted answer is that it must find and apply the rule which in all the circumstances appears most reasonable. . . ."

" Reasonable " he understands as

> " an ideal standard, which cannot be precisely defined, but is none other than that general consent of right-minded and rightly informed men which our ancestors in the profession called reason, and continental doctors the law of nature. . . . In modern terms, we say that the duty of the court is to keep the rules of law in harmony with the enlightened common-sense of the nation."[3]

In a nutshell, moral justice connotes conformity with positive morality.

This theory does not assume that a code of the morals subscribed to by the Englishmen of the day is always available. It is true that English moral philosophers have from time to time proposed schemes of morality,[4] but these have not been offered as representative of the positive morality of the author's day and society: nor do they agree in their schemes; they belong rather to that school of thought which we have labelled " natural justice ". At all events the legal practitioners have paid little or no attention to these schemes of very general moral precepts. A school of moral scientists

---

[1]*First Book of Jurisprudence* 6th edn. (1929), p. 33.

[2]*Ibid.*, p. 48.

[3]" Judicial Caution and Valour" (1929), 45 L.Q.R. 293, at pp. 294-295.

[4]*E.g.*, W. Paley, *Principles of Moral and Political Philosophy* (1785), Books II-IV; H. Sidgwick, *Methods of Ethics* (1874), Book III, Chaps. IV-VIII; H. Spencer, *Principles of Ethics*, 2 vols. (1879-1892), especially Vol. II; W. D. Ross, *The Right and the Good* (1930), Chaps. V-VII.

collecting the current moral opinions of righteous English citizens and publishing systematic codes thereof has never existed: indeed, Pollock suggests that it is part of the characteristic English moral sense that ethical judgments should not be organised into a system.[1] Nor does the theory assume that there is some ultimate human arbiter on moral questions, such as is recognised within the Roman Catholic Church. Of course, as Pollock admitted,[2] the moral sense of Englishmen has, in the eight hundred years of the history of the common law, been nurtured within the Christian tradition and has been continuously refined by Christian doctrine. The theory assumes, at most, that right-minded Englishmen at a given time are tacitly agreed upon certain principles of right and wrong. Or it assumes, at least, that such citizens if confronted with a particular problem or situation would, either by intuition or by casuistry, arrive at similar judgments that a certain solution was right. More often than not, when English lawyers have invoked the concept of moral justice they have had in mind as a standard this latter specific *ad hoc* formulation of right, rather than general principles applicable to broad categories of hypothetical situations. A corollary of these assumptions is that the criteria of moral justice are dynamic, developing with the changes of moral opinion within the community.

Pollock might insist in these discussions on using the moral standards of the right-minded members of the community, the standards of the best sort of citizens, of the select few. But this is not the only moral standard which the common lawyers have actually invoked over the centuries. It is in effect an intermediate standard. On the one hand the judges have as often appealed to " the prevailing morality ", *i.e.* the morality of the average member of the community, and on the other they have openly resorted to the dictates of their own refined moral sense.

Such moral criteria are applicable both to man's inner life and to his social life. It is with the latter only that lawyers are professionally concerned. They have applied these moral

---

[1] *Essays in Jurisprudence and Ethics*, p. 272.
[2] *First Book of Jurisprudence*, 6th edn., pp. 49-50.

criteria to the conduct of individuals, to legal process, to the judicial function and to the law itself. So by this criterion a man's conduct may be declared just, or unjust; a particular trial may be approved as just or condemned as the opposite; a judgment itself may be adjudged the just solution or otherwise; and even the positive law of the land is capable of evaluation thereby. As will be shown later, perhaps the most important application of the notion is in the sphere of legislation, particularly judicial legislation; for as Pollock stressed, in his valedictory essay on " Judicial Caution and Valour ",[1] in cases of first impression one of the sources from which common law judges have long been disposed to draw inspiration for the formulation of new law is the prevailing moral opinion of their society and day. Besides, the notion is particularly prominent in the actual administration of many rules of law, prescribed by statute or by case law, which lay down flexible standards or confer discretion on the judge.[2]

It has already been observed that according to some exponents of the theory of natural justice the precepts of natural law were of supreme obligation: that is to say, they were not only criteria for measuring the justice of positive law, but that laws which were unjust by these criteria were not binding. Is moral justice to be regarded likewise as of supreme authority, or is it to be regarded simply as a criterion for evaluating positive law and a source of inspiration for legislation and a guide for administering certain laws? Most English lawyers who have subscribed to the notion of moral justice have given the evolutionary rather than the revolutionary answer. The orthodox answer is given by Pollock, who while admitting that a given rule of common law may be condemned by reference to positive morality, enjoins on the lawyer to accept as of paramount obligation the rule of positive law: " such unfortunate accidents must be endured ".[3] But, exceptionally, an English judge has regarded the claims of moral justice as paramount.[4]

---

[1] (1929) 45 L.Q.R. 293.
[2] *Post*, pp. 84-85.
[3] *Genius of the Common Law* (1912), p. 114.
[4] See *post*, pp. 80-81 and 88-93.

§B

English judges have subscribed to and acted upon the notion of moral justice from the earliest days of the common law down to the present generation.

In the late twelfth century, when the royal judges were ostensibly collecting and consolidating the laws and customs common to the kingdom, on many occasions they in fact decided cases on principles of moral fairness.[1] BRACTON, writing in the middle of the next century, admitted that " it appertains to the king to apply a suitable remedy to restrain every injury whatsoever ",[2] and that " there may be as many forms of action as there are causes of action "[3]—admissions which reveal that new forms of action were being sanctioned by the royal courts to remedy what were regarded contemporaneously either by the judges or by the community as moral wrongs. A similar concept of justice underlies the *consimili casu* clause of the statute of Westminster the Second;[4] the deficiency " in doing justice to suitors ", which was to be obviated, has been interpreted as the absence of remedies in cases which shocked the moral sense of the community.[5]

In the Middle Ages and indeed down to the late eighteenth century the common lawyers were disposed to identify their law with " reason ". For instance in 1345 SHARSHULLE, J., observed that no precedent was of such force as reason,[6] and in the same case STONORE, C.J., rejected the opinion that law is the will of the judges and declared emphatically that " law is reason ".[7] St. Germain's Student of the Common Law explained the first ground of the law of England as " the law of reason ".[8] COKE in the early seventeenth century, in a

---

[1]Winfield, *Legal Essays* (1952), p. 4; Pollock and Maitland, *History of English Law*, 2nd edn. (1898), I, 197-198; Plucknett, *Concise History of the Common Law*, 5th edn. (1956), pp. 677-680.

[2]*De Legibus et Consuetudinibus Angliae* (*circa* 1256), ed. Woodbine, Vol. IV, p. 289.

[3]*Ibid.*, p. 286; Maitland, *Forms of Action* (1909), 1948 edn., p. 6.

[4]13 Edw. I, c. 24.

[5]Ames, " Law and Morals ", 22 H.L.R. 97, at p. 105.

[6]Y.B. 18-19 Edw. III Hil. Term 3, R.S., pp. 376-377.

[7]*Ibid.*, pp. 378-379: " Nanyl; ley est resoun. "

[8]*Doctor and Student* (1532), I, Chap. 5. See *ante*, pp. 54-55.

famous passage dilates on the notion—" Reason is the life of
the law, nay the common law itselfe is nothing else but
reason; which is to be understood of an artificiall perfection
of reason, gotten by long study, observation, and experience,
and not of every man's naturall reason; for *Nemo nascitur
artifex*. This legall reason *est summa ratio*. And therefore if all
the reason that is dispersed into so many severall heads, were
united into one, yet could he not make such a law as the law
in *England* is; because by many successions of ages it hath
beene fined and refined by an infinite number of grave and
learned men, and by long experience growne to such a perfection, for the government of this realme, as the old rule may
be justly verified of it, *Neminem oportet esse sapientiorem
legibus;* no man out of his own private reason ought to be
wiser than the law, which is the perfection of reason."[1] Since
Hume's penetrating analysis of the concept of " reason " and
his assignment of the intellectual faculty which properly
deserves that name to a rôle second to that of sentiment or
feeling in the sphere of morals[2] such eulogies of the common
law have rarely fallen from lawyers. BLACKSTONE repeated
the axiom that the common law was the perfection of reason,[3]
but half-heartedly, with an apologia. But if, following Hume,
we substitute the term " moral sense " for " reason " in these
contexts we will the more readily understand the boast of the
older lawyers. In a more modern idiom the same point was
made by FARWELL, L.J., in 1911: " The common law is, or
ought to be, the common sense of the community, crystallised
and formulated by our forefathers."[4]

The most prominent and consistent exponents of moral
justice in the judicial process in the formative era of the
English legal system were the Chancellors. During the
fifteenth century, adjudicating upon petitions in the Court of
Chancery, they avowedly gave judgment according to
" conscience ".[5] Lord Chancellor WOLSEY[6], describing his

---

[1]*Institutes*, I (1628), 97 b, § 138.
[2]*Treatise of Human Nature* (1738), Book III; *Enquiry Concerning the
Principles of Morals* (1751), Appendix I.
[3]*Commentaries* 3rd edn. (1768), Introduction § 3, pp. 69-70.
[4]*Barker* v. *Herbert*, [1911] 2 K.B. 633, at p. 644.
[5]*E.g. Anon.* (1468), Y.B. Trin. 8 Edw. IV. fo. 5, pl. 1.
[6]L.C. 1515-1529.

office, maintained that: " The King ought of his royal dignity and prerogative to mitigate the rigour of the law, where conscience hath the most force; therefore . . . he hath constitute a chancellor, an officer to execute justice with clemency, where conscience is opposed by the rigour of the law. And therefore the Court of Chancery hath been heretofore commonly called the Court of Conscience ".[1] While the earlier ecclesiastical Chancellors might rely upon the theological concept of conscience which revealed to them the precepts of the natural law, in the many instances where these precepts failed to indicate one clear-cut solution to the particular petition they must have resorted to the dictates of their own moral consciousness; and after the Reformation lay Chancellors relied more plainly on the dictates of their own moral sense directed to the facts of the concrete case, without claiming to consult eternal moral principles or descending to consult the positive morality of the ordinary citizen.[2] In retrospect Holdsworth concluded emphatically that from the fifteenth century well down into the seventeenth century, the Court of Chancery was actually, and not merely technically, a court of conscience.[3]

In the later eighteenth century Lord MANSFIELD as Chief Justice of the Court of King's Bench, 1756-1788, dominated the Common Law Bench. His fame rests not only on his performance of the office *jus dicere*, but on his exceptionally overt performance of the office *jus dare*. In his complex technique of judicial legislation the method of moral justice is prominent. In his monumental work of reducing the mercantile law into a system of cognizable principles Lord MANSFIELD leant heavily on morality, the positive morality of the class of merchants, which he attempted to establish objectively by empanelling special juries selected from the merchants of the City of London.[4] In the cases in which he

---

[1]Holdsworth, *History of English Law*, Vol. V, p. 219.

[2]*Ibid.*, pp. 215-338.

[3]*Ibid.*, p. 337.

[4]*E.g.*, in *Lewis* v. *Rucker* (1761), 2 Burr. 1167, at pp. 1168-1172, Lord MANSFIELD upheld a verdict of one of his special juries in these terms: " The special jury (among whom there were many knowing and considerable merchants) found the defendant's rule of estimation to be right, and gave their verdict for him. They understood the

(*continued at foot of next page*)

attempted to extend the sphere of obligation of agreements as contracts[1] he plainly invoked moral criteria—it might be the moral standards of the mercantile class[2] or his own estimate of current general morality.[3] The classic example of his attempt to reform the law of contract to conform with moral principles is his judgment in *Hawkes* v. *Saunders*[4] where he enlarged the scope of the concept of consideration: " Where a man is under a moral obligation, which no Court of Law or Equity can inforce, and promises, the honesty and rectitude of the thing is a consideration . . . In such instances . . . as the promise is only to do what an honest man ought to do, the ties of conscience upon an upright mind are a sufficient consideration."[5] In an important case on copyright, *Millar* v. *Taylor*,[6] MANSFIELD'S ultimate criterion was " whether it is agreeable to natural principles, moral justice and fitness, to allow him the copy, after publication, as well as before ". Moral criteria are as patently the premises of his reasoning in the cases[7] in which he not only attempted to but succeeded in extending the range of obligation of quasi-contract. In these cases Lord MANSFIELD was prone to use the terms " natural justice " and " eternal justice ", but it is evident that he did not rely on the primary precepts of the theological or rationalist doctrines of natural law, but on his own moral sense or that of his contemporaries.

In his use of moral criteria in the judicial process Lord MANSFIELD was not in his era unique. In most of his decisions in the Court of King's Bench he carried all his fellow judges

---

(continued from foot of previous page)
question very well, and knew more of the subject of it than anybody else present; and formed their judgment from their own notions and experience, without much assistance from any thing that passed. The moment the jury brought in their verdict, I was satisfied that they did right, in totally disregarding the particular circumstances of this case. . . . "

[1]*Pillans and Rose* v. *Van Mierop and Hopkins* (1765), 3 Burr. 1664; *Atkins* v. *Hill* (1775), 1 Cowp. 284; *Trueman* v. *Fenton* (1777), 2 Cowp. 544; *Hawkes* v. *Saunders* (1782), 1 Cowp. 289; see Fifoot, *Lord Mansfield* (1936), Chap. V, pp. 121-141.

[2]As in *Pillans and Rose* v. *Van Mierop and Hopkins, supra.*

[3]As in *Hawkes* v. *Saunders, supra.*

[4](1782), 1 Cowp. 289.

[5]*Ibid.*, at p. 290.

[6](1769), 4 Burr. 2303, at p. 2399.

[7]See *post*, pp. 96-101.

with him, including such not inconsiderable lawyers as
WILLES, ASHHURST, and BULLER, JJ. For instance in *Hawkes*
v. *Saunders*[1] BULLER, J., as emphatically based his concurring judgment on moral grounds; " The true rule is, that
wherever a defendant is under a moral obligation, or is liable
in conscience and equity to pay, that is a sufficient consideration."[2] And Lord MANSFIELD's successor as Chief Justice of
the Court of King's Bench, Lord KENYON, though in many
respects poles apart from his predecessor, allowed moral considerations to sway him to such an extent in cases of actions
for damages for adultery as to earn for himself the sobriquet
of " the legal monk ". In one of these cases he confessed: " I
had not been long in a court of justice before I felt that I
should best discharge my duty to the public by making the
law of the land subservient to the laws of religion and
morality ".[3] And, it was Lord KENYON who presided in the
famous case of *Pasley* v. *Freeman*[4] when the court in effect
created tortious liability for damages caused by fraudulent
statements. He admitted to being driven to his decision by
the broad consideration that law should " enforce moral and
social duties ". BULLER, J., affirmed that " if a man may
assert that which he knows to be false and thereby do an
everlasting injury to his neighbour and be not answerable for
it, that is as repugnant to law as to morality ". And ASH-
HURST, J., said that he had so great a veneration for the law
as to suppose that nothing could be law which was not
founded in common sense or common honesty.

In the nineteenth century the notion of moral justice was
not so plainly invoked by the lawyers. The prevailing mood
was positivism, taking the form of a firm devotion to legal
justice,[5] leavened by utilitarianism.[6] But this notion of
morality as the criterion for law and legal process was not
extinguished in the profession even in that period. The dour

---

[1](1782), 1 Cowp. 289.
[2]*Ibid.*, at p. 294.
[3]*Howard* v. *Bingham*, cited in CAMPBELL, *Lives of the Chief Justices*,
Vol. III (1857), pp. 67-68.
[4](1789), 3 Term Rep. 51.
[5]See *post*, Chap. 8.
[6]See *post*, Chap. 6.

Real Property Commissioners in 1829[1] resorted to positive morality in determining the merits and demerits of the law of inheritance. Thus, they approved of most of the rules of inheritance as " well suited to the habits and feelings of the people ", but the rule which excluded ascendants was found to be " at variance with the ordinary feelings and notions and has long been considered unjust ". It is arguable that a good part of the volume of criticism in the nineteenth century of the legal system which the lawyers actually did express in utilitarian terms might, but for Bentham, have been expressed in terms of moral justice.[2] For instance Chief Justice COCKBURN in his public criticism of a proposal to reorganise the judicature in 1870[3] wrote on one page that " Equity is but another name for law adjusted to the dictates of reason of general utility " and on the next that " Equity embodies the plain and simple principles of rational justice ". He admitted that " where law and equity differ, the principles on which justice is administered in equity are more consonant to rational justice than those of the common law and consequently the law ought to be adapted to the standard of equity ". What was his ultimate criterion, " rational justice ", if not the moral sense of Chancellors, fined and refined by experience? In 1874 Lord CAIRNS, L.C., could still expose the moral basis of a particular rule of equity: " Now, the rule of this court as I understand it, as to agents, is not a technical or arbitrary rule. It is a rule founded on the highest and truest principles of morality. No man can, in this court, acting as an agent, be allowed to put himself into a position in which his interest and his duty will be in conflict."[4] Bentham and Austin had tried—with considerable success for some decades —to expel the notion of moral justice from the common lawyers' legal philosophy, but so fundamental a notion could not be eliminated. To take a case at random: in 1888 in *Wilson* v. *Glossop*,[5] all the members of the Court of Appeal, Lord ESHER, M.R., FRY and LOPES, L.JJ., explicitly rejected

---

[1]First Report, pp. 10 *et seq.*
[2]See Stone, *Province and Function of Law* (1947), p. 296.
[3]*Letter from L.C.J. Cockburn to Lord Chancellor Hatherley* (1870).
[4]*Parker* v. *McKenna* (1874), 10 Ch. App. 96, at p. 118.
[5](1888), 20 Q.B.D. 354.

as an outrage to their moral sense the proposition that a husband, who had connived at his wife's adultery and subsequently turned her out of doors, could lawfully refuse to pay for necessaries supplied to her, and decided the appeal the way their moral sense indicated.

The moral criterion has been invoked more openly in judgments in the English courts in the twentieth century. It has re-emerged as a gloss upon the theory of social utility and has become one of the double criteria in the theory of social justice.[1] And the notion of moral justice *simpliciter* still plays a large part in the judicial process. Admittedly one judge did assert that in this century the High Court was no longer a court of conscience,[2] and another in the Court of Appeal did deny that the judges were not any longer free to administer " justice as between man and man ".[3] But the latter, Lord SUMNER, a year later in the House of Lords, when his own moral sense revolted against the logical application to the facts before him of principles well established by precedents, deliberately extended an equitable remedy so as to reach what he clearly regarded as the morally right solution of the case.[4] The truth of the matter is that even in the twentieth century, despite the accumulation of an immense range of precedents and statutes the English judge cannot perform his office without continuous resort to the notion of moral justice. Such elementary and regular matters as the award of costs in civil cases and the determination of the amount of punishments within prescribed maxima in criminal cases are left to be determined by " the discretion " of the judge. Many a principle laid down in authoritative precedents which the judge must apply, itself contains a general term or flexible standard—for instance the duty to use " reasonable care " in the law of negligence, the duty of trustees to conduct themselves " reasonably ", the notion of " reasonable user " in the law of nuisance, the various principles in the

---

[1] See *post*, Chap. 7.

[2] *In re Telescriptor Syndicate Ltd.*, [1903] 2 Ch. 174, at pp. 195-196, *per* BUCKLEY, J.

[3] *Baylis* v. *Bishop of London*, [1913] 1 Ch. 127, at p. 140, *per* HAMILTON, L.J.

[4] *Sinclair* v. *Brougham*, [1914] A.C. 398, at p. 458.

law of contract incorporating the concept of " reasonable time ", the concept of " possession " in the tort of conversion and the crime of larceny, and the elastic concept of " breach of the peace " in criminal law, to name only a few. A score of modern statutes expressly confer on the judge the mandate to decide " as he thinks fit " or as the court thinks " just and equitable " or simply " as the court considers just having regard to all the circumstances of the case ".[1] In such cases, according to one former member of the Court of Appeal, the judge does rely on the present state of social morality.[2] After examining such cases where the moral criterion *inter alia* is necessary to the judicial function, Professor Winfield concluded: " Where there is any scope for the application of morals . . . what they [the judges] do apply is the practical morality which is prevalent for the time being in the community. They have no general formula, whether utilitarian or otherwise, as to what the morality *ought* to be. It is enough for them if they can keep abreast of what it *is* now."[3] As Lord Justice DEVLIN has said recently: " In the administration of justice the choice always lies between the application of the fixed rule . . . and the investigation of each case on its merits."[4] " The justice of the case is the best compromise that can be obtained between the demands of the law and judgment on the merits."[5]

Outstanding modern exponents of the method of moral justice in the sphere of judicial legislation have been Lord ATKIN, and latterly Lord DENNING.[6]

---

[1]*E.g.*, Married Women's Property Act, 1882, s. 17 extended by Matrimonial Causes (Property and Maintenance) Act, 1958, s. 7; Judicature Act, 1873, s. 25 (8), re-enacted as Judicature Act, 1925, s. 45; Partnership Act, 1890, s. 35 (f); Law Reform (Married Women and Tortfeasors) Act, 1935, s. 6 (2); Inheritance (Family Provision) Act, 1938, s. 1; Law Reform (Frustrated Contracts) Act, 1943, s. 1 (2), (3), (6); Law Reform (Contributory Negligence) Act, 1945, s. 1; Companies Act, 1948, s. 222 (f); Adoption Act, 1950, s. 5 (2); Variation of Trusts Act, 1958, s. 1 (1).

[2]Sir Henry SLESSER, in *The Judicial Office* (1943), p. 127.

[3]" Ethics in English Case Law " (1931), 45 H.L.R. 112, at p. 133.

[4]*Carter* v. *Minister of Health*, [1950] 1 All E.R. 904, at p. 907.

[5]*Trial by Jury* (1956), at p. 152.

[6]*Cf.* the cautious use of the method by DEVLIN, J. in *Pyrene Co., Ltd.* v. *Scindia Steam Navigation Co., Ltd.*, [1954] 2 All E.R. 158; [1954] 2 Q.B. 402; see 19 M.L.R. 324.

Lord ATKIN'S speech in the House of Lords in *Donoghue*
(*or McAlister*) v. *Stevenson*[1] has been generally recognised in
the profession as the key judgment in one of the principal
cases decided in the English courts in this century. When he
delivered this judgment Lord ATKIN was no tyro but had
perfected his distinctive judicial technique after nearly
twenty years' experience on the Bench. The specific question
for determination was whether the manufacturer of an
article, sold by him to a distributor in circumstances which
prevent the ultimate consumer from discovering by inspection any defect, is under any legal duty to the ultimate consumer to take reasonable care that the article is free from
defect likely to cause injury to health. No pronouncement of
the House of Lords had precisely answered the question; a
few precedents indicated a possible affirmative answer, but
a considerable stream of English authorities pointed the
other way. Nevertheless Lord ATKIN gave an affirmative
answer to the question. While the larger part of his judgment
is devoted to a thorough analysis of precedents, this discussion is directed to showing that there was some pre-existing
authority for this affirmative answer and that the adverse
precedents did not unequivocally preclude him from reaching
this answer. The answer itself is dictated by arguments based
on other grounds, as three passages from the judgment reveal.
In the opening section he established a general principle of
liability in tort for negligence: " *The liability for negligence . . .*
is no doubt based upon a general public sentiment of moral
wrongdoing for which the offender must pay.[2] But acts or omissions which any moral code would censure cannot in a
practical world be treated so as to give a right to every
person injured by them to demand relief. In this way rules
of law arise which limit the range of complainants and the
extent of their remedy. The rule that you are to love your
neighbour becomes in law, you must not injure your neighbour; and the lawyer's question, Who is my neighbour?
receives a restricted reply. You must take reasonable care to
avoid acts or omissions which you can reasonably foresee
would be likely to injure your neighbour. Who, then, in law

---

[1] [1932] All E.R. Rep. I, at pp. 10-20; [1932] A.C. 562, at pp.
578-599.   [2] Italics supplied.

is my neighbour? The answer seems to be—persons who are
so closely and directly affected by my act that I ought reasonably to have them in contemplation when I am directing my
mind to the acts or omissions which are called in question ".[1]
Later, turning his attention to the specific question before
the court as to the extent of a manufacturer's duty to con-
sumers, Lord ATKIN characteristically conned the specific
facts and expressed a moral judgment upon them: " A manufacturer puts up an article of food in a container which he
knows will be opened by the actual consumer. There can be
no inspection by any purchaser and no reasonable preliminary inspection by the consumer. Negligently, in the course of
preparation he allows the contents to be mixed with poison.
It is said that the law of England and Scotland is that the
poisoned consumer has no remedy against the manufacturer.
If this were the result of the authorities, I should consider
the result a grave defect in the law, and so contrary to principle that I should hesitate long before following any decision
to that effect which had not the authority of this House."[2]
Finally Lord ATKIN laid down the proposition which has
become definitive of the law on this question: " That by
Scots and English law alike a manufacturer of products,
which he sells in such a form as to show that he intends them
to reach the ultimate consumer in the form in which they
left him with no reasonable possibility of intermediate
examination, and with the knowledge that the absence of
reasonable care in the preparation or putting up of the products will result in an injury to the consumer's life or property, owes a duty to the consumer to take that reasonable
care ", adding, illuminatingly, " *It is a proposition which I
venture to say no one in Scotland or England who was not a
lawyer would for one moment doubt. It will be an advantage to
make it clear that the law in this matter, as in most others, is
in accordance with sound common sense.*"[3] Patently, the main
argument is based principally on Lord ATKIN's own estimate
of current morality on the question; admittedly he invokes
the supreme axiom of Christ's social teaching, and in another

---

[1][1932] A.C. 562, at p. 580.
[2]*Ibid.*, at p. 582.
[3]*Ibid.*, at p. 599; italics supplied.

7

passage refers to current social interests;[1] but in the structure of his judgment these appear to be buttresses rather than foundations.

It was a characteristic of Lord ATKIN's judicial technique to state in the most succinct and luminous terms the facts of the social problem before the court and to express a moral judgment upon those facts.[2] However, it may be gleaned from these judgments and his few extra-judicial writings[3] that he was not disposed to rely on his own moral intuitions unless he was sure that his moral judgment corresponded with that of enlightened contemporary public opinion. He was alive to the dangers of giving too much rein to the " idiosyncratic inferences of a few judicial minds ".[4] And he was never prepared to give effect to the morally just solution of a case if the law had been laid down otherwise in a precedent case which was binding on the court in which he sat.[5] In the last two particulars his use of the method of moral justice differs from that of his successor Lord DENNING.

More recently Lord DENNING has made extensive use of the notion of moral justice in the judicial process and in extra-judicial lectures.[6] As a judge of first instance in 1947 in the *High Trees House* case[7] he startled the profession by the use of a moral proposition as an integral part of his reasoning in such a way as to appear to challenge a deep-rooted legal principle, and he has continued to use moral criteria liberally in the process of restating the law in the Court of Appeal and latterly in the House of Lords. While the

---

[1]*Ibid.*, at p. 583: see *post*, p. 150.

[2]*E.g., Hambrook* v. *Stokes Bros.*, [1924] All E.R. Rep. 110, at pp. 114-115; [1925] 1 K.B. 141, at pp. 152-154; *United Australia, Ltd.* v. *Barclays Bank, Ltd*, [1940] 4 All E.R. 20, at p. 32; [1941] A.C. 1, at p. 31; *Fibrosa Spolka Akcyjna* v. *Fairbairn Lawson Combe Barbour, Ltd.*, [1942] 2 All E.R. 122, at p. 130; [1943] A.C. 32, at pp. 50-51.

[3]" The Future Development of English Law ", Jo.S.P.T.L. (1925), pp. 12-15; Address to Holdsworth Club (1930), p. 9.

[4]*Fender* v. *Mildmay*, (1937] 3 All E.R. 402, at p. 407; [1938] A.C. 1, at p. 12.

[5]*Lord Atkin of Aberdovey*, Obituary by Lord WRIGHT, Proc. British Academy, XXXII, p. 317.

[6]*Freedom under the Law* (1949); *The Changing Law* (1953); *The Road to Justice* (1955).

[7]*Central London Property Trust, Ltd.* v. *High Trees House Ltd.*, [1956] 1 All E.R. 256; [1947] K.B. 130.

notion of moral justice is not the only notion of justice in Lord DENNING's juristic philosophy[1] it appears to be the dominant one. In his judicial technique the notion may be discerned operating in two ways. In some cases he overtly relies on some moral principle, the validity of which is assumed *a priori*, and which he applies casuistically to the facts before the court. In others he concentrates upon the facts before the court, setting them out not only in the narrow form disclosed in the pleadings but in their wider social context, and then, relying on an intuitive sense of right and wrong, pronounces a moral judgment *ad hoc*.

The pre-eminent example of the first method is his use of the proposition which he postulated in the *High Trees House* case—that promises intended to be binding, intended to be acted on, and in fact acted on, are binding.[2] The principle has been applied by the learned judge, through the medium of the legal categories of contract and estoppel, to a wide variety of factual situations. In the original case he was prepared to apply it (though the specific claim did not require him to do so) to prevent a landlord, who had promised to allow a tenant to remain in possession at half the contractual rent during war-time conditions, from going back on this promise at will several years later and exacting the full rent. In *Robertson* v. *Minister of Pensions*[3] he applied it to prevent the Minister of Pensions from denying a representation given to a soldier by the War Office, which would have entitled the soldier to a pension and on which he in fact relied. In *Charles Rickards, Ltd.* v. *Oppenheim*[4] he used it to prevent a buyer, who had

---

[1] See *ante*, pp. 30-33 and 63-64.

[2] [1956] 1 All E.R. 256; [1947] K.B. 130 at p. 134. Some legal authority can be found for the proposition in a limited form, involving waiver of rights: *viz.* Hughes v. *Metropolitan Rail. Co.* (1877), 2 App. Cas. 439, at p. 448, *per* Lord CAIRNS, L.C.; *Birmingham and District Land Co.* v. *London and North Western Rail. Co.* (1888), 40 Ch. D. 268. But the proposition is essentially ethical, analogous to that which Lord WRIGHT adopted *à priori* in his critique of the law of contract (see *post*, p. 158), and having close affinity with the principle of the inherent moral obligation of serious promises which moralists and theologians have advanced for centuries: see St. Germain, *Doctor and Student*, II, Chap. XXIV; Paley, *Principles of Moral and Political Philosophy* (1785), Book III, Chaps. V and VI.

[3] [1948] 2 All E.R. 767; [1949] 1 K.B. 227.

[4] [1950] 1 All E.R. 420, at p. 423; [1950] 1 K.B. 616, at p. 623.

agreed to accept delivery on a date later than that named in
the contract, from turning round and trying to hold the
seller to the original delivery date. More recently, in *Lyle-
Meller* v. *A. Lewis & Co. (Westminster), Ltd.*,[1] the defendants
had represented to the plaintiff that their goods did embody
his invention, and on that assumption promised to pay him
royalties. On the strength of these assurances the plaintiff
refrained from exploiting his invention elsewhere. When the
defendants discovered that their manufactures actually did
not embody the plaintiff's invention or infringe his patent,
they attempted to repudiate their assumed liability for
royalties. DENNING, L.J., relying fundamentally on this
same moral principle, held that the defendants could not
evade liability arising from their promise.[2]

Examples of the second method are becoming numerous.[3]
Lord Justice DENNING'S dissenting judgment in *Bonsor* v.
Musicians' Union[4] most clearly illustrates the method at
work. Bonsor, a professional musician, had joined the defendant union, a registered trade union, and had agreed to
observe its rules. When he fell into arrears with subscriptions,
the secretary of the local branch of the union purported to
expel him on the ground that he had thereby violated the
rules. Thereafter Bonsor was in fact excluded from the union

---

[1][1956] 1 All E.R. 247.

[2]*Ibid.*, at pp. 249-251. The potentialities of this principle in rational-
ising and modifying the various rules of the law of contracts and
estoppel have been expounded further by the same judge in lectures
and essays: *The Changing Law* (1953), pp. 53-60; "Recent Developments in the Doctrine of Consideration". 15 M.L.R. 1.

[3]*E.g.*, *Smith* v. *River Douglas Catchment Board*, [1949] 2 All E.R.
179, at pp. 188-189, [1949] 2 K.B. 500, at pp. 514-517; *Drive Yourself
Hire Co. (London), Ltd.* v. *Strutt*, [1953] 2 All E.R. 1475, at pp.
1480-1484; [1954] 1 Q.B. 250, at pp. 269-275; *Adler* v. *Dickson*,
[1954] 3 All E.R. 397, at pp. 399-403; [1955] 1 Q.B. 158 at pp.
179-185: *re* third party rights arising by way of contract. *Candler* v.
Crane, Christmas & Co., [1951] 1 All E.R. 426, at pp. 428-436;
[1951] 2 K.B. 164, at pp. 174-185; *re* duty of accountants. *Errington*
v. *Errington and Woods*, [1952] 1 All E.R. 149, at pp. 153-156;
[1952] 1 K.B. 290, at pp. 294-300; *Bendall* v. *McWhirter*, [1952]
1 All E.R. 1307, at pp. 1309-1316; [1952] 2 Q.B. 466, at pp. 474-485;
Woodcock (Jess B.) & Son, Ltd. v. *Hobbs*, [1955] 1 All E.R. 445, at
pp. 446-450; *re* deserted wife's rights in matrimonial home.

[4][1954] 1 All E.R. 822; [1954] Ch. 479.

for several years. He claimed (*a*) a declaration that his expulsion was wrongful, null and void, (*b*) an injunction restraining the union and its servants and agents from acting on the purported expulsion, and (*c*) damages for wrongful expulsion. The Court of Appeal (EVERSHED, M.R., DENNING and JENKINS, L.JJ.) unanimously held that the plaintiff was entitled to the declaration and the injunction as the branch secretary had no power under the rules to expel a member; but the majority of the Court of Appeal refused to grant Bonsor damages, holding themselves bound to follow a ruling to that effect by the Court of Appeal in *Kelly's* case.[1] Lord Justice DENNING'S statement of the facts at the beginning of his judgment on the question of damages is characteristic; this marshalling of the facts in their social context is the preliminary process in the moral judgment. " This case well illustrates the great power wielded by trade unions at the present day. This Union, the Musicians' Union, has the power to dictate both to employers and to workmen. It has in this case excluded the plaintiff from the occupation as a musician in which he has spent his life, and which is the only occupation he knows; and all because he fell into arrears with his subscriptions. It is, indeed, a grievous punishment to inflict upon him. He was reduced at one time to accepting employ· ment to remove rust from Brighton Pier. . . . This exclusion has lasted four years, and his loss of earnings must be considerable, to say nothing of the worry and trouble to which he has been put. And the exclusion was unlawful. . . . We have already held that this exclusion was a breach of contract." The moral judgment follows immediately: " Yet it is said that we cannot award the plaintiff damages for the injury done to him. If this is so, then it is a grievous thing; for I know of no other case where the law allows a party to break a contract with impunity. A man's right to work is just as important to him, indeed more important, than his right of property. If he is unlawfully deprived of his right to work, the courts should intervene to protect him."[2] As for the

---

[1] *Kelly* v. *National Society of Operative Printers* (1915), 113 L.T. 1055; see *post*, pp. 213-214.

[2] [1954] 1 All E.R. 822, at pp. 835-836; [1954] Ch. 479, at pp. 506-507.

ruling in *Kelly's* case, which stood in the way of this morally just solution of the problem before the Court, Lord Justice DENNING proceeded in effect to overrule that case, *inter alia* by demonstrating that the assumption on which it relied— that a trade union was not an entity distinct from its members—was inconsistent with statute-law and a series of decisions in the House of Lords, and that nowadays a registered trade union is a legal entity capable of entering into contracts with its own members.[1] Thus, he reached the conclusion that, as " no-one in this country should be in law fully excluded from his livelihood without having redress for the damage thereby done to him "[2] Bonsor was entitled to damages against the offending union.[3] That this conclusion was dictated by the initial moral judgment formed after conning all the facts seems incontestable.

Though a traditional common lawyer in his refusal to philosophise at length in the abstract about justice, Lord DENNING has attempted to formulate his own view of the nature of the concept. " I ask the question, what is justice? That question has been asked by many men . . . and no-one has yet found a satisfactory answer. All I would suggest is that justice is not something you can see. It is not temporal but eternal. How does man know what is justice? It is not the product of his intellect but of his spirit. The nearest we can get to defining justice is to say that it is what the right-minded members of the community—those who have the right spirit within them—believe to be fair."[4] Though Lord DENNING in his rationalisation of the concept professes thus to rely on positive morality, in the course of judgment and in juristic essays he never sets out any *evidence* of contemporary moral opinion other than his own. He trusts his own moral sense as representative of that of the right-minded members of the community in which he lives. In another lecture[5] he has in effect analysed this moral sense, and found it to be the product of the habits of thought of many genera-

---

[1]*Ibid.*, at pp. 836-840; 507-514 respectively.
[2]*Ibid.*, at pp. 840, 514 respectively.
[3]See *post*, pp. 213-214.
[4]*The Road to Justice* (1955), p. 4.
[5]*The Changing Law*, Chap. 5, " The Influence of Religion ".

tions of English lawyers, continuously informed by the precepts of Christianity.

If Lord DENNING is heterodox in this generation it is not in his allegiance to the notion of justice according to morality, but only in the priority he has been disposed to give to it on the Bench over the notion of justice according to established law. For it is orthodox enough amongst lawyers in modern England[1] to use current morality in criticising the positive law or in formulating proposals for parliamentary legislation. Thus moral justice appeared prominently among the canons of criticism employed by the practitioners and professors who constituted the Law Revision Committee[2] in their eight Reports, 1934-1939. For example, it appeared in their First Report[3] in which they examined the operations of the maxim " *actio personalis moritur cum persona* " in the sphere of tort. They showed that if A, a negligent driver, injures people, and A lives, the law entitled the injured to compensation: a result of which they approved. But if A, the negligent driver, injures people, but is himself killed, the operation of this maxim is such that the victims have no right to compensation, a result which they accounted " a defect in the law ", which " many lawyers have long felt involves great injustice ". Besides, if as a result of A's negligent driving, B is not just injured but killed, at common law (as distinct from statute) some classes of dependants could not recover compensation from A: another " defect in the law ". Why defects? The criterion evidently was a moral axiom assumed by the Committee—that persons who in fact suffer injuries or loss as the result of the wrongful conduct of others should receive adequate compensation from the wrongdoer or from his property. Again, in their last Report in 1939,[4] they used moral criteria in the course of their review of the doctrine of contributory negligence. Their approach was to consider on the one hand the established Admiralty rule, that where by fault

---

[1]*E.g.*, Professor Goodhart, in his Hamlyn Lectures, *English Law and the Moral Law* (1953), and in his editorial case notes in the Law Quarterly Review, uses the " generally recognised moral standards of the community " as a stock criterion for approving or disapproving of particular rules or decisions.

[2]See *post*, pp. 157-158. [3]1934, Cmd. 4540.
[4]Eighth Report, Cmd. 6032.

of two or more vessels damage is caused to one or more of
them the liability should be in proportion to the degree in
which each was at fault; and on the other hand the rule of
common law that if the fault of each party contributed to
the accident neither party could recover from the other; and
then to review fully many of the factual situations disclosed
in the reported cases in which each rule had operated. In
conclusion the Committee simply pronounced in favour of the
Admiralty rule " as in our opinion it is the fairer "—a classic
example of the moral judgment proceeding immediately from
a consideration of concrete factual situations by experienced
common lawyers. Similar criteria have been used almost as
readily by the Law Reform Committee since 1953, most
patently in their Third Report on Occupiers' Liability to
Invitees, Licensees and Trespassers,[1] in which the new Committee used both of the methods described above. They tested
the existing law against an assumed moral principle—that
the occupier of premises owes some duty of care in regard to
the safety of those premises to persons lawfully coming on
them[2]—a proposition which they thought " must command
universal acceptance ". They considered a series of factual or
hypothetical situations involving visitors, and offered what
they adjudged to be the right solution to each.[3] In using the
latter method they professed to give the view which " the
hypothetical reasonable man of ordinary prudence and with
an ordinary regard for the safety of others " would be likely
to take as to the degree of care due from occupier to visitor—
an attempt to assess positive morality on the question. Again
we may observe that the moral criterion invoked is ostensibly
the morality of the right-minded men of the community,
positive morality; but, as no evidence of that morality was
formally taken in the Committee's deliberations or cited in
their Report, we must conclude that the judges, counsel and
academic lawyers who constituted the Committee[4] fell back
on their own moral sense, fined and refined by experience. At
least the moral propositions and judgments were agreed on by
most of the members of the Committee.

---

[1]1954, Cmd. 9305.
[2]*Ibid.*, §§ 2, 46, 58.
[3]*Ibid.*, §§ 63-77.   [4]See *post*, p. 157.

§C

The notion of justice set out in this chapter, whether the criterion be the positive morality of the day, or the morality of the " best men " of the time, or the moral sense of the judge or jurist in question, has permeated most of the great branches of English law. It is not proposed to establish and elaborate here the connection between the many doctrines of positive law and this notion of moral justice.[1] It has inspired many doctrines of equity, the substratum and several refinements of the law of crimes, several branches of the law of torts and of the law of contracts and, not least, the ubiquitous doctrine of estoppel by conduct. It is only proposed to demonstrate the connection between the notion under discussion and one branch of the positive law, which is nowadays classified as quasi-contract or restitution. An examination of three particular rules of quasi-contract and their moral basis must suffice.

First, it is a firmly established rule of quasi-contract that when A has paid money to B under the influence of a mistake of fact, B is under an obligation to refund the money.[2] It was laid down dogmatically by PARKE, B., in *Kelly* v. *Solari* in 1841[3] that " where money is paid to another under the influence of a mistake, that is, upon the supposition that a specific fact is true, which would entitle the other to the money, but which fact is untrue . . . an action will lie to recover it back . . ." and this proposition has been approved and applied by the House of Lords and the Privy Council in modern cases.[4] Now in *Kelly* v. *Solari*, PARKE, B., himself appended to the above statement of the rule his opinion as to the basis of it: " and it is against conscience to retain it ";

---

[1]See Ames, " Law and Morals" (1908), 22 H.L.R. 97-112; Winfield, " Ethics in English Case Law" (1931), 45 H.L.R. 112-135; Goodhart, *English Law and the Moral Law* (1953), *passim*.

[2]Winfield, *Law of Quasi-Contracts* (1952), § 12.

[3](1841), 9 M. & W. 54, at p. 58. The rule can be traced back to earlier centuries: *Bonnel* v. *Foulke* (1657), 2 Sid. 4; *Framson* v. *Delamere* (1596), Cro. Eliz. 458.

[4]*Jones (R. E.), Ltd.* v. *Waring and Gillow, Ltd.*, [1926] All E.R. Rep. 36; [1926] A.C. 670; *Norwich Union Fire Insurance Society* v. *William H. Price, Ltd.*, [1934] All E.R. Rep. 352; [1934] A.C. 455.

and ROLFE, B., underlined this moral basis.[1] In *Sadler* v.
Evans, or *Lady Windsor's* case in the previous century[2] Lord
MANSFIELD, speaking for the unanimous Court of King's
Bench, had exhibited most plainly the moral basis of this and
related rules: " It [the action for money had and received to
the plaintiff's use] is a liberal action, founded on large principles of equity, where the defendant cannot conscientiously
hold the money. The defence is any equity which will rebut
the action."[3] Admittedly in 1912 HAMILTON, L.J., in *Baylis*
v. *Bishop of London*[4] reacted to an argument based on this
famous *dictum*, particularly to the last proposition about
equitable defences, with the now notorious *dictum*: " Whatever may have been the case 140 years ago, we are not now
free in the twentieth century to administer that vague jurisprudence which is sometimes attractively styled ' justice as
between man and man '." But in the preceding sentences he
clearly reasserted the original moral basis of the rule in
question; " In effect, therefore, both the equitable and legal
considerations applicable to the recovery of money paid
under a mistake of fact have been crystallised in the reported
common law cases. The question is whether it is conscientious
for the defendant to keep the money, not whether it is fair
for the plaintiff to ask to have it back. To ask what course
would be *ex aequo et bono* never was a very precise guide, and
as a working rule it has long since been buried in *Standish* v.
Ross[5] and *Kelly* v. *Solari* ".[6]

A second rule of positive law, nowadays classified as quasi-
contractual, is that where money is paid by A to B for the
performance of some undertaking by B, if B wholly fails to
perform his undertaking then B is obliged to return the
money to A;[7] in technical terms money paid upon a consideration which wholly fails is recoverable by an action for
money had and received to the plaintiff's use. It was evi-

---

[1](1841), 9 M. & W. 54, at p. 59.
[2](1766), 4 Burr. 1985.
[3]*Ibid.*, at p. 1986.
[4][1913] 1 Ch. 127, at p. 140.
[5](1849), 3 Exch. 527.
[6](1841), 9 M. & W. 54.
[7]Winfield, *Law of Quasi-Contracts* (1952), § 10.

dently recognised as far back as the thirteenth century[1] and was treated in *Holmes* v. *Hall* in 1704 as a familiar rule in cases where part-payment of the price of a bargain had been made and the " bargainer would not perform ", and in cases of insurance where premiums had been paid but the ships " did not go the voyage ". In the latter case[2] HOLT, C.J., indicated the basis of the rule when he declared that recovery was not possible upon a usurious contract " because it was not intended that it should be repaid or anything done for it ".[3] In *Dutch* v. *Warren*[4] the Court of Common Pleas evidently based such a right to recover on the notion of moral turpitude in the defendant: " If one man take another's money to do a thing, and refuses to do it; it is a fraud." In recent years in the *Fibrosa* case[5] the House of Lords unanimously applied the rule to a case in which A had paid money in advance to B under a contract which was eventually discharged under the doctrine of frustration, when B had not performed his undertaking before the frustrating event and A had accordingly received no benefit whatsoever. In this case Lord WRIGHT emphasised that the basis of this particular rule of quasi-contract was that the courts recognised that as there was in such circumstances no intention on the part of A to enrich B, B had no moral right to retain the money.[6]

A third rule of quasi-contract runs, according to Leake:[7] " Where the plaintiff has been compelled by law to pay, or being compellable by law has paid money which the defendant was ultimately liable to pay, so that the latter obtains the benefit of the payment by the discharge of his liability; under such circumstances the defendant is held indebted to the plaintiff in the amount "—a formula which has been

---

[1] Jackson, *History of Quasi-Contract* (1936), § 6, citing Y.B. 21 & 22 Edw. I, R.S. 598.

[2] *Holmes* v. *Hall* (1704), 6 Mod. Rep. 161.

[3] *Ibid.*, at p. 161.

[4] (1720), 1 Stra. 406: quoted by Lord MANSFIELD in 2 Burr. at p. 1011.

[5] *Fibrosa Spolka Akcyjna* v. *Fairbairn Lawson Combe Barbour, Ltd.*, [1942] 2 All E.R. 122; [1943] A.C. 32.

[6] *Ibid.*, at pp. 61-64.

[7] *Law of Contracts*, 1st edn. (1867), p. 41: Winfield, *Law of Quasi-Contracts* (1952), § 17.

adopted in the Court of Exchequer Chamber[1] and in the modern Court of Appeal.[2] The rule as formulated is itself a generalisation of several rulings in particular cases decided since the late eighteenth century.[3] In one of the earliest cases, *Exall* v. *Partridge*,[4] the defendants were lessees of premises who were bound to pay rent to W, and the plaintiff had left his coach on the premises in the possession of one of the defendants. When the defendants failed to pay the rent due W took the plaintiff's coach by way of distress. To recover his coach the plaintiff had to pay to W the rent due from the defendants. In the Court of King's Bench the plaintiff recovered the amount of the rent due from the defendants. GROSE and LAWRENCE, JJ., simply rehearsed the above facts and concluded that in such circumstances the defendants were bound to repay the plaintiffs, the latter saying: " The justice of the case indeed is, that the one who must ultimately pay this money, should be answerable here."[5] Leake cited this type of case under the rubric " Contracts implied in Law ", and observed the common characteristic: " that some undue pecuniary inequality exists in the one party relatively to the other which justice and equity require should be compensated ".[6] It is only in recent years that a judge has clearly expressed the basis of these particular rulings— these items of judicial legislation. Lord WRIGHT, in the Court of Appeal in *Brook's Wharf and Bull Wharf, Ltd.* v. *Goodman Bros.*,[7] *à propos* the general rule as formulated by Leake and applied in various cases, revealed in the plainest terms that the source of the rule has been the sense of moral justice in a succession of judges confronted with various combinations of facts: " The obligation is imposed by the court simply under the circumstances of the case and on what the court decides is just and reasonable, having regard to the relationship of the parties."

---

[1] *Moule* v. *Garrett* (1872), L.R. 7 Exch. 101, at p. 104, *per* COCKBURN, C.J.

[2] *Brook's Wharf and Bull Wharf, Ltd.* v. *Goodman Bros.*, [1936] 3 All E.R. 696, at pp. 706-707; [1937] 1 K.B. 534, at pp. 543-544.

[3] Jackson, *History of Quasi-Contract*, § 20.

[4] (1799), 8 Term Rep. 308.

[5] *Ibid.*, at p. 311.

[6] *Law of Contracts* 1st edn. (1867), p. 38.

[7] [1936] 3 All E.R. 696, at p. 707; [1937] 1 K.B. 534, at p. 545.

These are but three of the score of obligations imposed by
law, *i.e.* by the judges from time to time, which go to make
the doctrine of quasi-contract or restitution in modern
English law.[1] Some evidence from the relevant case-law has
been cited to demonstrate that several of these obligations
derive principally from the judges' notions of moral justice.
But can the doctrine as a whole be regarded as a historical
precipitate of this notion? Lord MANSFIELD, as Chief Justice
of the Court of King's Bench, speaking *ex cathedra* at a time
when the doctrine was still in the process of being laid down
in particular decisions, evidently thought so. In 1760 in
Moses v. *Macferlan*[2] he listed six of these obligations arising
" as it were upon a contract ", which were enforceable by
actions of *indebitatus assumpsit* for money had and received
to the plaintiff's use, and explained: " This kind of equitable
action, to recover back money, which ought not in justice to
be kept, is very beneficial. . . . It lies only for money which,
ex aequo et bono, the defendant ought to refund. . . . In one
word, the gist of this kind of action is, that the defendant
upon the circumstances of the case, is obliged by the ties of
natural justice and equity to refund the money."[3] In another
case[4] he spoke of the action as " founded on principles of
eternal justice ". Now this invocation of natural justice
seems unwarranted: the rulings he was advocating do not
appear as primary or secondary precepts in the doctrine of
natural law advanced by the mediaeval theologians or the
seventeenth century rationalists.[5] But the phrases used were
probably no more than rhetorical expressions for the dictates
of the moral sense of particular judges confronted with
particular situations. Even on this interpretation Lord
MANSFIELD'S exposition of the basis of the doctrine was
heterodox, being too candid for most common lawyers in the
era of the dominance of the forms of action in legal thinking.
As the form of action for the enforcement of such obligations
was, from the late seventeenth century until the Common

---

[1]See Winfield, *Law of Quasi-Contracts, passim.*
[2](1760), 2 Burr. 1005.
[3]*Ibid.*, at p. 1012.
[4]*Towers* v. *Barrett* (1786), 1 Term Rep. 133, at p. 134.
[5]See *ante*, Chap. 4.

Law Procedure Act of 1852, *indebitatus assumpsit*, and as this procedure necessitated the allegation of a promise to pay by the defendant, which promise would in this type of case be " implied ", *i.e.*, be a legal fiction, the more orthodox view of these obligations was that they depended on implied promises or contracts implied by law: and this theory of quasi-contract has died hard within the profession[1] in spite of the Act of 1852.[2] But this " theory " is formulated *à posteriori:* it is comprehensive of the cases that were decided since the late seventeenth century. The crucial and prior question for the judges in the actual cases in which the obligations were recognised was—should we imply, *i.e.* invent, a promise to pay on the part of the defendant in these circumstances? Lord MANSFIELD's theory provided a general answer to that fundamental question. Modern research substantially confirms his answer though disapproving of its references to " natural law " and " equity " as oratorical flourishes. Professor Winfield[3] concludes that the basic concept in this branch of positive law is " unjust benefit ".[4] By " just " in the context Winfield refers to the flexible standard of " what is reasonable ";[5] and the standard of reasonableness is seen as resolving itself into the decision by the judge in the particular case of what is reasonable on the facts as between the parties confronting him, the judge representing the " highest common factor of public sentiment and intelligence ".[6] In a nutshell, the historical basis of quasi-contract has been the notion of moral justice operating in the minds of a series of

---

[1]*Sinclair* v. *Brougham*, [1914] 1 A.C. 398, *per* Viscount HALDANE and Lord SUMNER; *Halsbury's Laws of England*, 2nd edn., Vol. VII, p. 274; *cf.* Landon, 8 *Bell Yard* (1931), p. 27.

[2]Section 49 expressly enacted that " All statements which need not be proved, such . . . as promises in indebitatus counts . . . shall be omitted " (from pleadings).

[3]*The Province of the Law of Tort* (1931), Chap. VII, entitled " Tort and Quasi-Contract " covers most of the ground explored more fully by the author in his later work *Law of Quasi-Contracts* (1952).

[4]" Genuine quasi-contract may be defined as follows. Liability, not exclusively referable to any other head of law, imposed on a particular person to pay money to another particular person on the ground that non-payment of it would confer on the former an unjust benefit ": *Law of Quasi-Contracts*, pp. 1-2.

[5]*Op. cit.*, p. 20.

[6]*Op. cit.*, p. 13.

judges. Lord Wright has endorsed this conclusion in his extra-judicial essays,[1] and on the Bench. In the House of Lords in the *Fibrosa* case[2] he asserted: " It is clear that any civilised system of law is bound to provide remedies for cases of what has been called unjust enrichment or unjust benefit, that is to prevent a man from retaining the money or some benefit derived from another which it is against conscience that he should keep. Such remedies in English law are generically different from remedies in contract or in tort, and are now recognised to fall within a third category of the common law which has been called quasi-contract or restitution. . . . The standard of what is against conscience in this context has become more or less canalised or defined, but in substance the juristic concept remains as Lord Mansfield left it."

§D

The notion of moral justice has been under running fire from within the legal profession for centuries. The objection most often voiced has been that the essential criterion is subjective and variable: not only that the criterion may vary from generation to generation, but that in the same decade or in the same year or in the very same case the judges who use this criterion may reach contrary conclusions. It was on this ground that the older common lawyers railed against the practices of Chancellors in the new Court of Chancery. As the Serjeant, in a replication to St. Germain's Doctor, acidly observed " divers men, divers conscience ".[3] Hence Selden's gibe that conscience in Chancery varied with the Chancellor: " 'Tis all one . . . as if they should make the standard for the measure we call a foot to be the Chancellor's foot."[4] Later

---

[1] *Legal Essays and Addresses* (1939), pp. 1-65.
[2] [1942] 2 All E.R. 122, at pp. 135-136; [1943] A.C. 32, at pp. 61-63.
[3] Anon. " Two Pieces concerning Suits in Chancery by Subpoena ", *circa* 1529, published in Hargrave, *Law Tracts* (1787), 321, p. 326.
[4] Selden, *Table Talk* (*circa* 1654; pub. 1689: ed. Pollock 1927) title " Equity ", p. 43.

Bentham attacked the notion on the same score, with characteristic verbal venom: the doctrines of moral sense or common sense he regarded as resolving into the principle of
sympathy and of antipathy, which could become the principles of caprice or of phantasy, as they depended on the
mere opinion of the individual concerned: such doctrines he
condemned " as a cloke, and pretence, and aliment, to
despotism ".[1] John Austin maintained the attack in the
nineteenth century.[2] He rejected the individual's moral sense
as the primary index of justice on the ground that it was
notorious that " the respective moral sentiments of different
ages and nations and of different men in the same age and
nation have differed to infinity ".[3] The gravamen of the objection of these English lawyers is that this moral criterion is the
negation of an objective measure or standard, which they
regard as of supreme importance in the administration of
justice in courts. Moral justice is thus condemned by the
exponents of legal justice, the disciples of Austin, in so far
as it promotes uncertainty in the legal process. The prognosis
is borne out to some extent by the law reports. On occasions
where the judges have resorted to their moral sense as the
canon of decision they have been sharply divided in their
conclusions.[4] But exponents of moral justice could cite as
many if not more reported cases in which the judges each
reached similar conclusions on moral grounds. The result of
this inveterate objection on the part of many common
lawyers to moral justice has not been to exterminate the
notion in the judicial process. Rather, after a case in which
a judge has openly invoked the notion as the basis of his
decision the tendency has been for succeeding courts to treat
his specific answer as a rule of positive law, and thus the

---

[1]*Introduction to Principles of Morals and Legislation* (1789), Chap.
II, §§ 14, 22.
[2]*Province of Jurisprudence Determined* (1832), ed. Hart (1954),
pp. 34-37 and 87-99.
[3]*Ibid.*, ed. Hart (1954), Lecture IV, p. 98.
[4]*E.g.*, in *United Australia, Ltd.* v. *Barclays Bank, Ltd.*, [1940] 4 All
E.R. 20; [1941] A.C. 1, Lord ATKIN and Viscount SIMON, giving
judgment *against* the Bank, professed to reach the morally just
solution: in the Court of Appeal [1939] 2 K.B. 53, at p. 60, giving
judgment *for* the Bank, the whole court expressed satisfaction that
this result accorded with " the general principles of right ".

notion of legal justice, involving the value of certainty,[1] comes into operation to confine the effects of the notion of moral justice—as we have observed in the preceding discussion of the law of quasi-contract.[2]

To meet this objection exponents of moral justice in more recent times have contended that the moral criterion which the judge applies is not his own individual moral sense but the positive morality of his day. Though they may profess to apply an objective moral criterion it is doubtful whether any of the judges (Lord MANSFIELD only excepted) has ever gone further than to trust to his own moral principles or moral reactions to a given situation as representative of the morality of his contemporaries. In the late nineteenth century Pollock considered that though ethical judgments are not organised they nevertheless make a body of fairly uniform tradition the contents of which are known to most men for most purposes.[3] But it may be observed that Pollock was speaking in the context of Victorian England when there was probably a wider measure of agreement on moral questions than in the English society which has been profoundly disturbed by two world wars. Very recently Lord Justice DEVLIN, while defending the system which provides for the enforcement of some sectors of public morality by legal sanctions, relied on the institution of the jury as a mechanism for ascertaining the moral judgment of the community: ". . . the moral judgment of society must be something about which any twelve men or women drawn at random might after discussion be expected to be unanimous ".[4] But this mechanism is not available to judges in the vast majority of civil cases in these days. Lord Justice SCRUTTON in the Court of Appeal in 1930[5] confessed to the

---

[1]See *post*, Chap. 8.

[2]" We may set out to administer the law with " moral justice " as a guide, but we always find that it turns into " justice according to law " before we reach the journey's end ". Winfield, " Ethics in English Case-Law " (1931) 45 H.L.R. 112, at p. 134.

[3]*Essays in Jurisprudence and Ethics* (1882), Chap X, " The Casuistry of Common Sense ".

[4]" The Enforcement of Morals " (1959), Maccabean Lecture in Jurisprudence of the British Academy, at p. 16.

[5]*Watt* v. *Longsdon*, [1929] All E.R. Rep. 284, at pp. 286-288; [1930] 1 K.B. 130, at pp. 139-144. *Cf.* Lord HEWART, who admitted

(continued at foot of next page)

8

greatest difficulty in ascertaining the existence of a moral duty as distinct from a legal duty in a given situation, and to being perplexed whether to give effect to his own views, which might differ from those of a considerable proportion of the community, or to endeavour to ascertain what view the great mass of " right-minded " men would take on the moral question before the court. Even if the judge does attempt to determine the morality of his contemporaries he is faced with considerable practical difficulties. No authoritative code of morality is open to him. No evidence from social scientists is normally admissible in court. Counsel may argue from moral principle but this is but a second individual opinion, which may be contradicted by his opponent. The judge's knowledge of other people's opinions may be limited to his professional or social set and the sample may not correspond with the opinions of most citizens from Alnwick to Penzance. Further, on a novel question conflicting opinions crystallising into various schools of thought may emerge and it may be a decade or more before one school of moral opinion prevails in the community; yet the judge may be seised of a case involving a decision on the novel moral question within the first year. The " objective " criterion invoked turns out to be either a legal fiction or a rough and fallible estimate of public opinion.

A more fundamental objection to this theory of moral justice arises from the assumption that the majority of righteous men in a society at any time are the ultimate arbiters of right and wrong. Most Englishmen approved of slavery, in the form of villeinage, in early mediaeval England. In the eighteenth century " the best sort of citizens " in Parliament and in the counties approved of the death penalty for scores of petty criminal offences. In the early nineteenth century most Englishmen believed it right that a married woman should be the inferior of her husband in legal powers. Yet to-day the vast majority of Englishmen reject all these moral judgments. So it is difficult to believe that the

---

(*continued from foot of previous page*)
to a deep mistrust of that sense of duty which enables a man to perceive, or to think he perceives, with extraordinary clearness the duty of someone else: *Essays and Observations* (1930), pp. 53-54.

current moral opinion is infallible. Besides, as Dr. Allen has pointed out, the popular judgment on a question is apt to be treacherous, concentrating on only one aspect of a complex situation, and subject to gusts of passion.[1] The assumption may be challenged on another ground. It is questionable whether the majority opinion is the better opinion on every question. At least one moral philosopher has recorded that " moral progress has been possible just because there have been men in all ages who have seen the difference and have practised, or at least preached, a morality in some respects higher than that of their race and age ".[2] Those who hold to the absolute doctrine of justice, as the conformity of human affairs to divine law including natural law, would reject this assumption that *vox populi* is the primary authority on questions of justice, though they would still assign to conscience the subsidiary rôle of supplementing the precepts of the revealed or the natural law.[3]

Even the lawyers who nevertheless accept this notion of moral justice cannot claim that it is a complete theory. Given that the function of law is to achieve justice, this objective cannot be moral justice in every case, as there are so many cases which are without moral significance. Many questions which fall to be decided in courts are such that a decision either way is morally indifferent. Whether traffic should drive on the left or right side of the road or within a speed limit of 30 or 50 m.p.h. is not a moral question. The formula used in a conveyance or will to effect a transfer of property is a matter for the law to prescribe, but positive morality is silent on the point. The question whether the period of limitation of actions in contracts should be six or twelve years is one on which a moral opinion is irrelevant. Legal rules determining where the loss shall fall when both parties are innocent are without moral counterparts. In dealing with such questions the lawyer who aims to do justice must rely on some other notion than moral justice.

---

[1]Allen, *Law in the Making*, 6th edn. (1958), p. 370; *cf.* AVORY, J., summing up in *R.* v. *Browne & Kennedy* (1928): " Public opinion is often, like rumour, a lying jade ": reported in Lang, *Mr. Justice Avory* (1935), p. 35.

[2]Ross, *The Right and the Good* (1930), p. 12.

[3]See *ante*, Chap. 4.

CHAPTER 6

INDIVIDUAL UTILITY

§A

A general standard for a system of judicature and for substantive law which has been prominent in English legal thought is the principle of utility. The term " utility " is used here not to connote usefulness with reference to any purpose whatsoever, but to express shortly that first principle in a system of moral philosophy which evaluates actions with reference to their tendency to produce pleasure or reduce pain in the human beings concerned. The same principle is invoked by the lawyers on occasion under the name " convenience ", and is referred to as " expediency " more often by its opponents than by its supporters.

In England nowadays the principle of utility is indelibly associated with Jeremy Bentham. Bentham certainly did not originate this first principle for morals and law[1] nor was he the first to introduce it into English moral philosophy. BACON,[2] Hume,[3] Priestley,[4] and Paley[5] had advanced such a principle in England before Bentham proclaimed it in his *Principles of Morals and Legislation* in 1789.[6] But what

---

[1]The notion is discussed by ancient and mediaeval philosophers; see Cicero, *De Legibus, I, XV;* Aquinas, *Summa Theologica,* II, I, 2-5.

[2]" The end and scope which laws ought to regard and to which they should direct their commands and sanctions, is nothing else than that citizens may live happily." *De Augmentis Scientiarum* (1623), Book VIII, Chap. 3, § 2, on " Universal Justice ", aphorism V; ed. Heron (1852), p. 4.

[3]*Treatise of Human Nature* (1738).

[4]*Essay on the First Principles of Government* (1768).

[5]*Principles of Moral and Political Philosophy* (1785).

[6]Bentham had outlined his theory earlier in his *Fragment on Government* (1776).

Bentham did was to consider in prodigious detail[1] over the next forty years the consequences of this principle within the province of law, particularly within the English legal system. He wrote primarily for men of affairs, parliamentarians and lawyers, rather than for the cloistered student of moral philosophy. He has been described aptly as " the man of one idea ".[2] That one idea, as worked out in detail by Bentham himself, and operating as a motive for the activities of many disciples inside and outside Parliament, has proved to be a dynamic force in the subsequent development of the English legal system. It has been Bentham the legal philosopher, rather than Paley the divine or Hume the pure philosopher who has been the father of utilitarian doctrine for the common lawyer. In Bentham's own words:

" By the principle of utility is meant that principle which approves or disapproves of every action whatsoever, according to the tendency which it appears to have to augment or diminish the happiness of the party whose interest is in question ";[3]

or, more succinctly, " the greatest happiness principle ".[4] Equally the principle of utility approves or disapproves of every action according to its tendency to diminish or augment pain or mischief or unhappiness in the persons whose interests are in question.[5] Bentham advanced this principle as the basic criterion not only for laws but also for morals. While the happiness-maximising principle may be more appropriate in the sphere of morals, it is the pain-minimising corollary which has proved more significant in the sphere of law.

To determine whether a particular action is conformable to utility Bentham would have the human agent concerned make a calculation. He should consider the tendency of the action in question, its probable consequences in pleasure and pain to the persons involved, and making allowances for

---

[1]*Works*, ed. Bowring, 11 vols. (1843); these volumes by no means exhaust his manuscripts, *e.g.*, *Limits of Jurisprudence Defined*, ed. Everett (1945).

[2]Leslie Stephen, *The English Utilitarians*, (1900), Vol. I, p. 234.

[3]*Principles of Morals and Legislation* (1789), ed. Harrison (1948), Chap. I, § 2.

[4]*Op. cit.*, Chap. I, § 1, note by Bentham added in 1822.

[5]*Op. cit.*, Chap. I, § 3.

quantity, such as duration and intensity and for the various degrees of sensibility in the persons involved, determine whether on balance the action is likely to augment the sum of their happiness or diminish the sum of their pain.[1]

When the axiom of utility is applied to the subject of laws it takes the form of the maxim, " it is the greatest happiness of the greatest number that is the measure of right and wrong ".[2]

> " The general object which all laws have, or ought to have in common, is to augment the total happiness of the community; and therefore in the first place, to exclude, as far as may be, everything that tends to subtract from that happiness; in other words, to exclude mischief."[3]

In the process of evaluating a positive law the critic, and in the process of legislating the legislator, should make a calculation, on the lines indicated above, to determine whether the law in question on the whole is likely to create more happiness than pain or at least to reduce pain in the persons concerned, that is in certain sections of the community or indeed in the whole community. In such a social question the pain or pleasure of *all* concerned is to be considered. Bentham himself insisted that " the dictates of utility are neither more nor less than the dictates of the most extensive and enlightened benevolence ".[4] So Bentham was disposed to define the objective of law not as " justice "[5] but as

---

[1]Bentham himself provides a detailed scheme for this " felicific calculus " in *Principles of Morals and Legislation*, Chaps. IV, V and VI. To counter the charge of hedonism which has so often been levelled at Bentham's utilitarianism it is worth emphasising that amongst the fourteen species of pleasure which Bentham enumerated he included not only those of the senses and of wealth, but also the pleasures of amity, piety and benevolence, and amongst pains not only those of privation and of the senses but also enmity and malevolence.

[2]*Fragment on Government* (1776), ed. Harrison (1948), Preface, § 2.

[3]*Principles of Morals and Legislation*, Chap. XIII, § 1.

[4]*Op. cit.*, Chap. X, § 36.

[5]For the most part Bentham avoided the term " justice ", mainly on account of its association in eighteenth century thought with natural law. " Justice, in the only sense in which it has a meaning, is an imaginary personage, feigned for the convenience of discourse, whose dictates are the dictates of utility, applied to certain particular cases ". *Principles of Morals and Legislation*, Chap. X, § 40, note. *Cf.* " I am a partisan of the *principle of utility* when I measure
(*continued at foot of next page*)

" the greatest possible happiness of the community ".[1]

The axiom of utility as applied in the sphere of law was conceived by Bentham as a first principle for parliamentary legislation. The whole of Bentham's writing for lawyers is orientated towards the reform of the legal system by Acts of Parliament and the establishment of complete codes of mandatory laws. The possibility of piecemeal judicial legislation on utilitarian principles or of adjudication with reference to them rather than the established law was discounted in Bentham's own works; and most utilitarians in the nineteenth century, whether in Parliament or in the legal profession accepted this emphasis. But it is by no means impossible to apply the utilitarian criterion in adjudication or in judicial legislation and on occasion its influence can be detected in the judicial process.[2]

These generalities mask a major problem. Assuming that the proper aim of the law-giver should be the diminution of pain and the promotion of happiness for the community as a whole, how is that state of affairs to be achieved? Who is the best judge of the happiness of the many individuals who constitute the community—the individuals themselves, or the government?

Bentham himself dogmatically asserted that the individual rather than the government could best judge his own happiness:

> " As a general rule, the greatest possible latitude should be left to individuals, in all cases in which they can injure none but themselves, for they are the best judges of their own interests."[3]

(continued from foot of previous page)
my approbation or disapprobation of a public or private act by its tendency to produce pleasure or pain; when I employ the words *just, unjust, moral, immoral, good or bad*, simply as collective terms including the ideas of certain pains or pleasures ".—*Theory of Legislation*, ed. Ogden (1931), p. 3.

[1]*Theory of Legislation*, ed. Ogden (1931), pp. 95 *et seq.* Within this general objective he saw four particular objectives of law—subsistence, equality, abundance and security, and he made plain his view of the relative importance of these objectives: that security was " the pre-eminent object ", subsistence " necessary for life ", and the other two " the ornaments of life ".

[2]See *post*, pp. 122-124 and 126.

[3]*Theory of Legislation*, ed. Ogden (1931) at p. 63; *Truth* v. *Ashurst, Works*, Vol. V, p. 234.

But this proposition is not itself logically part of the theory of utility. It is a distinct notion, a notion very much in vogue in England in the late eighteenth century and well into the nineteenth century,[1] a notion simply assumed by many Englishmen in that era without being elaborated in a formal theory by any one political philosopher or jurist, but having deep roots in English political[2] and juristic tradition.[3] The notion in its political form exalts individual liberty, and gave rise to the political dogma of *laissez-faire*. In its juristic form it gives rise to the dogma that legislation should aim at the removal of all those restrictions on the free action of an individual which are unnecessary, *i.e.*, not necessary for securing an equal freedom for other individuals. Bentham in effect fused with his general theory of utility this prevailing individualist notion. The composite doctrine, which has been labelled " individual utilitarianism ", is the version of utility which was in the ascendency in Parliament in England in the middle of the nineteenth century[4] and we shall see that this doctrine became the criterion of justice for many of the English lawyers.

But this is not the only possible answer to the problem posed. Alternatively it is arguable that the individual is not the best judge of his own happiness, or even if he is, that he is not always in a position to secure his own happiness, so that the enlightened governor rather than the governed should determine what is best for the latter. This answer coupled with the principle of utility leads to the conclusion that the law-giver best serves the end of the happiness of the community by legislating extensively for the benefit of the many individuals. This composite doctrine, which has been labelled " social utilitarianism ", superseded the individualist doctrine in Parliament in the late nineteenth

---

[1]See Leslie Stephen, *The English Utilitarians* (1900), Vol. I, pp. 130-136.

[2]Locke, *Treatises of Civil Government* (1690), *passim*.

[3]"The faith of the utilitarians in the supreme value of individual liberty . . . owes far more to the traditions of the common law than thinkers such as John Mill, who was no lawyer, are prepared to acknowledge. Bentham is heavily indebted to Coke . . ." Dicey, *Law and Public Opinion in England*, 2nd edn., (1914), at p. 176.

[4]See Dicey, *Law and Public Opinion*, Lecture VI.

century and since,[1] and bulks large in the modern English lawyers' notions of justice; it will be considered more fully in the next chapter.

Bentham himself applied the doctrine of individual utilitarianism to numerous branches of the law of England: to the constitution, to criminal procedure, to the law of punishments, to civil procedure and evidence, to the institutions of property and marriage and to the doctrine of contract. It is not proposed to consider in any detail Bentham's criticism of all these branches of law, but only, by way of illustration, to mention some of the more particular principles —" sub-principles "—which this process yields in two branches of the law, namely contracts and civil procedure. It has been at this intermediate level of abstraction that the common lawyers have the more readily absorbed utilitarian doctrine.

The doctrine of individual utility applied to the subject of the law of contracts yielded for Bentham the sub-principle of the maximum freedom of contract:

> " The sovereign should give his authority to all contracts proposed by individuals. . . . For no private contracts would be made, except with a view to reciprocal advantage, and they cannot be restrained, without in the same proportion injuring the happiness of individuals. Entire liberty for contracts—such would be the general rule."[2]

Exceptionally, he admitted, legal sanction should be refused to particular agreements, as when they are contrary to the public interest or the interests of the parties.[3]

The subject of civil procedure was prominent in Bentham's later detailed work, as he was acutely aware that no branch of English law stood more in need of extensive reform. As the object for law in general was the greatest happiness of the greatest number, he laid it down that

> ". . . the whole of the adjective branch taken together may be said to have two specific ends: the one positive, maximising the execution and effect given to the substantive branch; the other negative, minimising the evil, the

---

[1]See *ibid.*, 2nd edn., Lectures VII and VIII.
[2]*Works*, Vol. III, p. 190; see Dicey, *Law and Public Opinion*, 2nd edn. (1914), pp. 150-151.
[3]*Works*, Vol. III, p. 190.

hardship in various shapes necessary to the accomplishment of the main specified end."[1]
He enumerated several particular mischiefs which are liable to develop in any system of civil procedure, the diminution or reduction of which should be the constant aim of the legislator and administrator: (1) the frustration of well-grounded claims; (2) the allowance of ill-grounded claims; (3) expense; (4) vexation; (5) delay; (6) precipitation; and (7) complication.[2] Only when such mischiefs are minimised and the whole system of procedure gives full effect to the substantive law, which defines rights and wrongs, is " justice rendered ".[3] Applying these criteria to the English system of civil proceedings in the early nineteenth century Bentham found it to be grossly defective. There then existed several systems of courts—Common Law Courts, Courts of Chancery, Admiralty Courts and the archaic County Courts, and within the common law system itself there were the separate Courts of King's Bench, Common Pleas, Exchequer and the Assize Courts—all with overlapping jurisdictions. The County Court system was so inadequate that in effect civil jurisdiction was confined to the superior courts in London or on assize, so that the ordinary citizen had no forum in which he could effectively vindicate his legal rights to small debts or damages. The superior courts of common law operated not one procedure but scores of forms of action, barbed with technicalities, beset with fictions, and involving the most intricate patterns of pleading. In the result the honest litigant often suffered the frustration of a well-grounded claim on a technicality of jurisdiction or pleading, and was likely to incur excessive expense in complex proceedings perhaps necessarily pursued through several courts; and the delays in the Common Law Courts and even more notoriously in the Courts of Chancery were such as often to go beyond vexation to the point of ruining the parties who had recourse to them. The gravamen of Bentham's charge against the prevailing system was that it protected the " sinister " interests of the lawyers, " Judge and Co.", " at the expense and by the

---

[1]*Principles of Judicial Procedure*, written 1820-1827, published 1837; *Works*, Vol. II, p. 8.
[2]*Op. cit.*, p. 19.
[3]*Op. cit.*, p. 20.

sacrifice of the universal interest ".[1] In place of this system which so often " rendered injustice " Bentham proposed a relatively unified system of judicature based on several principles. On the principle of " single-seatedness " the major courts would be constituted of a single judge without a jury; on the principle of " omnicompetence " each of the major courts would have general jurisdiction over civil causes, so having power to deal with questions of common law or equity within the one proceeding.[2] Bentham proposed to substitute one uniform rational system of procedure for the multiplicity of archaic forms of action.[3] Legal fictions, "wilful falsehoods uttered by a judge for the purpose of giving to injustice the colour of justice ", he would sweep away; pleadings he would retain but reduce to a minimum necessary to define an issue.[4] For the various parts of the country he proposed a system of minor courts, located with regard to population and distance, with limited jurisdiction to entertain suits for small sums.[5] Of the host of minor reforms proposed one may be singled out. Dealing with the mischief of the expense of " litiscontestation " he advocated that

> ". . . with ample precaution against abuse, the necessary expense of evidence and professional assistance [should be] provided by the public for those who are not themselves in a condition to defray it."[6]

Most of these sub-principles of utility became orthodox principles for reform of the system of civil procedure in the course of the nineteenth century, even among the successors of " Judge and Co.".

§B

While Bentham's articulate theory of utility only captured the allegiance of the English common lawyers in the nineteenth century, traces of the notion can be found in the legal literature and the law reports of earlier centuries.

[1] *Op. cit.*, p. 7.
[2] *Op. cit.*, p. 22.
[3] *Op. cit., passim.*
[4] *Rationale of Judicial Evidence* (1827); *Works* VII, pp. 270 *et seq.*
[5] *Op. cit.*, pp. 236 *et seq.*
[6] *Principles of Judicial Procedure*; *Works* II, pp. 7-8.

In the fifteenth century LITTLETON, in his treatise *Of Tenures*,[1] had adopted as a criterion for rejecting certain rules their " inconvenience ". In St. Germain's *Doctor and Student*[2], the Doctor insisted that for positive law to be just the lawgiver must have wisdom " to judge after reason what is to be done for the communalty and what is expedient for a peaceful conversation [conservation?] and necessary sustentation of them "[3]; the Student replies that the common law provides that to avoid inconvenience to many some inconvenience may be visited on one,[4] giving specific examples. With COKE the consideration of the convenience of the community becomes more prominent. For instance, discussing frankalmoign tenure and the rule that a tenant in frankalmoign shall do certain services for his land, and LITTLETON's argument *ab inconvenienti* relating to these, COKE commented: " an argument drawne from an inconvenience is forcible in law, as hath beene observed before, and shall be often hereafter: *nihil quod est inconveniens est licitum.* And the law, that is the perfection of reason, cannot suffer any thing that is inconvenient. It is better, saith the law, to suffer a mischief that is peculiar to one than an inconvenience that may prejudice many "[5] Elsewhere[6] COKE reports that in the Court of King's Bench he and his brethren resolved that in interpreting a statute " the law will never make an interpretation to advance a private [benefit?] and to destroy the public [benefit?] but always to advance the public and to prevent every private, which is odious in law in such cases ". Later, Sheppard,[7] discussing the validity of conditions annexed to estates, included in his categories of void conditions " such as are against the public good ", giving as an example a condition that a man being a husbandman shall not sow his arable land. Such passages indicate that even the earlier common lawyers took into account at least occa-

---

[1] See *Coke on Littleton, Institutes*, I, §§ 138 and 231.

[2] *Dialogues between a Doctor of Divinity and a Student of the Common Law*, Revised edn. (1532).

[3] *Op. cit.*, First Dialogue, Chap. IV, 1709.

[4] *Op. cit.*, First Dialogue, Chaps. XII and XVIII.

[5] *Institutes* (1628), I, 97 a and b, § 138; *cf.* § 231.

[6] *Magdalen College Case* (1614) 11 Co. Rep. 66 b at 73 b.

[7] *Touchstone of Common Assurances* (*circa* 1641), p. 132.

sionally as *one* factor in law-making and the judicial process, their own estimate of what was agreeable to citizens generally or to the majority of the class of persons affected.

Bentham's theory of individual utility, though directed at English legislators and lawyers, did not take the legal profession by storm at the turn of the nineteenth century. Indeed in the revolutionary context of 1793 the Chief Justice of the King's Bench, Lord KENYON, once gave a strong direction to a jury that a newspaper proprietor who had advocated " that all true government is instituted for the general good . . . and all its actions are or ought to be directed for the general happiness and prosperity of all honest citizens " had uttered a gross seditious libel.[1] His successor, Lord ELLENBOROUGH, had spoken in Parliament derisively of some of Bentham's theories as " speculative and modern philosophy ".[2] Nevertheless the doctrine of utility gradually gained in popularity in England in the early nineteenth century as a result of the exertions of Bentham himself and the group of personal disciples, politicians and philosophers, who gathered round him in the latter part of his long life, notably Grote, Roebuck, Molesworth, James and John Stuart Mill. Through such men the doctrine became in different degrees part of the political creed first of the Philosophical Radicals, then of the Whigs and eventually of the Tory party, so that by 1850 moderate utilitarianism was the accepted and orthodox political faith.[3] It is less well known that several of the lawyers were among his personal disciples; Sir Samuel Romilly,[4] John Austin,[5] Henry BICKERSTETH, a future Master of the Rolls,[6] Joseph Parkes, a prominent solicitor and law reformer.[7] The meteoric BROUGHAM, if not

---

[1]*R. v. Lambert and Perry and Gray* (1793), 22 State Tr. 953; the jury however brought in a verdict of " not guilty ".

[2]CAMPBELL, *Lives of Chief Justices* (1857), Vol. III, p. 232.

[3]Dicey, *Law and Public Opinion*, 2nd edn. (1914), p. 182; *cf.* Halévy, *The Growth of Philosophic Radicalism* (English edn. 1928).

[4]K.C., 1800 S.-G., 1806. Romilly, though leader of the Chancery Bar, never reached the Bench in a superior court, though he held office as Chancellor of the Court Palatine of Durham, 1805-1815.

[5]See *post*, pp. 176-179.

[6]See *post*, p. 122.

[7]Author of *A History of the Court of Chancery* (1828).

an intimate, was on friendly terms with the aged Bentham
in his last years. Through such disciples the doctrine gradually infiltrated that most conservative stronghold, the English
legal profession.

An event which gave considerable impetus to the
utilitarian movement in the sphere of English law was
BROUGHAM's famous six-hour speech in the House of
Commons in 1828,[1] in which he focussed the attention of the
House and the country on many features of the legal system
which he adjudged defective and for which he proposed a
stream of specific reforms. This massive criticism of the legal
system, particularly the procedural sector, from one of the
leaders of the Bar, though avowedly based on " experience "
and " notorious abuses ", was in truth mounted from several
of the particular sub-principles of utility as applied to civil
procedure worked out by Bentham.[2]

An immediate and direct result of BROUGHAM's indictment

---

[1] 7th Feb., 1828; *Hansard*, 2nd series, Vol. 18, cols. 127-256.

[2] In the preparation of this very speech BROUGHAM had consulted
Bentham himself: see correspondence in Bentham, *Works*, Vol. X,
pp. 574-575, in which Bentham offered the Whig leader " some
nice sweet pap of my own making ". Characteristically Bentham was
dissatisfied with BROUGHAM's eventual proposals in the Commons:
—" Mr. Brougham's mountain is delivered, and behold! the mouse ":
Works, Vol. X, p. 588:—for BROUGHAM had only attacked a few
aspects of the whole legal system. Later the octogenarian Bentham
wrote amiably to BROUGHAM—in the year the latter became Lord
Chancellor—upbraiding him for what Bentham regarded as his
moderation in this speech: " When will you have learnt your
primer? When will you be able to spell—*greatest happiness principle;
non-disappointment principle; ends of justice—main end giving
execution and effect to the substantive branch of law;* collateral ends,
avoidance of delay, expense, and vexation—evils produced by the
adjective branch? When you have got that by heart, you may then
be fit to be breeched and sent to a grammar-school ". *Works*, Vol. XI,
pp. 36-37. Bentham was preaching to the converted. Later BROUG-
HAM acknowledged the inspiration of Bentham: " The age of Law
Reform and the age of Jeremy Bentham are one and the same. . . .
He it was who first made the mighty step of trying the whole provisions of our jurisprudence by the test of expediency . . . how far its
arrangements were framed according to the principle which should
pervade a Code of Laws—their adaption to the circumstances of
society, to the wants of men, and to the promotion of human happiness ". *Speeches* (1838), Vol. II, p. 287.

was the appointment of two Commissions[1] to consider the reform of particular branches of the legal system, one on procedure in the Common Law Courts, another on real property.

In 1828 Commissioners were appointed to enquire into proceedings in the Courts of Common Law and to determine whether any parts might conveniently and beneficially be discontinued or improved. At first only five Commissioners were appointed, all of them practitioners experienced in these courts, four of them future judges: BOSANQUET, ALDERSON, PARKE and PATTESON. But later five other counsel were added, including J. S. POLLOCK who came to preside and WIGHTMAN. Thus the Commissioners were men drawn from the heart of the profession, eminently practical, experienced, long-headed lawyers. Between 1829 and 1834 they submitted six extremely detailed, critical and constructive Reports.[2]

Our concern is not with the specific defects which these lawyers observed in the system nor with the specific remedies they proposed for each, but rather with the grounds on which they adjudged a rule of procedural law to be defective and equally those on which they based a proposal for a better rule. Their own initial observations are illuminating.[3] Their objective is stated as " to render proceedings shorter, cheaper and more certain ". " We shall have no hesitation in proposing the abolition, as far as practicable, of fictions, circuitous courses and matters of mere form . . . as have ceased to be necessary to purposes for which they were introduced, but which increase the length and consequently the cost of proceedings. . . ." A glance at two of the specific topics will reveal the grounds of criticism. With regard to initial

---

[1]The various royal Commissions on the Courts of Chancery and Common Law and particular branches of the law, which were appointed in the early part of the nineteenth century are considered in detail by Holdsworth in 56 L.Q.R. 33, 208 and 240: " Reform in the Law (1793-1832) ".

[2]First Report, Parlt. Papers (1829), Vol. IX, 1 et seq. Second Report, Parlt. Papers (1830), Vol. XI, 547 et seq. Third Report, Parlt. Papers (1831), Vol. X, 375 et seq. Fourth Report, Parlt. Papers (1831-1832), Vol. XXV, 1 et seq. Fifth Report, Parlt. Papers (1833), Vol. XXII, 195 et seq. Sixth Report, Parlt. Papers (1834), Vol. XXVI, 1 et seq.

[3]First Report, p. 7.

process,[1]—*viz.* by writ served on the defendant to compel an appearance by him before the plaintiff could declare his cause,—the Commission regarded the general principle as justifiable, but they commented adversely on the great variety of species of writs used, showing that most of them were outmoded, and holding that the variety now only produced unnecessary complexity and consequently was conducive to chicanery and expense. To combat these evils they proposed the reduction of primary writs of process to two simple forms. With regard to the limited power of the Common Law Courts in trial procedure, compared with the Court of Chancery,[2] they recommended such new powers be conferred on the former as the power to examine parties by way of discovery and to examine witnesses by way of interrogatories and a system of verification of written documents before trial, " to avoid enormous expense ", " to diminish the vexation of suitors " and " to save time ". An examination of the reports reveals that the Commissioners invoked many diverse criteria, some deriving from the notion of justice as fair trial,[3] as that parties should be on equal terms, that both parties be properly heard, and that a man should not be judge in his own cause. But pervading all the reports are these three criteria: that proceedings should not be unduly delayed, that expenses be reduced, and that the vexations of suitors and defendants should be diminished. These as we have seen are sub-principles of utility, *i.e.,* utilitarian criteria applied to the subject of civil procedure. Yet these Commissioners were not admirers of Brougham, or disciples of Bentham, or otherwise doctrinaire utilitarians. They would probably have said these criteria derived from their common-sense and experience. But the common-sense and experience of the leading practitioners even thirty years before[4] had not driven them actively to criticise the law on these grounds. It is difficult to resist the conclusion that the

---

[1]First Report, pp. 70-78.
[2]Second Report, Part V.
[3]See *ante*, p. 35.
[4]Yet much earlier, in the middle of the seventeenth century, some of these criteria had been used by law reformers; see Nourse, " Law Reform under the Commonwealth and Protectorate ", 75 L.Q.R. 512.

actual contemporary inspiration, though unacknowledged, was the principle of utility.

At the same time another group of lawyers was acting on the mandate " to make inquiry into the law of real property, and to make known what improvements can be made therein. . . ." The first Commissioner was John CAMPBELL, a future Chief Justice and Lord Chancellor, and with him were several much more experienced and more learned real property lawyers.[1] They in turn consulted scores of serjeants, barristers and solicitors, in the preparation of their four Reports, 1829-1833.[2] Nowadays it is the first and least part of their Report which is the most quoted, to the effect that the rules with regard to the *enjoyment* (*i.e.* rights of use and disposition) were satisfactory. But the bulk of the four full Reports is devoted to an extremely detailed examination of the law relating to the *transfer* of real property, a branch which the Commissioners found to be " exceedingly defective ". Our concern is only with the criteria manifestly used by the Commissioners in their adverse criticisms and constructive proposals. Such general observations as that law should satisfy the wants of mankind, and that it should conform to the feelings of the people, and that law should be adapted to the current state of society so that rules which have outlived their social function should be abrogated, are to be found in these highly technical documents.[3] The general objective to which all these rules of law should be orientated is defined as " the public good " or " the general convenience ". Particular principles directed to that end are: that maximum freedom of alienation be achieved;[4] that title obtained by a purchaser be secure;[5] that transfer of land be expeditious and

---

[1]Tinney, Hodgson, Duckworth, Brodie; later Sanders, Duval and Tyrell were appointed.

[2]These Reports have been published separately: *Real Property Commissions; First Report* 1829 (*re* power of inheritance, dower etc., fines and recoveries, prescription and limitation of actions). *Second Report* 1830 (*re* registry of deeds and instruments relating to land). *Third Report* 1832 (*re* tenures, contingent remainders, perpetuities etc.). *Fourth Report* 1833 (*re* wills).

[3]*E.g.*, First Report, Introduction and *re* dower and tenure.

[4]*E.g.*, *Ibid.*, *re* dower; Third Report, *re* perpetuities.

[5]*E.g.*, First Report, Introduction, *re* transfer of realty; Third Report, *re* registry of deeds and documents.

inexpensive;[1] that litigation be reduced to a minimum;[2] that the outcome of disputes should turn on the merits of the claims, not on technical rules and fictions.[3] If these principles were implemented in the law, it was argued, then the " general convenience " should be advanced in that the following states of affairs are likely to ensue; public wealth should increase; agriculture should be improved; the misery and loss and, indeed, ruin resulting from the failure of an insecure title should be avoided; the vexation and expense of unnecessary litigation should be reduced; and the demand for property in the open market should be satisfied. With regard to a specific problem, when the public good points to one solution and individual interests to another, the former should prevail.[4] But still, sectional interests, as those of purchasers, owners or widows, should be implemented as far as this is consistent with the public good. The basic criterion in these Reports is manifestly the " happiness-maximising and disappointment-minimising " principle. These Commissioners, too, have in a rough and eminently practical way applied the " felicific calculus " to the positive law and actual practice relating to the transfer of land in England in the early nineteenth century.[5]

---

[1]*E.g.*, First Report, *re* fines and recoveries and limitation of action of ejectment.

[2]*E.g.*, *Ibid.*, *re* limitation of actions; Third Report, *re* tenures.

[3]*E.g.*, First Report, *re* dower.

[4]*E.g.*, *Ibid.*, *re* successive disabilities and period of limitation; Third Report, *re* perpetuities and *re* compensation for heriots.

[5]Actually the octogenarian Bentham was among the many lawyers consulted by the Commissioners in the preparation of their Report on a registry of deeds and instruments. His reply reached them only in time for inclusion in the appendix to the Third Report on tenure, etc. In this he re-affirms the axiom of utility, applies it to the subject shortly, and tacitly approves of the general scheme for a registry, stresses such details of a registry as the expense of running it, and pours streams of captious criticisms on the plans proposed by the Commissioners, and indulges in an elaborate excursus on the use in such a registry of a " manifold writing machine! " It ends—" *Dixi*, J. Bentham ". This is typical of the man; he could never himself carry his eminently practicable idea into workable, practical, detailed schemes. The paradox is that it is the Benthamite notion of justice which evidently inspired Campbell and his co-Commissioners in their many practical proposals in these Reports, most of which were adopted into the law by statutes in succeeding years.

Several of the criteria for reforming civil procedure, which were used by the earlier Commissioners recur time and time again in the Reports of other Commissioners later in the nineteenth century. For instance, the second group of Common Law Commissioners, who prepared three Reports, 1851-1860,[1] the first of which recommended the radical pruning of pleading and the abolition of the many forms of action, constantly invoked the following four now familiar criteria: (i) avoid unnecessary expense; (ii) avoid unnecessary delay; (iii) save litigants from vexation or frustration; and (iv) ensure that suits be decided on issues of fact or of substantive right, not on technicalities. The members of this Commission again were amongst the staunchest of the common lawyers, senior experienced counsel, shortly to be judges, as JERVIS, MARTIN, BRAMWELL, WILLES, and COCKBURN. In the late 1860's an even more formidable array of judges and senior members of the Common Law and Equity Bars, under Lord CAIRNS, and including BLACKBURN, PALMER, WILDE, ERLE and COLERIDGE, constituted the Judicature Commission. Their First Report[2] in 1869 recommended the consolidation of all the superior courts of common law and equity into one Supreme Court, so that all the elements of a complete remedy involving common law and equity should be available to a plaintiff in the same court, with a simplified system of pleading. These Commissioners too invoked as their principal criteria for these fundamental reforms the same four criteria listed above.

These various reports demonstrate the extent to which some of the sub-principles of utility, especially those relating to civil procedure had come to be accepted as orthodox principles amongst the leading English lawyers. Such principles had become accepted dogma for law reform within the legal profession.[3] Dicey wrote of the form of utilitarianism which prevailed in the mid-nineteenth century as " the

[1]First Report, Parlt. Papers (1851), Vol. XXII, pp. 567 *et seq.* Second Report, Parlt. Papers (1851-1853), Vol. XL, pp. 705 *et seq.* Third Report, Parlt. Papers (1860), Vol. XXXI, pp. 341 *et seq.*

[2]Parlt. Papers (1869), Vol. XXV, pp. 1 *et seq.*

[3]In the spate of periodical literature which appeared after BROUGHAM's speech in 1828—*viz.* The Law Magazine (1828-1856); The Law Review (1844-1856); The Law Magazine and Law Review (1856-

(continued at foot of next page)

Benthamism of common sense . . . This liberalism was the
utilitarianism not of the study but of the House of Commons
or of the Stock Exchange "[1]—and he might have added " of
the Inns of Court ".

By the middle of the century even the Bench included
judges who if not partisans of the doctrine of utility in all its
applications were certainly sympathetic to many of its sub-
principles. BROUGHAM,[2] who had been the Whig Lord Chancellor 1830-1834, continued to sit in the House of Lords in
a judicial capacity for more than twenty years thereafter.
Henry BICKERSTETH had become Master of the Rolls in 1836
as Lord LANGDALE[3] and held that office for fifteen years.
John CAMPBELL,[4] who had presided over the Real Property
Commission in the thirties came to preside over the Court of
King's Bench in the fifties, and became Lord Chancellor
1859-1861. Undoubtedly these judges gave fuller rein to
their utilitarian doctrine when advocating various reforms of
the law in the House of Lords in its legislative capacity, and
on the Bench were disposed to administer the positive law
irrespective of whether it was justifiable on utilitarian principles. But it is to be presumed that when sitting as judges
in cases on which there existed no precedents, or the authorities were inconclusive, or the common law or equity permitted the exercise of discretion by the judge, they were
similarly actuated by their utilitarian doctrine. For instance,
in *R.* v. *Millis*[5] when the House of Lords was confronted with
a question of matrimonial law, Lord BROUGHAM rejected the
solution which would have the effect of declaring void a vast
number of marriages and declaring bastard the numerous

(*continued from foot of previous page*)
1915); Transactions of the Juridical Society (1855-1873); Journal of
Social Science (1865-1866)—numerous particular aspects of the legal
system were exposed to criticism, *inter alia*, on utilitarian grounds.
Cf. Joshua Williams, *Letters to John Bull, Esq., on Lawyers and Law
Reform* (1857).

[1]*Law and Public Opinion*, 2nd edn., p. 170.
[2]See Garratt, *Lord Brougham* (1935); Aspinall, *Lord Brougham and
the Whig Party* (1927).
[3]See his " Reform of the Court of Chancery " (1836), a reprint of
his speech in the Lords, June 13, 1836, *Hansard*, 3rd Series, Vol.
34, cols. 440-474.
[4]See *Life of John, Lord Campbell* (1881), 2 vols., ed. Hardcastle.
[5](1843-1844), 10 Cl. & Fin. 534, at pp. 699-742.

progeny of such liaisons and unsettling a host of titles to real property, and adopted the solution which would promote the security of these *de facto* marriages and be conducive to " the peace and happiness of society ".

Later in the nineteenth century the outstanding protagonist of the Benthamite doctrine of justice in the legal profession was George BRAMWELL. Created a Baron in the Court of Exchequer in 1856, he remained conspicuous on the Bench and in Parliament for another thirty-five years. He has been described as " a perfect fanatic about justice ".[1] He himself disbelieved in supra-legal ethical systems; he had the typical common lawyer's contempt for metaphysics, cherishing rather the most robust " good sense ". But in his judgments, his speeches in the Lords, and his extensive correspondence and articles, several principles consistently appear. He championed the maximum freedom of contract expressed in the terse maxim " a bargain is a bargain "; he stood firm in opposition to the growing volume of socialistic thought on property in defence of the system of private property;[2] and there was no more vigorous champion of individual liberty of body and mind—in the context of industrial strife—on the Bench in the last half of the nineteenth century.[3] The assumption underlying these principles is made explicit in an informal address he gave in 1873:[4] " Of all the good things which this world gives us the best, in my judgment, are liberty and independence; liberty for each man to think and act for himself, and independence which gives him the power to do that which he deems best for his own happiness, and for the happiness of those he cares for." It is more than a coincidence that BRAMWELL's " robust good sense " led him to affirm many a principle which flows from the notion of individual utility.

Again, the subtle operation of individual utilitarianism in the judicial process can be detected in some of BRAMWELL's

---

[1]Fairfield, *A Memoir of Baron Bramwell* (1898), p. 362; *cf.* Fifoot, *Judge and Jurist in the Reign of Victoria* (1959), pp. 15-16.

[2]*Nationalisation of Land* (1884). Published by Liberty and Property Defence League.

[3]*R. v. Druitt, Lawrence and Adamson* (1867), 10 Cox C.C. 592.

[4]Fairfield, *op. cit.*, p. 55.

judgments. For example, in *Manchester, Sheffield and Lincoln-shire Railway Co.* v. *Brown*[1] the specific issue before the House of Lords was the validity of an exemption clause in a contract between a fishmonger and a railway company. The Railway and Canal Traffic Act, 1854, s. 7 allowed such a clause to be valid if it was such " as shall be adjudged by court or judge . . . to be just and reasonable ". Lord BRAM-WELL was not prepared to press his views of freedom of contract to the extreme position where he would hold that it was an impossibility that a contract entered into knowingly and voluntarily could be unjust and unreasonable. But he did affirm that in the case of voluntary contract the onus is on the man who says it is unreasonable and that he would require " the strongest possible evidence to show . . . that a [voluntary] agreement was unreasonable ".[2] After professing how ill-qualified a judge was to decide what is reasonable between fishmongers and fish-carriers, he considered the business realities as best he could, and held that the immunity term decided on by the parties was valid. Manifestly Lord BRAMWELL is giving effect to the principle that the maximum freedom of contract be allowed so that parties can secure their own well-being—a dictate of individual utility.

While the notion of individual utility remained the main criterion of justice for some English lawyers in the latter half of the nineteenth century, many more favoured utilitarian solutions of specific social problems without accepting the allied individualist principle, which assumed that the happiness of the majority of people would on the whole be best secured by leaving to all persons the maximum freedom for self-help. On the contrary, they had increasingly been driven to hold to the alternative allied principle that the general happiness is to be achieved and distress most effectively mitigated by limiting the freedom of individuals—in the spheres of industry, commerce, proprietary rights, general services—by legislating more extensively for the benefit of the distressed classes or for the community as a whole. The swing has been from individual utility to social utility.

---

[1](1883), 8 App. Cas. 703. *Cf. Abrath* v. *North-Eastern Railway Co.* (1886), 11 App. Cas. 247, at pp. 250-254.
[2](1883), 8 App. Cas. at pp. 717-719.

The social and individual versions of utility while cognate are not identical notions of justice. Applied to social questions they may point to opposing solutions. For instance, should a workman receive compensation from his employer for injuries received as a result of the negligent conduct of a fellow-employee? Individualist opinion if it did not originally inspire the negative answer laid down by the Court of Exchequer in *Priestley* v. *Fowler*[1] certainly supported it[2] on the ground that the well-being of masters and servants was best served by leaving them to determine their liability *inter se* by private contracts. But collectivist opinion, concerned to protect the whole class of workers, fought long and in the end successfully for the imposition of inescapable statutory liability on the employer in such cases.[3] The notion of social utility has much more in common with social justice, into which it has been merged in the twentieth century. Accordingly it will be considered more fully in the next chapter under that title.

Still, the doctrine of social utility has not altogether displaced the notion of individual utility from the common lawyers' thinking in the twentieth century. An English lawyer will still on occasions reach a conclusion as to the justice or injustice of a particular matter by an *ad hoc* invocation of some sub-principle of utility, though he may not always appreciate its source. For example, the sub-principle of individual utilitarianism—that the law should encourage the maximum freedom of contract—which came to be regarded as the paramount policy by the judges in cases involving the law of contracts in the nineteenth century[4] has

---

[1] (1837), 3 M. & W. 1.

[2] *E.g.*, Bramwell in " The Times " and the House of Lords: see Fairfield, *Memoir*, pp. 333-355.

[3] Employers' Liability Act, 1880 (9 Halsbury's Statutes, 2nd edn., 30); Workmen's Compensation Act, 1897 (60 & 61 Vict., c. 37); Workmen's Compensation Act, 1900 (63 & 64 Vict., c. 22).

[4] " If there is one thing which more than another public policy requires it is that men of full age and competent understanding shall have the utmost liberty of contracting, and that their contracts when entered into freely and voluntarily shall be held sacred and shall be enforced by courts of justice ", *per* Jessel, M.R. in *Printing and Numerical Registering Co.* v. *Sampson* (1875), L.R. 19 Eq. 462, at p. 465.

become a dogma upon which many an English judge relies in the twentieth century, notwithstanding that a contrary policy (derived from considerations of social utility) has been implemented by Parliament throughout this century. Lord ATKIN may be singled out as one of the modern exponents of this dogma. So, in his well-known judgment in the leading case, *Bell* v. *Lever Bros., Ltd.*[1] in which he minimised the effect of mistake as to facts in the formation of contract, the dogma appears as his major premiss: " It is of paramount importance that contracts should be observed, and that if parties honestly comply with the essentials of the formation of contracts—*i.e.*, agree in the same terms on the same subject-matter—they are bound, and must rely on the stipulations of the contract for protection from the effects of facts unknown to them."[2] Further, the judges, professors and counsel[3] who constituted the Law Revision Committee in the 1930's evidently assumed, as one of their criteria for the law of limitation of actions that a case should be decided on its merits, not on obsolete technicalities,[4] and expressly rejected the trust concept as a solution to the problem of the *jus quaesitum tertio* on the grounds that it has led to " unnecessary and vexatious delay and expense "[5]—now traditional criteria for law reform committees, but criteria first formulated, as we have seen, within the profession by the early nineteenth century law reform commissioners who were directly influenced by Benthamite doctrine. Besides, between the World Wars, Lord HEWART, when Lord Chief Justice of England, never lost an opportunity of championing the individualist principle which was woven into the Benthamite doctrine, but continuously spoke out against the modern tendency of benevolently despotic governments to restrict

---

[1][1931] All E.R. Rep. 1; [1932] A.C. 161.

[2][1931] All E.R. Rep. 1, at p. 31; [1932] A.C. 161, at p. 224; likewise in *Fender* v. *Mildmay*, [1937] 3 All E.R. 402; [1938] A.C. 1, the gist of Lord ATKIN's exposition of the relevant law is that *pacta sunt servanda*, unless the harm to the public caused by that particular type of contract is incontestable: " In popular language, following the wise aphorism of Sir George JESSEL cited above, the contract should be given the benefit of the doubt ": *ibid.*, at p. 12.

[3]See *post*, pp. 157-158.

[4]Law Revision Committee, 5th Interim Report, Cmd. 5334, pp. 6-8.

[5]Law Revision Committee, 6th Interim Report, Cmd. 5449, p. 29.

the freedom of individuals to conduct their lives and seek happiness according to their own lights.[1]

The basic principle of general utility has been positively advocated afresh by jurists addressing law students. Salmond, whose textbook *Jurisprudence*[2] has reached most students of English common law in the last fifty years, defined law in terms of justice[3] and proceeded to define justice in terms of the theory of utility.[4] He identified the concept of justice with moral right, and accepted the philosophy that the business of men is to be happy, so that everything is good so far as it produces happiness and evil so far as it produces pain. The general welfare, as Salmond conceived it, consists in the abolition so far as may be of suffering and sorrow and the increase of all forms of desirable consciousness. " The rule of justice determines the sphere of individual liberty in the pursuit of individual welfare, so as to confine that liberty within the limits which are consistent with the general welfare of mankind."[5] And a contemporary constitutional lawyer[6] has pleaded for a consideration and development of Bentham's principle of utility as applied to legislation in contemporary England. Affirming that our governments are *de facto* guided by the general principles of utility, he argues that those concerned with the science of jurisprudence should assist the legislative organs in their functions by providing the appropriate social data to enable them to determine more intelligently which measures are likely to reduce the distress and advance the happiness of the governed. A recent symposium on Bentham and his influence in the sphere of law, published in 1948[7] on the occasion of the bi-centenary of his

---

[1] *The New Despotism* (1929); *Essays and Observations* (1930); *Not Without Prejudice* (1937).

[2] 1st edn. (1902); 7th edn. (1924)—the last by the author; 11th edn. (1957) ed. Glanville Williams. *Cf*. Markby, *Elements of Law*, (1st edn. 1871), (6th edn. 1905), §§ 49 and 54.

[3] *Op. cit.*, 7th edn., § 15.

[4] *Op. cit.*, 7th edn., § 19.

[5] *Op. cit.*, 7th edn., § 19, p. 66; 11th edn., § 21, p. 63.

[6] Ivor Jennings, " A Plea for Utilitarianism ", 2 M.L.R. (1938), p. 22.

[7] *Jeremy Bentham and the Law*: ed. Keeton & Schwarzenberger on behalf of the Faculty of Laws of University College, London.

birth, to which ten academic lawyers contributed, is illuminating. It reveals that the doctrine of utility is not only of far-reaching importance in the history of English law as the inspiration of extensive statutory law reforms in the nineteenth century, but that even in the middle of the twentieth century if not uncritically accepted it is still sympathetically treated by members of the academic branch of the profession. Summing up, Professor Graveson wrote " he would be rash, indeed, who said that Jeremy Bentham . . . had ceased to influence the development of English law ", for this principle of general utility could still be detected at work in modern English legislation, and " Bentham's faith in individual freedom . . . embodied, consciously or unconsciously, the living spirit of the common law . . ."[1]

§C

The notion of justice as the conformity of law with the principle of utility has in the long run left deep imprints on many branches of the modern English legal system. In the middle of the nineteenth century, during the era of the flood of law reform by statute, participants such as BROUGHAM[2] and observers such as Maine[3] attributed the whole range of law reforms in Parliament to Bentham's inspiration. Dicey, the historian of legislative opinion in the country during that century, endorsed this judgment.[4] Much more recently doubts have been expressed whether utilitarian doctrine caused or only facilitated some of these reforms.[5] But an

---

[1]*Op. cit.*, pp. 113-122.

[2]See *ante*, p. 112.

[3]" I do not know of a single law-reform effected since Bentham's day which cannot be traced to his influence ". *Early History of Institutions* (1875), p. 397.

[4]" From 1825 onwards the teaching of Bentham exercised so potent an influence that to him is fairly ascribed that thoroughgoing though gradual amendment of the law of England which was one of the main results of the Reform Act ". *Law and Opinion*, 2nd edn., p. 126. *Cf.* Holdsworth, *History of English Law*, Vol. I, pp. 633-650 and " Reforms in the Law (1793-1832)," 56 L.Q.R. 33, 208 and 340.

[5]Stone, *Province and Function of Law* (1947), p. 294.

examination of Bentham's sub-principles for reform of particular branches of the law and the criteria adopted by various law reform Commissions in the nineteenth century and the resultant statutes reveals that utilitarian doctrine was undoubtedly a potent factor in many of these particular reforms. It is not proposed to examine here in detail the many developments in the English law of contract, real property and conveyancing, succession, evidence, family law, trade union law and poor law, or the political developments which led to the modification in the law of the constitution, all of which were in greater or lesser degree inspired by the theory of justice as utility,[1] but simply to note the influence of that theory on the English law of civil procedure.

The maze of courts and the labyrinth of forms of action and formulae which constituted the law of civil procedure in the early nineteenth century and Bentham's sub-principles for the reconstitution of the system were mentioned in the first section of this chapter. The effect of utilitarian doctrine on the law of civil procedure in England may be gauged by a glance at the system a century later. The several ancient superior courts have gone: in their place is one comprehensive Supreme Court of Judicature, with a High Court sitting in various divisions and a Court of Appeal.[2] In civil cases trial is usually before a single judge without a jury: *cf.* Bentham's sub-principle of " single-seatedness ". In the provinces there is now an effective system of county courts with jurisdiction to hear civil disputes involving comparatively small sums of money;[3] *cf.* Bentham's proposal for a system

---

[1]See Dicey, *Law and Public Opinion*, 2nd edn., Lecture VI, pp. 184-210 for a summary of the nineteenth century developments; and *Jeremy Bentham and the Law, A Symposium*, (1948) ed. Keeton & Schwarzenberger, for several modern studies of the influence of the utilitarian philosophy on divers branches of the private and public law; and Radzinowicz, *History of English Criminal Law since 1750*, 3 Vols. (1948-1956), for a detailed study of the influence of the doctrine on the criminal law and its administration and on the law and theory of punishments.

[2]Supreme Court of Judicature Act, 1873 (following on a series of Court of Chancery Amendment Acts, 1841-1862, and the Exchequer Chamber Act, 1830); now Supreme Court of Judicature (Consolidation) Act, 1925 (5 Halsbury's Statutes, 2nd edn., 337).

[3]County Courts Acts, 1846-1888; now County Courts Act, 1959 (39 Halsbury's Statutes, 2nd edn., 102).

of minor local courts. The whole of the law of the land, whether common law or equity, is administered in one and the same court, *viz.* the Supreme Court;[1] *cf.* Bentham's subprinciple of " omnicompetence ". Procedural fictions have for the most part been abolished by Act of Parliament.[2] The many distinct procedures—forms of action—have given way to what is in effect a single code of procedure in the High Court.[3] Pleading remains a necessary part of procedure to define issues for trial, but the process is more flexible, and errors are less liable to frustrate well-grounded claims: so that a Lord Justice of Appeal could assert that " it is not *possible* in the year 1887 for an honest litigant in her Majesty's Supreme Court to be defeated by any mere technicality, any slip, any mistaken step in his litigation ".[4] One of the principal objects of the Judicature Act of 1873 was to reduce unnecessary costs for the litigants by fusing the administration of common law and equity. Only recently a bold move has been made to reduce " the mischief of costs " by a scheme which allows the poorest litigants free legal aid and those with modest means assistance in the payment of their costs out of a central fund:[5] *cf.* Bentham's proposal that the public should bear the expense of " litiscontestation " for the poor. The most remarkable change in the legal system inspired by utilitarian doctrine, is not, however, to be found on the statute book. The result of these procedural reforms has been the gradual relegation, during the nineteenth century, of detailed matters of procedure, which used to dominate the legal scene, to a rôle subordinate to that of the substantive law, so that the procedural law is seen even by the lawyers to be no more than the means whereby rights established by

---

[1]Judicature Act, 1873, ss. 16-25; now Judicature Act, 1925, ss. 18-29 (5 Halsbury's Statutes, 2nd edn., 347 *et seq.*). *Cf.* County Courts Act, 1959, ss. 39-54 (39 Halsbury's Statutes, 2nd edn., 126 *et seq.*).

[2]Common Law Procedure Act, 1852, s. 49.

[3]Uniformity of Process Act, 1832; Real Property Limitation Act, 1833; Common Law Procedure Acts, 1852-1860; now Rules of the Supreme Court, 1883, made under the Judicature Act, 1873, Part IV and Judicature Act, 1925, s. 99 (18 Halsbury's Statutes, 2nd edn., 511).

[4]Bowen, L.J., " The Administration of the Law " in *Reign of Queen Victoria* (1887), Vol. I., ed. Ward, p. 310.

[5]Legal Aid and Advice Act, 1949.

the substantive law are to be safeguarded: the proportion commended by Bentham in the light of utility.[1]

§D

The principle of utility has been subjected to withering criticism by moral philosophers,[2] and more recently by psychologists.[3] But few lawyers have echoed this destructive criticism or attempted in print to refute the principle of utility as a criterion for law on grounds of their own choosing. In part this relative dearth of criticism is no doubt due to the reluctance of the common lawyers to philosophise. But it may be regarded as indirect evidence of the extent to which utilitarian doctrine is acceptable to the members of the legal profession. Besides, as Dicey judiciously observed,[4] the principle of utility is far less objectionable as a first principle for law than for morals, as law is more concerned with social conduct than with private motives.

Of course the common lawyer has been quick to criticise the principle of utility on the ground of its over-great generality. For instance, it was pointed out by one critic[5] a hundred years ago that the principle of utility by itself is a mere truism from which no right-minded legislator would dissent, but it leaves unsolved the great question—what is the best mode of securing the greatest happiness to the greatest number?[6] Yet couple the principle of utility with the principle of individual liberty or the principle of collectivism and

---

[1]See *ante*, pp. 111-112.

[2]Leslie Stephen, *The English Utilitarians* (1900), 3 vols., *passim*; Moore, *Principia Ethica* (1903), pp. 59-109; Ross, *The Right and the Good* (1930), pp. 16-47.

[3]See Stone, *Province and Function of Law* (1947), pp. 288-291; Stephen, *op. cit.*, Vol. I, pp. 269 *et seq.*

[4]*Law and Public Opinion*, 2nd edn., p. 137.

[5]Best, *Transactions of the Juridical Society* (1855-8), Vol. I, p. 399; " The Common Law of England; with an Examination of some False Principles of Law Reform ".

[6]*Op. cit.*, p. 430; *cf.* Glanville Williams' criticism of Salmond's definition of justice, as a vague formula from which particular rules can hardly be deduced: Salmond, *Jurisprudence*, 10th edn., at p. 525.

apply the composite doctrine to the facts of a given community, then practicable sub-principles for legislation can be deduced, or at any rate such sub-principles were deduced in abundance in the process of statutory law reform in the nineteenth century.

It has been remarked that legislation is a feeble instrument of happiness: that laws and their administration are in the nature of things unlikely to promote positive feelings of pleasure in citizens. Rather the value of law is to be measured not by the happiness it procures but by the misery from which it preserves us.[1] This is however not to deny but to affirm the principle of utility as a value for law, emphasising the pain-minimising rather than the happiness-promoting aspect of the principle.

Bentham himself assumed that the maximum happiness for all members of the community would follow from laws which freed the individual to pursue his own happiness. The former condition might indeed result from the latter state of affairs if individuals found a large part of their own happiness in active benevolence towards their fellows or suffered deeply in sympathy for the distress of their fellows. But neither in logic nor in life does the happiness of the many follow necessarily from the pursuit of it by individuals.[2] Experience shows that a few aggressive and unsympathetic individuals in pursuit of their own selfish happiness may severely increase the misery of many of their fellows. This criticism is properly directed against the individualist principle in Bentham's doctrine rather than against the principle of utility itself, and the development of social utility with its emphasis on safeguarding the interests of the community has been an attempt to overcome this objection.

The lawyer like the layman must often have condemned utilitarianism for confusing justice with selfish pleasure-seeking and with materialism. The criticism is apt in so far as those professing utilitarianism have emphasised the pleasures of the senses and of wealth. But it is not apt as

---

[1] Markby, *Elements of Law*, 6th edn. (1905), §§ 57-58.
[2] Friedmann, *Legal Theory*, 4th edn. (1960), p. 273; Lloyd, " The Law of Associations " in *Law and Opinion in England in the Twentieth Century* (1959), ed. Ginsberg, Lecture VI, p. 99.

applied to Bentham's original theory or to Mill's version thereof, which emphasised spiritual and altruistic pleasures and the pains of sympathy for the suffering of others, as important factors to be taken into account in the " felicific calculation " which indicates the right act or the right law.

The typical common lawyer, usually an extremely busy man of affairs, is liable to treat derisively the felicific calculus. He would find it impracticable to take into account on every occasion of legislation or adjudication the whole range of pleasures and pains which are likely to occur in an immense number of people and make allowance for intensity etc., and so calculate the predominant effect. A James Mill or a John Stuart Mill might have the inclination and the leisure to attempt the calculation, though even they would lack the full range of data for its perfect solution. But a busy parliamentarian or a judge with a full list would have neither. However, the proposition—that a state of affairs, which to one's own knowledge causes widespread distress to thousands or millions of people without creating any obvious compensating benefits, should be remedied by a law reform, when this is likely on the whole to remove or at any rate to diminish the distress—is one which would be accepted by the same busy practitioner. Yet this proposition is the " felicific calculus " reduced to a rule of thumb.

A more fundamental objection to the doctrine under review is its equation of utility with morality. Those who believe in a system of eternal moral precepts immanent in nature, revealed to man in Christian doctrine or ascertained by him by reason, would deny the validity of this equation,[1] and would certainly restrict the valid operation of the principle of utility to those sectors of social life to which no moral precepts apply. But more lawyers would reject this equation not on such ultimate principles but rather because their own experience has made them aware of the rectitude of certain moral principles or of moral judgments *ad hoc*, which do not always tally with the utilitarian principle or utilitarian solu-

---

[1] See *ante*, Chap. 4.

tion of a given case.[1] As a modern English moral philosopher has expressed it: the rightness of an act is not determined by the ordinary man by a mental assessment of its tendency to produce happiness, but is self-evident to mature minds in civilised society; an act is not right because it is likely to produce happiness or reduce pain, but because it is known to be intrinsically right irrespective of consequences.[2] This is but to say that those who are partisans of the notion of natural justice[3] or moral justice[4] are not partisans of utility, at least in that range of cases where moral principles conflict with the dictates of utility.

---

[1] *E.g.*, Stone, *Province and Function of Law* (1947), p. 289: " Hedonism revolts the general intuition of men ". *Cf.* Potter, *The Quest of Justice* (1951), p. 73.

[2] Ross, *The Right and the Good* (1930).

[3] See *ante.*, Chap. 4.

[4] See *ante.*, Chap. 5.

CHAPTER 7

SOCIAL JUSTICE

§A

The term " social justice " is used nowadays in a variety of senses. Here it is used to refer to a theory of an order of society which takes into account as the guiding factors current human claims and current morality. Accordingly, it is closely related to the notions of utility and moral justice which we have considered in earlier chapters. While this rather more complex notion has deep roots in English legal thought it has come into particular prominence in the twentieth century. Yet it is only rarely that the English lawyer has actually referred to it under the label " social justice "; more frequently this notion or some facet of it is invoked by him under such names as " expediency ", " social convenience ", " social utility ", " public policy " or " the public interest ".

A theory of social justice has been advanced and elaborated in this century by the American jurist, Roscoe Pound, which is congenial to the modern English common lawyer on several accounts. Pound wrote for the lawyer rather than the student of politics and philosophy, and he speaks from within the legal profession, having been a practitioner before becoming a whole-time professor of law and Dean of the Harvard Law School.[1] While primarily professing legal philosophy Pound made himself master of the detail of many branches of the common law in its modern and historical forms, and thus

---

[1]Admitted to the Bar of Nebraska, 1890; in practice 1890-1901 and 1904-1907; Judge (Commissioner of Appeals) of the Supreme Court of Nebraska 1901-1903. At Harvard Law School, Story Professor of Law 1910-1913, Carter Professor of Jurisprudence 1913-1936, Dean 1916-1936, Professor 1936-1946.

approached legal philosophy from within the common law tradition. Though avowedly his theory of justice was inspired by German sociological jurisprudence,[1] yet his theory expressed tendencies clearly recognisable in English as well as American judicial and legislative practice in the modern era. Moreover, as Pound's theory of social justice is in effect a development of Bentham's theory of utility as applied to the sphere of law the many common lawyers who have recieved the tradition of utilitarian doctrine are disposed in its favour.

Pound's theory of justice is interwoven in his work with his general theory of law, and runs through his many publications over the last forty years.[2] It is epitomised in his lectures on *Social Control through Law*, published in 1942:

> " As the saying is, we all want the earth. We all have a multiplicity of desires and demands which we seek to satisfy. There are very many of us but there is only one earth. The desires of each continually conflict with or overlap those of his neighbors. So there is, as one might say, a great task of social engineering. There is a task of making the goods of existence, the means of satisfying the demands and desires of men living together in a politically organised society, if they cannot satisfy all the claims that men make upon them, at least go round as far as possible. That is what we mean when we say that the end of the law is justice. We do not mean justice as an individual virtue. We do not mean justice as the ideal relation among men. We mean a regime. We mean such an adjustment of relations and ordering of conduct as will make the goods of existence, the means of satisfying human claims to have things and to do

---

[1] See Pound, " Scope and Purpose of Sociological Jurisprudence " (1911-1912), 24 H.L.R. 591, 25 H.L.R. 140, 489. Pound acknowledged his debt to Ihering—*Der Zweck im Recht* (1877-1883), 2 vols.: Vol. I translated as *Law as a Means to an End*, by Husik (1924); and to Kohler—*Lehrbuch der Rechtsphilosophie* (1908): English edn. *Philosophy of Law*, Albrecht, (1914).

[2] Particularly the following: *The Spirit of the Common Law* (1921), Lecture VIII; *Introduction to the Philosophy of Law* (1921), Lecture II; " A Theory of Social Interests "—(1921), 15 Proc. American Sociological Society 16; " The Theory of Judicial Decision " (1923), 36 H.L.R. 641, 802 and 940; " A Survey of Social Interests " (1943), 57 H.L.R. 1; *Social Control Through Law* (1942), Lecture III; *Justice According to Law* (1951), Lecture I; *Jurisprudence* (1959), 5 vols., especially Parts 2-4.

things, go round as far as possible with the least friction and waste."[1]

Elsewhere he spoke of the objective as giving effect to

" the greatest total of interests or to the interests that weigh most in our civilisation, with the least sacrifice to the scheme of interests as a whole."[2]

More recently, in 1951 in *Justice According to Law*, he has expressed the theory more succinctly. After discussing the essence of earlier theories of justice he concluded:

". . . . we come to an idea of a maximum satisfaction of human wants or expectations. What we have to do in social control, and so in law, is to reconcile and adjust these desires or wants or expectations, so far as we can, so as to secure as much of the totality of them as we can."[3]

Thus the general axiom of justice; but how is this general objective to be achieved in practice in a given society?

Pound, like Bentham, has not been content only to advocate a general theory, but has proceeded to implement his theory in immense detail over many years. Pound made himself master of the facts of the life in as well as the positive law of, his society. As the interests of the actual living human beings of the time and place are the cardinal elements in the administration of justice, he prescribes for the jurist the task of drawing on the data provided by lawyers' experience and by contemporary social science and of compiling an inventory of the claims men in his society are in fact making, be it loudly in political spheres or tacitly in home or workplace.[4] Such claims or interests he would arrange into three

---

[1]*Op. cit.*, pp. 64-65.

[2]" A Survey of Social Interests " (1943), 57 H.L.R. 1, p. 39.

[3]*Op. cit.*, p. 31.

[4]Pound undertook the most formidable task of formulating schemes of interests which he regarded as valid for his own time and place, *viz.* American society in various decades of the twentieth century, and his findings are among the major contributions to sociological jurisprudence: " Interests of Personality " (1915), 28 H.L.R. 343 and 445; " Individual Interests in the Domestic Relations " (1916), 14 Mich. L.R. 177; " A Theory of Social Interests " (1921), 15 Proc. Am. Sociological Socy. 16; " A Survey of Social Interests " (1943), 57 H.L.R. 1; " Individual Interests of Substance " (1945), 59 H.L.R. 1. Summaries are given in: *Outlines of Lectures on Jurisprudence*, 5th edn., (1943), Part IV, in *Social Control Through Law* (1942), Lecture III, and in *Jurisprudence* (1959), Part 4. This scheme of interests is valid (if at all) only for the society which the

(continued at foot of next page)

classes:[1] individual interests—claims made by individuals on their own behalf for their private life; public interests—claims made by or for governments relating to political life; and social interests—claims made by individuals on their own and others' behalf relating to their social life, when such claims are made by the whole or the majority of the social group as such. Of these classes of interests the first is of particular importance in private life though many of the interests within the class come within the sphere in which private law can effectively operate; the second is of prime concern in public life, in the sphere of government and is especially important in questions of public law; the third comprises the basic material for the achievement of justice in social conflicts through both private and public law. In dealing with a specific social problem Pound stressed that the just solution could only be achieved if the interests involved were assembled within *one* of these classes, and he was inclined to resolve most social problems by weighing or adjusting the relevant *social* interests.

Pound's theory of justice, far from disregarding moral values, assigns to them a key function. In *Law and Morals*[2] Pound insisted that:

> " a body of received ideals of what legal precepts should be and what they should achieve . . . form a part of the authentic materials by which justice is administered ".

Experience tells us that every claim which say several million people in State A may make cannot be satisfied

---

(*continued from previous page*)
jurist has studied, *viz.* American society (or some American states) in certain decades in this century. To assume as some writers have done that Pound's scheme of interests is valid for some other society, *e.g.*, England in the 1950's, is to misunderstand Pound's philosophy of law.

[1]Pound defined *individual interests* as " claims or demands or desires involved immediately in the individual life and asserted in title of that life "; and *public interests* as " claims or demands or desires involved in life in a politically organised society and asserted in title of that organisation. They are commonly treated as the claims of a politically organised society "; and *social interests* as " claims or demands or desires involved in social life in civilised society and asserted in title of that life. It is not uncommon to treat them as the claims of the whole social group as such ": " A Survey of Social Interests ", 57 H.L.R. 1-2.

[2](1924), 2nd edn. (1926), preface.

in full. Some of the claims may be accounted trivial and not deserving recognition. Many will conflict so that all cannot be satisfied in full. Before a just order of that society can be achieved some selection of the interests which are to be satisfied must be made. The decision that a particular type of claim is too trivial to deserve recognition involves a value judgment. Granting one type of claim to the exclusion of another, or giving priority to one type of claim to the partial frustration of another, these no less involve value judgments. The moral values to be employed in this process of selection and adjustment are not necessarily those propounded in any one religious doctrine, or those postulated or deduced *à priori* in a particular ethical system, but rather the values which happen to be generally accepted in the society in question: " the ethical custom " alias " the received ideals " of the time and place.[1]

In his later works[2] at least Pound was not an advocate of

---

[1]Pound set himself the task of determining the moral values which prevailed in American society in the early twentieth century, and produced his famous " jural postulates " in 1919: *Introduction to American Law*. He would have judge and legislator in that society use these general principles as guides in the evaluation of interests. But twenty years later in *Social Control Through Law* (1942), Lecture IV, when he came to review the position in his American society he was forced to admit that the jural postulates could no longer be determined with any precision: ethical custom was not settled for the time being. Further, seeking a dominant ideal, he found that in the nineteenth century American society a prevailing belief in " individual freedom of action ", but in the society of his day he found competing and inconsistent general ideals namely " individual freedom of action " and " co-operative organised activity ": *Social Control Through Law* (1942), Lecture IV. In such a society without commonly accepted beliefs in particular or general values Pound was forced to concede that justice must be done without such moral guides. In his later works, *The Ideal Element in Law* (Tagore Law Lectures, 1948, published 1958), pp. 84-107 and in *Justice According to Law* (1951), pp. 22-23, after observing totalitarian régimes in Europe, Pound re-emphasises the importance of values in the administration of justice though he still does not commit himself to definitions of the ideals valid for his society.

[2]In 1912 he had written: " In general the sociological jurists stand for what has been called the equitable application of law; that is, they conceive of the legal rule as a general guide to the judge, leading him toward the just result, but insist that within wide limits he should be free to deal with the individual case, so as to meet the demands of justice between the parties and accord with the general reason of ordinary men ": 25 H.L.R., p. 515.

justice without law in a civilised society. As a master of the common law, a law which he aptly defined as " a taught tradition of experience developed by reason and reason tested by experience "[1] he appreciated the many advantages of the administration of justice according to this positive law.[2] But knowledge of and respect for the common law has not obscured for Pound its defects as the sole criterion of justice. The principal defect, in his view, is that in a developing society the positive law is liable to reflect the interests and morality of previous generations, and to fail to recognise current interests and moral opinion of contemporary living human beings. On balance, Pound would have judges in the course of adjudication on concrete cases apply the pre-existing law, except when it was abundantly clear that such a decision would offend against social justice, *i.e.* frustrate more interests than it would satisfy or frustrate those interests which ethical custom indicates are the more valuable. Only in the latter event should the judge reformulate the law for that type of case according to the principles of social justice.[3]

In short, social justice is realised in a particular community when judges and legislators, faced with concrete social problems or conflicts, perform their respective rôles so as to give effect to the greatest total of interests or the interests which weigh most in this community with the least sacrifice of the scheme of interests as a whole. They will be guided to a choice between or reconciliation of interests by the prevailing moral values in their society, if there is a general consensus on these ethical matters. Failing such consensus, they must resort to the method of finding out by experience and developing by reason solutions which will give the maximum effect to the whole scheme of interests with the least friction and waste. So, more often than not, justice involves ultimately the striking of a balance between competing interests and values.

It cannot be claimed that this doctrine amounts to a blue-

---

[1] *Justice According to Law*, p. 60.
[2] *Outlines of Lectures on Jurisprudence*, 5th edn. (1943), p. 88.
[3] "Theory of Judicial Decision", 36 H.L.R. 940 *et seq*; *Social Control Through Law, passim; Justice According to Law, passim.*

print of the ultimate ideal order of society. It is not a plan for the best of all possible worlds, as the theological or rationalist doctrines of natural right claim to be, but it is a plan for a tolerable order of actual societies of men as they are. It makes due allowance for the highest aspirations of men and due allowance for the other sides of human nature, within the sphere of the practicable. It prescribes a method for arriving at just solutions of social problems in this generation, through existing legislative and judicial institutions. Pound only claimed to offer to the lawyer a " working idea " of justice, " even if that working idea is not metaphysically or logically or ethically convincingly ideal ".[1]

Pound's notion of social justice is easily confused with the notions of social justice to be found in the political theories of socialism. In Britain where there has never been any one authoritative doctrine of socialism but many diverse formulations of related political doctrines[2] the term " social justice " is used in these political contexts usually to denote the conformity of some social structure with some principle of socialism. Pound's theory of justice has features in common with that of such a leading modern British socialist as Laski.[3] Both regard law as a means of realising " social justice "; both assume that social justice can best be achieved by a government exercising a comparatively high degree of social control through law; both insist that this law should meet current human interests. To this extent Pound's theory of justice is socialist as opposed to individualist. But Pound's theory does not import the whole range of political and economic doctrine which pass under the title of socialism. For example, Pound's theory of justice does not necessarily require that the state should take over the ownership of the means of production, distribution and exchange or that edu-

---

[1] *Justice According to Law*, p. 29.
[2] In *Socialism, a Short History* (1949), N. Mackenzie refers at p. 11 to some 200 definitions of " Socialism " by leading British Socialists. See Max Beer, *History of British Socialism* (1940); *cf.* G. D. H. Cole, " The Growth of Socialism ", in *Law and Opinion in England in the Twentieth Century* (1959), ed. Ginsberg, Lecture V.
[3] *Studies in Law and Politics* (1932), Chap. XII; *A Grammar of Politics*, 4th edn. (1938).

cation, health services and unemployment relief should be government responsibilities, or that wealth should be more nearly equalised by taxation—to mention only some of the political and economic principles of the socialism of the modern British Labour Party. On Pound's theory such principles would not even be factors in social justice in a given society, unless the majority of citizens asserted them on behalf of all and thus constituted them as social interests. Accordingly the juristic notion of social justice should not be identified with the political notions which pass under the same name.

The theory of social justice advanced by Pound has more affinities with the theory of utility, more particularly with social utility.[1] Both treat human interests as the cardinal element in justice and lay down that the satisfaction of these interests is the function of law; both accept as just those solutions of concrete social problems which amount to a compromise between competing interests. Both allow that just solutions vary with the time, place and persons affected. But social justice diverges from social utility in three directions. (1) Theoretically, at least, the utilitarian takes into account in his just solution of social problems only those human claims which are likely to produce pleasure and reduce pain, whereas the exponent of social justice would take into account the whole range of claims made by the persons in question irrespective of their estimated effect on happiness. (2) In the theory of social justice a prominent function is assigned to prevailing moral values, as guides to the selection of and delimitation of interests. Social utility does not so clearly involve moral values but concentrates attention on the relevant interests. Yet it should not be forgotten that in the utilitarian scheme of pleasures and pains the pleasures of observing positive morality and the pains of ostracism are not excluded. So the difference is one of degree. If in the solution of a problem positive morality is invoked as a major factor along with the relevant interests, it is a useful shorthand to say that the notion of social justice rather than that of social utility is at work. (3) Social justice is a more com-

---

[1] See *ante*, pp. 110, 124-125 and *post*, pp. 146-147.

plex and professedly a more scientific theory than social utility. The social utilitarian would have the governor estimate approximately the interests of the governed. But Pound in his theory of social justice would have the governor invoke data organised by the jurist, drawn from the findings of the current social sciences.

§B

To what extent does Pound in formulating this theory of justice speak for the English common lawyer? It is certainly not the case that the English Bench and Bar have been converted from their traditional opinions to this version of justice by Pound's writings. The theory of social justice which pervades Pound's works has probably been more widely disseminated in England through the lectures of Cardozo[1] and the more recent jurisprudential work of Pound's disciple, Professor Stone,[2] and the popular modern text-book on Jurisprudence by Professor Paton,[3] than by Pound's own lectures and articles. Nevertheless Pound's version of social justice is important for the student of English legal thought because it rationalises and refines one of the traditional methods of adjudication and legislation used by English judges.

The embryo of this notion can be discerned in the occasional incidental reliance placed by the older common lawyers on the " public convenience ", which we have already remarked upon in the previous chapter.[4] It developed within the doctrine of utility, so that the preceding account of that doctrine, discounting only the individualist principle, is a necessary preface to this chapter.

The notion of social utility, with its emphasis on social rather than individual interests and its assumption that the

---

[1]*Nature of the Judicial Process* (1921), Lectures II and III; *The Growth of the Law* (1924); *Paradoxes of Legal Science* (1928).
[2]*Province and Function of Law* (1947).
[3]*A Text-Book of Jurisprudence*, 2nd edn. (1951), Part V.
[4]*Ante*, p. 114.

governor knows better than the governed the interests of the latter, is recognisable as the core of the judicial doctrine of public policy. In certain types of cases, at least since the Elizabethan period, the judges' estimate of the public interest becomes more than a factor in judgment; it becomes the decisive factor. The new emphasis is forcefully expressed in a *dictum* of Lord Chancellor HARDWICKE in the mid-eighteenth century: " Political arguments, in the fullest sense of the word, as they concern the government of a nation, must be, and always have been of great weight in the consideration of this court, and though there may be no *dolus malus*, in contracts as to other persons, yet if the rest of mankind are concerned as well as the parties, it may properly be said, that it regards the publick utility."[1] This priority given to the public interest is to be found in a variety of cases decided in the old courts of Common Law as well as Chancery, involving questions of property and contract. The names of several of the great English judges in the seventeenth and eighteenth centuries are associated with the formation of this doctrine of public policy, as for instance Lord NOTTINGHAM,[2] Lord MACCLESFIELD,[3] Lord MANSFIELD.[4]

When a judge is prepared to lay down a rule of law having regard primarily to what he conceives to be the contemporary interests of the public he is subscribing to a dynamic conception of public policy, and acting on the notions of social utility or social justice. But when a judge is only prepared to give effect to public policy so far as one of his predecessors has laid down a rule based thereon and that rule is the essence of the earlier decision, he is subscribing to a static conception of public policy, and in effect acting on the notion of legal justice. The English Bench has long been divided into two such schools of thought on the subject of public policy.

---

[1] *Earl of Chesterfield* v. *Janssen* (1750), 1 Atk. 301, at p. 352. The *dictum* occurs in the course of Lord HARDWICKE's classic survey of the doctrine of equitable fraud, with specific reference to bargains to procure offices, which, though neither party is defrauded, were rescinded in courts of equity since they introduce unworthy objects into public affairs.

[2] *Duke of Norfolk's Case, Howard* v. *Duke of Norfolk* (1683), 3 Cas. in Ch. 1, at pp. 25-54; see *post*, pp. 165-166.

[3] *Mitchel* v. *Reynolds* (1711), 1 P. Wms. 181; see *post*, pp. 107-108.

[4] *Lowe* v. *Peers* (1768), 4 Burr. 2225.

These divergent approaches are vividly illustrated in the opinions of the judges in 1853 in *Egerton* v. *Earl Brownlow*.[1] The specific question which eventually faced the House of Lords in that case was whether a devise of property (worth more than two million pounds) by the Earl of B. to Z, was invalidated by provisions to the effect that if Z did not acquire the title of Duke or Marquis his estate should be absolutely void. The solution of this question turned *inter alia* on whether such provisions were void as contrary to public policy. The House of Lords, in accordance with the old practice, consulted the judges of the common law courts. Of the eleven judges consulted nine advised that the provisions were *not* void as contrary to public policy. Baron PARKE proved to be the most vigorous defender of the static approach to public policy; in the absence of a clear precedent on the question he absolutely declined to declare the provision invalid on the ground of his own estimate of the public good.[2]

In sharp contrast, the minority opinion of the Chief Baron, POLLOCK, epitomises the dynamic approach. He examined the extent to which earlier lawyers had recognised public policy or " the good of the state " as a ground of decision, and dwelt on and attributed a wide import to the *dicta* of COKE that *nihil quod est inconveniens est licitum* and of Lord HARDWICKE that the court should regard the public utility in cases where the public are concerned.[3] He also considered the lines of cases which establish certain species of contract as against public policy and therefore void. On his interpretation of these authorities he felt justified in saying " that were I to discard the public welfare from my consideration I would abdicate the functions of my office—I should shrink from the discharge of my duty ".[4] The Chief Baron pointed out distinctly the factual position in the instant case and predicted the probable consequence; *viz.* that as some branches of the Duke of B.'s family had a strong financial motive for obtaining and others for opposing the grant of a

---

[1](1853), 4 H.L.Cas. 1.
[2]*Ibid.*, at p. 123: see *post*, p. 171.
[3]See *ante*, p. 144.
[4](1853), 4 H.L.Cas., at p. 149.

dukedom the departments of state were likely to be besieged by these interested parties and the sovereign herself was liable to be affected. He concluded that in the determination of a matter which ought to be decided by the executive on its merits the public good should prevail over the caprice of a testator. Accordingly he adjudged that it was against the public interest for any one to create any pecuniary interest or other bias of any sort in the decision of a matter of a public nature which involves the public welfare.[1] Hence he advised that the provisions were void. Although a seemingly overwhelming majority of the judges had advised to the contrary, the majority of the House of Lords agreed with POLLOCK, C.B., in his conclusion that the provisions were void, and, what is more significant for our enquiry, in reaching these conclusions Lord TRURO[2] and Lord LYNDHURST,[3] and to a lesser extent Lord ST. LEONARDS,[4] accepted the dynamic view of the function of the courts in cases involving public policy. The dynamic element in the opinions which prevailed in this case was plainly the notion of social utility.

Social utility as a *theory* of justice has had in England no single outstanding protagonist. Apparently the English lawyers in the later nineteenth century were oblivious of the theory of social utilitarianism which was being elaborated in German legal philosophy.[5] But John Stuart Mill, whose writings profoundly influenced the rising generations in England, must have led many of the younger generations of lawyers towards the notion of social utility as the measure of justice. For Mill, the great apologist of individualism (*On Liberty*, 1859) and of utilitarianism (*Utilitarianism*, 1863), in his later works moved distinctly towards socialism.[6] Collectivism alias socialism, as a political doctrine, evolved in the latter half of the nineteenth century in England, not as the result of the inspiration of any one political theorist, but, as

---

[1] (1853), 4 H.L.Cas., at p. 150.
[2] *Ibid.*, at pp. 195-197.
[3] *Ibid.*, at pp. 160-161.
[4] *Ibid.*, at pp. 233-239.
[5] Ihering, *Der Zweck im Recht* (1877-1883).
[6] *Autobiography* (1873); *Political Economy*, 2nd edn. (1874). Leslie Stephen, in *The English Utilitarians* (1900), Vol. III, p. 230, shrewdly observed that " Mill was well on the way to state socialism ".

Dicey has explained,[1] as the resultant of divers social forces in England. The lawyers of the day were not impervious to the ideas engendered in the great political debate. The pronounced swing towards social utilitarian solutions to specific questions among lawyers in England in the later nineteenth century can surely be attributed in part to their own experience of the grim facts of industrial and agricultural conditions of life which had materialised under the earlier *laissez-faire* régime, with which they were brought face to face daily in their practice in and out of court, at Nisi Prius in the county and industrial towns as well as in London.

In the last half of the nineteenth century critical opinion in the English legal profession inclined more and more towards social utility and social justice. The Juridical Society was launched in 1855 to develop the science of jurisprudence and to promote social, moral and political subjects having relation to law. A Queen's Counsel addressing the Society in 1856[2] described law as " an endeavour to meet and provide for the never-ending and ever-varying combinations of human interests, as they spring from the wants and wishes, follies and weaknesses, the virtues and vices, of human nature ". The proper criterion for laws he declared to be " the welfare of man in the social state ". But welfare he saw not as human happiness *simpliciter*, or the mere satisfaction of the wants and wishes of the humans concerned, but as that human welfare prescribed by morality—the morality of the Bible. Richard Bethell, later Lord WESTBURY—whom a contemporary had characterised as " a law reformer who was terribly in earnest "[3]—in an address to the same Society in 1857 complained that law as a science was falling behind the moral sciences and every part of the physical sciences. In the latter the method of induction was dominant; they employed continuous experiments and observation, and when at length

---

[1]See *Law and Public Opinion*, Lecture VII; *cf.* Ginsberg, " The Growth of Social Responsibility " in *Law and Opinion in England in the Twentieth Century* (1959), Lecture I.

[2]W. T. S. Daniel, Q.C.: " On Change as an Inherent Necessity in Every System of Municipal Law ", Transactions of the Juridical Society, Vol. I (1855-1858), pp. 95 *et seq.*

[3]Atlay. *Victorian Chancellors*, Vol. II, p. 256.

a great quantity of facts were ascertained the boundary of such science was advanced. " Why is not that applied to law? Take any particular department of the common law; take, if you please, any statute. Why is there not a body of men in this country whose duty it is to collect a body of judicial statistics, or in more common phrase, make the necessary experiments to see how far the law is fitted to the exigencies of society, the necessities of the times, the growth of wealth and the progress of mankind?"[1] In the same year the National Association for the Promotion of Social Sciences was launched by Lord BROUGHAM, and from the first it included a strong department of " Jurisprudence and the Amendment of the Law " which enlisted the support of leading members of the legal profession in the succeeding decades.[2]

A belief that law should serve the interests of the living generation and reflect moral principles evidently actuated one of the most acute and learned of the English judges in the later nineteenth century, Lord BOWEN. Although a supreme master of the detail of the positive law, BOWEN was nevertheless strongly disposed to take, in his own words, a bird's-eye view of a legal subject, and to treat the rules of positive law not according to their letter but as dynamic means of controlling society. In a lecture in 1884 on the value of the historical school of jurisprudence he spoke of law as the application of certain rules to a subject-matter which is constantly shifting, namely, English life and English business. The rules themselves, he argued, must and do gradually change, undergo evolution and move as human intelligence moves. So legal authorities, each the product of its own particular time, need to be studied with reference to it.[3] On the Bench, when occasion permitted, notably in his judgment in

---

[1]Nash, *Life of Lord Westbury* (1888), Vol. I, p. 191.

[2]See Transactions of the National Association for the Promotion of Social Sciences, 1857-1884. Besides BROUGHAM several other judges or future judges took an active part in its proceedings, *e.g.* PAGE WOOD, WILDE, PHILLIMORE, J. D. COLERIDGE, J. FITZJAMES STEPHENS. In 1867 this department had a standing committee of fifty, mostly lawyers, including fourteen Q.C's.

[3]Cunningham, *Lord Bowen, A Biographical Sketch* (1897), pp. 165-166.

the Court of Appeal in *Nordenfelt's* case[1] in 1893, he manifestly acted on these precepts. The basis of his approach to legal problems is most clearly revealed in his essay on " The Administration of the Law, 1837-1887 ".[2] " There is and can be no such thing as finality about the administration of the law. It changes, it must change, it ought to change, with the broadening wants and requirements of a growing country, and with the gradual illumination of the public conscience."

In the early twentieth century Viscount HALDANE, as Lord Chancellor, was advocating similar fundamental notions in the sphere of law. In 1913 in an address to lawyers[3] he stressed the importance of that social force which the Germans called *Sittlichkeit* (*i.e.* the standard of right conduct prevailing in a given society) as a factor in social control. Law is inevitably and properly affected by this force; for law has grown through the influence of the opinion of society, guided by its skilled advisers. To understand law fully one must go to the moralist and the sociologist. On this score HALDANE accounted Austin and Bentham deficient and Montesquieu as having a deeper insight. HALDANE conceived of the common law system of justice as something which lawyers are progressively and co-operatively evolving. Therefore he would have the lawyers more consciously attend to this *Sittlichkeit* (or ethical custom or positive morality) and " think in terms of society itself ".[4]

Roscoe Pound's theory of social justice brings into sharper focus these notions of justice subscribed to by this school of thought in the English legal profession in the late nineteenth and early twentieth centuries. Indeed it may well be that Pound in formulating his theory was inspired as much by the

---

[1]*Maxim Nordenfelt Guns and Ammunition Co.* v. *Nordenfelt*, [1893] 1 Ch. 630, at pp. 651-668; *cf. Dashwood* v. *Magniac*, [1891] 3 Ch. 306, at p. 367.

[2]Printed in *The Reign of Queen Victoria*, 2 vols., ed. Ward, Vol. I, pp. 281-329, at p. 329.

[3]*Higher Nationality, A Study in Law and Ethics* (1913): an address delivered to the American Bar Association.

[4]A few years later HALDANE was Chairman of the Committee on the Machinery of Government which recommended that fuller provision should be made for the continuous acquisition of scientific—including social—data to provide a proper basis for the formulation of government policy: Report of Machinery of Government Committee (1918), Cd. 9230, paras. 12, 13 and 56.

precepts and practice of such enlightened judges as BOWEN and HALDANE as by German jurisprudence. The theory which has rationalised and refined these tendencies has in turn served to strengthen them.

In this century many of the judges in the English courts have acted on the principles of social justice without professing to be partisans of that theory.[1] But several members of the English Bench have actually professed such principles and have demonstrably acted on them within the strict limits prescribed by statutes and the more flexible limits set by the doctrine of judicial precedent.[2] Outstanding among the latter is Lord WRIGHT.

[1]*E.g.* Lord ATKIN in *Donoghue (or McAlister)* v. *Stevenson*, [1932] All E.R. Rep. 1 at p. 13; [1932] A.C. 562, at p. 583; Lord McDERMOTT in *London Graving Dock Co., Ltd.* v. *Horton*, [1951] A.C. 737, at p. 765. Winfield observed that the judicial practice in acting on statutory mandates to do what is " just " or " just and convenient " has been to take into account all the conflicting interests put before the court in any particular case and to strike a balance between them: *Select Legal Essays* (1952), p. 281. A striking illustration is to be found in the speech of Viscount SIMON, L.C. in the House of Lords in *Blunt* v. *Blunt*, [1943] 2 All E.R. 76, at p. 78; [1943] A.C. 517, at p. 525. The Matrimonial Causes Act, 1937, s. 4, conferred discretion on the courts to dismiss a petition for divorce if the petitioner himself has been guilty of a matrimonial offence. Viscount SIMON interpreted this section as follows: " The utmost that can properly be done is to indicate the chief considerations which ought to be weighed in appropriate cases, as helping to arrive at a just conclusion. . . . These are (a) the position and interest of any children of the marriage; (b) the interest of the party with whom the petitioner has been guilty of misconduct, with special regard to the prospect of their future marriage; (c) the question whether, if the marriage is not dissolved, there is a prospect of reconciliation between husband and wife; and (d) the interest of the petitioner, and, in particular the interest that the petitioner should be able to remarry and live respectably. To these four considerations I would add a fifth of a more general character, which must, indeed, be regarded as of primary importance, namely the interest of the community at large, to be judged by maintaining a true balance between respect for the binding sanctity of marriage and the social considerations which make it contrary to public policy to insist on the maintenance of a union which has utterly broken down ".

[2]*E.g.*, Viscount HALDANE: *cf. Higher Nationality, A Study in Law and Ethics, supra*, pp. 31-45; *Kreglinger* v. *New Patagonia Meat and Cold Storage Co., Ltd.*, [1914] A.C. 25, at pp. 35-45, and *Rodriguez* v. *Speyer Bros.*, [1919] A.C. 59, at pp. 77 *et seq.*; McCARDIE, J.: *cf. The Law: The Advocate: The Judge* (1927), A Reading at the Middle Temple, and *Naylor, Benzon & Co., Ltd.* v. *K.I.G.*, [1918] 1 K.B. 331, and *Place* v. *Searle*, [1932] All E.R. Rep. 84; [1932] 2 K.B. 497.

Lord WRIGHT has expressly invoked the concept of justice more often and has considered its nature more fully in extra-judicial essays[1] than any other modern English judge. He speaks with rare authority having acted as a judge of first instance in the King's Bench Division for seven years (1925-1932), as Master of the Rolls presiding in the Court of Appeal (1935-1937), and as Lord of Appeal in Ordinary in the ultimate English court of appeal for some thirteen years (1932-1935 and 1937-1947). A characteristic invocation of the concept occurs in his essay on *The Common Law in its Old Home* (1936):[2] " I repeat that law must be regarded as a living organism; its rules are subsidiary to justice and must, so far as precedent and logic permit, be moulded so as to conform with justice. The judge can do much; when he can do no more, recourse must be had to Parliament." But while the concept of justice is most prominent in his judgments and writings, even Lord WRIGHT, the most articulate of modern English judges, has not attempted definition. He confessed, " I have not found any satisfactory definition of justice, but whatever it is, it is the quality of what is just. And what is just in any particular case is what appears to be just to the just man, in the same way as what is reasonable is what appears to be reasonable to the reasonable man ".[3] The observer may conclude that Lord WRIGHT deliberately left the concept at large rather than confine it within the strait-jacket of a verbal formula. But he may nevertheless discern the pattern of reasoning which Lord WRIGHT avowedly adopted when he acted upon the concept. Elsewhere he has given a distinct indication of his views of the essential principles of justice: " But it is difficult to define justice. We think we know what it means in any particular case. But there again we are merely acting on the *current sociological and moral ideas*. . . ."[4] Even clearer indication of his views on

---

[1]*Legal Essays and Addresses* (1939)—a volume which contains various lectures and essays written 1936-1939; " Precedents ", 8 C.L.J. (1942) 118-145; "Lord Atkin of Aberdovey", Proc. British Academy, Vol. XXXII, pp. 307-324.
[2]*Legal Essays and Addresses*, p. 344.
[3]*Ibid.*, p. 382.
[4]*Ibid.*, pp. 196-197; italics supplied.

the essential principles appear in his more recent obituary of Lord ATKIN. There he said " [laws] at whatever level they are taken they are not dry or abstract principles; they are for use and service in the aid of justice. . . . They must be tested and examined by the *criterion of social utility*, and the consensus of the human instinct and the *sense of right and wrong* "[1]. Running through his many judgments and essays are these two criteria. The first appears in a score of apparently synonymous phrases—for instance " social needs ", " social ideas of today ", " social policy ", " modern social view ",[2] " social welfare ", and perhaps the most significant, " social convenience ".[3] Lord WRIGHT explained his use of this key term " convenience " as meaning " not a mere opportunism or narrow practicality, but a wise regard to practical consideration. . . . Perhaps it was something like this which Holmes had in mind when he said that experience and not logic was the life of the law, or when he said that judges must think facts not words. He may have meant that law is not a self-contained system of rules and concepts *bombinans in vacuo* but a function of human life, only capable of justifying itself in so far as it meets the requirements of men and affairs ".[4] Patently this criterion belongs to the theory of social rather than individual utility. For the most part in estimating the justice or injustice of a particular rule of law or a decision Lord WRIGHT uses this criterion alone. But on occasions he called in aid the second, moral, criterion under various synonyms: " moral conceptions ", " shocking to the man in the street ", " the ordinary sense of mankind revolts

---

[1]Proc. British Academy, Vol. XXXII, p. 309; italics supplied.

[2]For example, *à propos* the principle established in *Rylands* v. *Fletcher* (1868), L.R. 3 H.L. 330. " I think it is sound because it accords with the modern social view that one who maintains a potential danger for his own benefit ought to compensate . . . those who suffer if in fact the danger evades control and does damage ".

[3]*Re* the rule that the House of Lords is bound by its previous rulings: " Can anyone doubt that on balance of social convenience and public welfare it would have been better to have refused to perpetuate the erroneous and unjust rule [in *R.* v. *Millis*]?": 8 C.L.J., p. 122.

[4]*Legal Essays and Addresses*, Preface, pp. xvii-xviii.

from such a result " or simply " moral values ":[1] it resolves into an active consideration of current morality in English society. In applying these criteria Lord WRIGHT insisted that the judge should not give effect to his own views but should attempt to gauge the social needs and moral opinion objectively.[2] In using these criteria and in insisting on some degree of objectivity Lord WRIGHT is acknowledging, if not his allegiance to Pound's theory of social justice,[3] at least that his own views on justice correspond to a striking extent with those advanced by the American jurist.

Ex cathedra Lord WRIGHT'S judgment in *Fender* v. *Mildmay*[4] was patently guided by such fundamental considerations. F had accepted M's promise to marry her at a time when M was still a married man: a decree nisi for the dissolution of his marriage had been pronounced but this had not been made absolute. Eventually M refused to marry F and married another woman. F sued M for damages for breach of promise of marriage. The question before the House of Lords was whether such a contract to marry was void as contrary to public policy, a question on which there was no precedent ruling precisely in point. The House, by a majority of three to two, decided that the contract was not void on this ground and accordingly that F was entitled to damages for breach of the contract to marry. Lord WRIGHT, one of the majority, considered the problem in its widest social setting. He saw it as involving an apparent conflict between two general policies of the law (*i.e.* social interests), namely the policy of upholding the sanctity of contract and the policy of upholding the marriage status. " The primary duty of a court of law is to enforce promises which parties have made and to

---

[1] *Re* the power of a court to make a new rule of law: it does so " by applying its standards of moral and social values and of justice " to the particular problem in a case of first impression: 8 C.L.J. 118, p. 124.

[2] *Legal Essays and Addresses*, p. 95.

[3] Lord WRIGHT acknowledged the stimulus he had received from Pound in *Interpretations of Modern Legal Philosophies* (1947), Essay XXXVIII, p. 794. Lord WRIGHT has not been a disciple of Pound, nor *vice versa*; rather the ideas of the English judge and the American professor have developed contemporaneously within the ethos of the modern common law.

[4] [1937] 3 All E.R. 402; [1938] 1 A.C. 1.

uphold the sanctity of contract which is the basis of society. But in certain cases the court dispenses parties from keeping their plighted word because of some rule of law founded on what is called public policy. It is said here that there is such a rule of law requiring the court to say the respondent's promise was not binding. . . . What is advanced as the basis of this particular new rule is that it involves the public interest in upholding the married state. That there is in general such a public interest I should be the last to deny. But the provisions of English law recognise civil marriage and divorce. . . . The question in the present case is whether after decree nisi there is any public interest in seeking to preserve, at the expense of the solid detriment of sanctioning a breach of contract, the transitory and unsubstantial form of a marriage which by the decree of the court is practically doomed to extinction in a brief period of months ".[1] Looking to the social realities in the type of case before him Lord WRIGHT observed that such an agreement commonly follows upon divorce proceedings when the guilty party and the co-respondent (or it might be the innocent party and some other person), were anxious to stabilise their position against the time when the decree absolute should take effect. The decree nisi has put an end to the common home and to the *consortium vitae* and to conjugal rights. The possibility of reconciliation at this stage is extremely slight, for in the vast majority of cases the decree absolute follows the decree nisi in due course. A mere possibility of reconciliation could not counterbalance the solid and certain considerations which he had indicated. " If realities are to be looked at and not mere form, by the court . . . the marriage is at an end, and the parties are entitled to provide for their future. . . . How can the public interest in regard to marriage be prejudiced if the innocent petitioner then desires to enter into an engagement, conditional on the decree absolute, for a fresh marriage? . . . Again, how can the public interest be prejudiced if the respondent seeks to make a conditional engagement to terminate or atone for an immoral association with the intervener or co-respondent?"[2] In short, in this type of case the

---

[1][1937] 3 All E.R. 402, at p. 423; [1938] I A.C. I, at p. 36.
[2]*Ibid.*, at pp. 430, 46, respectively.

public interest in the fulfilment of promises is to prevail, as the public interest in the security of marriage is not seriously subverted. Considerations of current morality entered into Lord WRIGHT's judgment, tilting the scales in favour of the public interest in the fulfilment of promises; for à *propos* the engagements to re-marry, whether made by the guilty or innocent parties to the subsisting marriage, he observed: " These new relations are not in their nature bad on the ground of immorality or likely to lead to immorality any more than the engagement of affectionate couples who have not suffered the miseries of an ill-assorted union ":[1] In short, moral opinion in England in the 1930's, far from condemning, would approve of such engagements.

Paradoxically, in this speech[2] Lord WRIGHT professed to prefer the conservative opinions of PARKE, B., on public policy to those expressed by POLLOCK, C.B., in *Egerton* v. *Earl Brownlow*:[3] yet Lord WRIGHT in this case in effect acted upon the dynamic conception of public policy advocated by the Chief Baron. The key to this paradox is that Lord WRIGHT was at pains to emphasise that in judicially determining public policy the judge should not act on his individual views or predilections, but should interpret prevailing contemporary opinion, and seek definite proof that the interests of the public are involved; " the matter must be decided on tangible grounds, not on mere generalisations ". Looking to the facts of this type of case, he adjudged that the decree nisi in truth determined the status of the parties and ended the marriage. An engagement to re-marry in such circumstances, he concluded, is not contrary to the public interest, and is therefore not void as contrary to public policy.

A more cryptic use of the method of social justice is to be found in Lord WRIGHT's speech in *Radcliffe* v. *Ribble Motor Services, Ltd.*[4] A, a bus driver, was negligently knocked over and killed by B, another bus driver, employed by the same

---

[1][1937] 3 All E.R. 402, at p. 423; [1938] 1 A.C. 1, at p. 37.
[2]*Ibid.*, at pp. 424-425, 38-42, respectively.
[3]See *ante*, pp. 145-146.
[4][1939] 1 All E.R. 637, at pp. 650-662; [1939] A.C. 215, at pp. 237-254.

company. A's widow, claiming damages from her husband's employer under the Fatal Accidents Act, 1846, was met by the plea of common employment, *i.e.*, the rule stemming from *Priestley* v. *Fowler*[1] to the effect that a master was not liable to his servant for any injury received as a result of any act or default of a fellow-servant. In a case in the previous year[2] Lord WRIGHT had castigated the rule as depending on an assumption which had " little regard to reality or to modern ideas of economics or industrial or social conditions ", and had said that the rule had only survived because of statutory remedies given to employees to minimise what to modern ideas appeared as an obvious injustice. But in *Radcliffe's* case, when counsel invited him to abrogate the rule on the ground that it was based on industrial and social conditions which had changed, and that it was the duty of the common law to mould and adapt itself from time to time so as to do justice under the new and changed conditions, Lord WRIGHT expressed sympathy with the argument but resisted the invitation to abrogate the rule entirely. A limitation on the flexibility and progressive character of the common law which he accepted while sitting judicially in the House of Lords was that the House was bound by its own decisions, and the rule in question had been affirmed by the House in 1858 in the *Bartonshill Coal Co.* cases.[3] But reading between the subsequent lines[4] the modern observer can detect that these very considerations of justice drove Lord WRIGHT to limit the scope of the rule to those cases where the injured men and the negligent co-employee are engaged in the same common work. Thus he was able to reach the specific conclusion that in such a case as the one before the court the rule did not operate to bar the plaintiff's claim.

These criteria of social justice are to be found at work in various branches of the English legal profession in the middle of this century. They run through the Reports of the Law

---

[1](1837), 3 M. & W. 1.
[2]*Wilsons and Clyde Coal Co., Ltd.* v. *English*, [1937] 3 All E.R. 628, at p. 641; [1938] A.C. 57, at p. 80.
[3](1858), 3 Macq. 266 and 300.
[4]See " Precedents ", 8 C.L.J. 118, at p. 123.

Revision Committee, 1934-1939. The Committee which produced the first four reports comprised five judges,[1] under the chairmanship of Lord HANWORTH and including Lord WRIGHT, two academic lawyers[2] and seven senior counsel and solicitors.[3] In their First Report[4] the Committee recommended radical modifications in the law epitomised in the maxim *actio personalis moritur cum persona*. Specifically they proposed that where a wrong-doer dies before or after action is commenced the victim should be allowed to maintain or continue proceedings against the deceased wrong-doer's personal representatives. Various reasons were advanced for this law reform, but principal among these was the consideration that in the new conditions of motor car travel when a negligent driver, A, was himself killed, the person whom he injured was barred by the maxim from recovering compensation from A's estate or his insurance company. The argument given—that " the greater frequency of deaths on the road due to negligent driving has made the reform . . . a matter of urgent national importance " might equally have been phrased " there is an urgent wide-spread current interest which the law frustrates and should satisfy ". In their Fourth Report[5] the Committee recommended the removal of the limits which the law still imposed on the liability of married women in contract and in tort, so that a married woman should bear liability to the same extent as a single woman or a man. The Committee looked to current social facts and noted that married women nowadays engage in most professions, trades and business, and are eligible to hold and do in general hold every sort of public and official post as much as men. "Differentiation cannot be regarded as being in accord with modern ideas or conditions." *A propos* the doctrine of restraint upon anticipation they proceeded to consider the various interests involved. On the one hand

---

[1]Lord HANWORTH, M.R., Lord WRIGHT, ROMER, L.J., SWIFT, J. and GODDARD, J.
[2]Professors Gutteridge and McNair.
[3]C. Asquith, W. E. Mortimer, T. J. O'Connor, K.C., R. Poole, S. L. Porter, K.C., C. Schuster, K.C., A. F. Topham, K.C.
[4]1934, Cmd. 4540.
[5]1934, Cmd. 4770.

married women have an interest in protecting their own property from extravagant husbands. On the other hand
creditors have an interest in securing full satisfaction out of
the married women's capital for debts incurred by married
women, and the married women themselves need on occasions to realise their capital for business enterprises. The
Committee concluded that the balance of convenience
pointed to the removal of the restraints upon anticipation.
In the Sixth Report[1] of the Law Revision Committee—now
under the chairmanship of Lord WRIGHT[2] the criteria of
social justice are even more plainly invoked. The Statute of
Frauds, 1677, s. 4, was the first target of the Committee's
criticism. It was condemned, *inter alia*, on these grounds:
(*a*) it was a product of conditions which had long passed
away, and had become an anachronism, *i.e.*, it no longer
served a current social need; (*b*) currently it promoted dis-
honesty and enabled men to break promises with impunity,
i.e., it offended the moral sentiment of the community; (*c*) the
classes of contracts caught by the statute were by modern
reckoning arbitrary, so that the operation of the statute in
one case and its non-operation in an analogous case offended
the moral sense at least of members of the Committee, and
(*d*) above all, this section of the statute defeated the expectations of ordinary honest men of affairs. When the Committee
turned to consider the various rules which constitute the
doctrine of consideration they reported adversely on some of
these, as " causing serious business inconvenience ", as " ir-
reconcilable with business expediency or common sense " or
as offending " the general conscience of mankind ". Their
principles for a reformed law of consideration are plainly
stated. In the first place the law on the subject should conform to the basic principle that if the parties intend the
promise to be one which will be effective in law it should be
enforced, a moral axiom assumed by the Committee.[3] In the

---

[1] 1937, Cmd. 5449.

[2] Lord HANWORTH had retired in 1935; a third academic lawyer,
Professor Goodhart, had now joined the Committee.

[3] Cmd. 5449, pp. 12 and 18; *cf.* Lord WRIGHT, " Ought the Doctrine
of Consideration to be Abolished " (1936) in *Legal Essays and
Addresses*, pp. 287-326, where this axiom is affirmed *à priori* as the
proper first principle for the law of contract.

second place the law on the subject should be such as would be " most likely to serve the needs of our modern community ".[1] While Lord WRIGHT's hand is evident in this last Report it remains the agreed report of fourteen eminent common lawyers.

Similar criteria are to be found in several of the recent Reports of the Law Reform Committee (1953-current).[2] For example, in their Report on occupiers' liability to invitees, licensees and trespassers[3] the grounds of criticism included (a) a moral proposition " which must command universal acceptance ", viz. that the occupier of premises owes some duty of care in regard to the safety of those premises to those persons lawfully coming on them, and (b) the question whether the law corresponds with the reasonable claims to protection of the classes of persons using property occupied by others. Even the one dissenting member[4] conceded that reforms were needed in some particulars " where the doctrine of stare decisis has prevented the common law from adapting itself to current social and ethical conceptions ". And in their Report on innkeepers' liability for property of travellers, guests and residents[5] the Committee concentrated on actual

---

[1]Cmd. 5449, p. 18.

[2]The Committee was constituted in 1952 of five judges: JENKINS, L.J., Lord GODDARD, C.J., Lord ASQUITH, DEVLIN, J. and PARKER, J.; three academic lawyers, Professors Goodhart, Hughes Parry and Wade; and six leading counsel and solicitors, viz. R. J. F. Burrows, W. J. K. Diplock, Q.C., G. Gardiner, Q.C., J. N. Gray, Q.C., R. E. Megarry, R. T. Outen.

[3]Third Report, 1954, Cmd. 9305: see post, pp. 210-211.

[4]K. Diplock, Q.C., now DIPLOCK, J.

[5]Second Report, 1954, Cmd. 9161. Cf. Sixth Report, 1957, Cmnd. 310 on court's power to sanction variation of trusts. The Committee condemned the positive law, as laid down in Chapman v. Chapman, [1954] 1 All E.R. 798; [1954] A.C. 429 as denying to older settlements " the flexibility which modern conditions demand ". After considering the various interests involved, the individual interests of different classes of beneficiaries (adults, children and potential objects), the individual interests of settlors and the public interest in revenue, the Committee pronounced that " Justice . . . demands that the court should have an unlimited jurisdiction to vary trusts ". Thus it would be left to the discretion of the judge in the Chancery Division to make allowance for the individual interests in a particular case while refusing to sanction any scheme " which as a citizen and taxpayer he would not think it right to enter into with regard to his own property ".

claims and expectations of the various classes of persons concerned and endeavoured to strike a balance between these
interests. In the course of their investigations of the facts and
the claims of the persons affected by this branch of the law
the Committee were not content to rely on their own experience and estimates but actually conducted a limited
social survey *ad hoc* by receiving evidence from associations
of persons affected by the laws in question.[1]

In the academic branch of the legal profession in England
—as distinct from the other parts of the common law world, *e.g.*,
America or Australasia—no disciple has been directly preaching Pound's theory of social justice. Nevertheless many an
English academic lawyer employs fragments of that theory
in his criticism of particular laws and cases. For instance, it
is commonplace to find a text-writer approving of a rule of
law as " consonant with the needs of a civilised community "[2]
or as " compatible with business conditions of the twentieth
century "[3] or condemning a rule as " inadequate to modern
needs ",[4] or asserting as a general axiom that the law ought
to " adjust itself to the novel condition of social life ".[5]

So far in this chapter we have demonstrated that several
modern English judges, most members of the committees for
law reform, and leading academic lawyers, have on occasions
employed criteria which correspond with those postulated in
Pound's theory of social justice. But this is not to say that
these lawyers have fully adopted Pound's philosophy of
justice or that they are implementing it fully in their professional activities. The " interests " which they so readily

---

[1]*Viz.* The Brewers' Society, The British Hotels and Restaurants
Association, the Standing Joint Committee of the R.A.C., the A.A.
and the R. Scottish A.C., etc. In their Eighth Report, Cmnd. 622,
in 1958, on the sealing of contracts made by bodies corporate, the
Law Reform Committee paid attention to memoranda submitted to
them by some forty bodies, *e.g.*, the Association of Municipal Cor-
porations, the B.B.C., the Chartered Institute of Secretaries, the
Committee of Vice-Chancellors and Principals of University Institutions in England, the L.C.C. and the Institute of Hospital
Administrators.

[2]*E.g.*, Winfield, *Torts*, 5th edn. (1950), p. 553.
[3]*E.g.*, Cheshire, *Modern Real Property*, 8th edn. (1958), p. 570.
[4]*E.g.*, Cheshire and Fifoot, *Law of Contract*, 5th edn. (1960), p. 370.
[5]*E.g.*, Goodhart, *Law Reform—Judicial and Legislative* (1954), p. 4.

invoke are not those which have been ascertained scientifically by jurists co-operating with social scientists, but rather
more often than not they are no more than the individual
lawyer's private estimate of the expectations or wants of the
persons in question, drawn from his own experience of the
society in which he lives. Nor are these estimated interests
balanced only on the same plane, *i.e.*, only individual interests
or only social interests, as Pound advised; as often as not the
lawyer who invokes interests will attempt to strike a balance
between the relevant private and public interests. Again, the
moral opinion on which he relies is his own private estimate
of what right-minded Englishmen of his day would think.*
These moral considerations have usually been called in aid
simply to buttress a conclusion arrived at by a rough compromise between what he considers to be the competing
interests, rather than used as arbiters between competing
interests in a complex calculation. While the experience of
judges like HALDANE and WRIGHT in the course of a long
career at the Bar and on the Bench must have provided them
with some data on current interests, it still falls far short of
the immense range of data required for the full operation of a
scientific system of social justice. In short, only a rule of
thumb version of social justice is acted on within the English
legal profession so far in the twentieth century.

Although in the 1930's Viscount SANKEY, L.C., stressed
the connection between law and other social sciences[1] and
although the Modern Law Review was launched in 1937 " to
deal primarily with English law in its relation to contemporary English conditions " and to take sociology within its
field of study, still by 1960 very little has been accomplished
of the enormous task for English sociological jurisprudence—
the correlation of the positive law with the data of English
social life.[2] So academic lawyers still have good cause to

---

[1] See Jo. Society of Public Teachers of Law (1933), at p. 23.

[2] In its first twenty years the Modern Law Review has only
exceptionally carried an article or note in which data from the social
sciences have been fully considered in the discussion of a legal
problem. The Editor admitted in 1957 that this attempt to bridge
the gap between law and the social sciences was petering out: 4 Jo.
Society Public Teachers of Law (New Series), 1957, at p. 73. Indeed
the English lawyers seem to have even less interest in sociology in
(*continued at foot of next page*)

plead afresh for the greater integration of the social sciences
in legal teaching and research and for more extensive use of
the data provided by the social scientist in the administration
of justice in the courts.[1] No single jurist, let alone a school of
jurists, has produced a scheme of interests and of positive
morality valid for English society for the current decade.[2]
Nor have the ordinary courts admitted evidence from the
social sciences[3] of the social implications of a specific issue
which, though affecting directly only the parties before the
court, may indirectly affect a large section of the community.
Nor, in contrast with the legislators in Parliament, have the

---

(*continued from foot of previous page*)
this century, when it has graduated to the level of an important
science, than their predecessors did in the last half of the nineteenth
century. The Sociological Review (1908-current), and latterly the
British Journal of Sociology (1950-current), have rarely carried contributions from the English professional or academic lawyers, and
these journals are not to be found on the bookshelves of the orthodox
common lawyers. In contrast, BROUGHAM's National Association for
the Promotion of Social Sciences, enjoyed more extensive support
from the practising lawyer. See *ante*, p. 148, n. 2.

[1]Street, " Law and Administration: Implications for University
Legal Education " (1953), *Political Studies*, pp. 97 *et seq.*

[2]Of course it is of the essence of Pound's theory that a scheme of
interests is only valid for a society at a particular time. So the
scheme of interests which he himself worked out (see *ante*, pp. 137 *et
seq.*) are only valid, if at all, for the American society which he studied
in the decade before he completed his survey. Stone's massive and
important contribution to sociological jurisprudence, *The Province
and Function of Law* (1947), contains an elaborate scheme of interests
at pp. 487-603. Though Stone wrote " for the common law of our
times " with " English law as the point of departure " it may be
doubted whether this scheme is valid for England in the 1940's (and
a fortiori for the 1960's) for several reasons: (i) the individual and
social interests in this scheme are those listed by Pound in his surveys
of American society 1915-1942; (ii) the evidence for these interests
is drawn extensively from American and Australasian experience as
well as English; (iii) the primary evidence for the interests is that of
lawyers rather than the findings of social scientists studying contemporary English society. Likewise the scheme of interests outlined
by Professor Paton of Australia in his *Text-book of Jurisprudence*,
2nd edn. (1951), pp. 101-137, though relevant, is hardly definitive of
the current interests in England.

[3]As the American Supreme Court has done in a limited range of
constitutional cases since *Muller* v. *Oregon* (1908), 208 U.S. 412. This
" Brandeis Brief " procedure is elaborated by Frankfurter in 29
H.L.R. 353, at pp. 362 *et seq.*, and by Biklé in 38 H.L.R. 6, at pp. 12
et seq.

English judges overtly considered the findings of fact and recommendations of the many *ad hoc* social surveys which are available in the authoritative form of Reports made by Royal Commissions or Departmental Committees. But the procedure of the new Restrictive Practices Court,[1] constituted of High Court judges and non-lawyers experienced in commerce or industry or public affairs, and the growing practice of the Law Reform Committee in receiving evidence from the professional associations whose members' interests are affected by the law under review,[2] are significant developments.

§C

The notions of social utility and social justice—or rather the various practical considerations which stem from such notions—have been the inspiration of many developments in the positive law of England, through parliamentary and judicial legislation. It is proposed to exhibit only a few of these historical precipitates.

The notions of social utility and social justice, sometimes operating in concert with political doctrines of socialism have actuated Liberal and even Conservative as well as Labour Governments in many items of parliamentary legislation since the middle of the nineteenth century. The individualist principle of freedom of contract which was substantially realised in the English law of contract in the mid-nineteenth century has since been gradually eroded by numerous statutes with the object of protecting the interests of particular classes of persons, such as employees,[3] infants,[4] tenants of leasehold property,[5] or those who take goods on

---

[1]See *post*, pp. 170-171.
[2]See *ante*, p. 160.
[3]Truck Acts, 1831-1940.
[4]Infants Relief Act, 1874.
[5]Landlord and Tenant Acts, 1927 and 1954; Rent and Mortgage Interest Restrictions Acts, 1920-1939; Landlord and Tenant (Rent Control) Act, 1949.

hire-purchase.[1] The traditional rights of ownership of land have been continuously cut down by a variety of statutes to protect the health of the community[2] or to control the development of town and country[3] or to stimulate agriculture,[4] all ostensibly designed to advance the interests of the public as a whole at the expense of the interests of individual owners of land. The expectations or hopes of the extensive class of workmen have been advanced at the expense of the interests of employers in many statutes—such as those which have granted status and privilege to trade unions,[5] and have guaranteed workmen against utter poverty,[6] as well as those which have abrogated piecemeal the rule of common employment.[7] These are but a few of the streams of parliamentary legislation over the last century flowing from the sources indicated.[8] Lord WRIGHT observed the general direction: " The old individualism which was so great a feature of the common law, has been cut into by more socialistic ideas ".[9]

The notions of justice which have been examined in this chapter lie at the back of innumerable rules of law which have been laid down in the course of adjudication by the judges themselves. The influence of these notions is most

---

[1]Hire Purchase Acts, 1938 and 1954; Advertisements (Hire-Purchase) Act, 1957.

[2]Public Health Acts, 1875-1936; Sale of Food and Drugs Acts, 1875-1927, now consolidated by Food and Drugs Act, 1955.

[3]Town and Country Planning Acts, 1947-1954.

[4]Agriculture Act, 1947, ss. 9-19.

[5]Trade Union Acts, 1871-1913; Conspiracy and Protection of Property Act, 1875; Trade Disputes Act, 1906, s. 4, as interpreted in *Vacher & Sons, Ltd.* v. *London Society of Compositors*, [1913] A.C. 107, which grants to trade unions immunity from tortious liability.

[6]National Insurance Act, 1911; now National Insurance Act, 1946 and National Assistance Act, 1948.

[7]Employers' Liability Act, 1880; Workmen's Compensation Acts, 1897-1945; now National Insurance (Industrial Injuries) Act, 1946; Law Reform (Personal Injuries) Act, 1948.

[8]The nineteenth and early twentieth century legislation with a collectivist bias is examined in Dicey, *Law and Public Opinion*, 2nd edn. (1914), Lecture VIII and Introduction. The later English legislation is reviewed in Friedmann, *Law and Social Change in Contemporary Britain* (1951), and in *Law and Opinion in England in the Twentieth Century* (1959), ed. Ginsberg, Lectures VI-XIII.

[9]Proc. British Academy, Vol. XXXII, p. 307.

patent in those various principles, woven into several of the great branches of the " unwritten law ", which have been cross-classified as principles or heads of public policy. This rubric " public policy " only underlines the fact that they stem from notions of justice which emphasise the public interest. Professor Winfield, after a re-examination of most of these cases down to 1928, confirmed this inspiration when he pronounced public policy in the common law to be no more than " a principle of judicial legislation or interpretation founded on the current needs of the community ".[1] In the course of a re-appraisal of this case-law in 1953[2] Professor Lloyd observed that the English legal system in general recognised that law is developed and applied with regard to the exigencies of the public interest and of overriding moral considerations, and that the doctrine of public policy is only distinctive in that there the *ethos* of the community has been erected into an explicit doctrine. Here only a few of these lines of cases are selected to illustrate the influence of these notions of justice in the formulation by the judges of principles of the substantive law of property and of contract.

One principle which looms large in the field of property, which is founded on the judicial consideration of the public good in preference to but making allowance for private interests, is the rule against perpetuities. In the Middle Ages and ever since the great landholders in England have endeavoured to tie up land within their families for generations and indeed for centuries ahead. The judges have as persistently limited the power of the landholders to do so " in perpetuity " by evolving various devices and doctrines,[3] in particular the modern rule against perpetuities, more accurately called the rule against remoteness of vesting. This rule was in effect initiated in the late seventeenth century by Lord NOTTING-HAM, L.C., in *The Duke of Norfolk's Case*,[4] and eventually

---

[1] " Public Policy in the English Common Law ", 42 H.L.R. 76, p. 92.

[2] *Public Policy, A Comparative Study in English and French Law* (1953), at pp. 4 and 147.

[3] See Morris and Leach, *The Rule Against Perpetuities* (1956); Holdsworth, *History of English Law*, Vol. VII, pp. 193-238.

[4] (1683), 3 Cas. in Ch. 1, at pp. 26-54.

defined in its final form by the House of Lords, on the advice
of the judges, in 1833 in *Cadell* v. *Palmer*.[1] The classic formulation runs: " No interest is good unless it must vest, if at all,
not later than twenty-one years after some life in being at
the creation of the interest ".[2] Our concern is with the
grounds on which the judges have evolved this rule. In
the leading case it is plain that in Lord NOTTINGHAM'S view
the law's objection to perpetuities rested on "inconvenience",
a notion which he did not define and of which he refused to
give hypothetical examples.[3] But he evidently regarded
" perpetual clogs upon the estate " as one form of " inconvenience ", presumably because they ran counter to " the
necessity of commerce between man and man ".[4] In other
words—the public convenience requires that land should be
relatively freely alienable and not be tied up indefinitely
within one family. Some fifty years later JEKYLL, M.R., was
more explicit. He explained the reasons for the law's abhor-
rence of perpetuities as " the mischief which would arise to
the public from estates remaining for ever, or for a long time
unalienable or untransferable from one hand to another,
being a damp to industry, and a prejudice to trade, to which
may be added the inconvenience and distress that would be
brought on families whose estates are so fettered ".[5] Here the
rule was expressly justified on the ground of the public
interest in promoting industry and trade and the individual
interests of land-holders in disposing of their land according
to their actual needs. It is pertinent to observe that while the
rule operates to advance the public interest in economic progress it does not do so to the utter frustration of the interests
of the individual landholders who wish to provide for the
generations who come after them; the rule treats as valid
dispositions which in effect restrict alienation provided the
interest must vest within twenty-one years after the death
of specified contemporaries (however young) of the grantor.
It thus strikes a balance between these competing interests.

[1](1833), 1 Cl. & Fin. 372.
[2]Gray, *The Rule Against Perpetuities*, 4th edn. (1942), s. 201;
Morris and Leach, *The Rule Against Perpetuities* (1956), p. 1.
[3]*Duke of Norfolk's Case, Howard* v. *Duke of Norfolk, supra*, at p. 49.
[4]Cas. in Ch. 1, at p. 31.
[5]*Stanley* v. *Leigh* (1732), 2 P. Wms. 686, at p. 688.

Within the sphere of contract the principle relating to agreements containing covenants in restraint of trade is largely the product of the notions of justice considered in this chapter. The rulings within this principle have varied from time to time, as judges have acted on their observations that commercial and industrial needs in England have changed. In Elizabethan times, and earlier, the common law judges[1] had pronounced that all restraints of trade were unlawful. In the sixteenth century the Court of King's Bench in *Colgate* v. *Bacheler* grounded such a ruling on " the benefit of the commonwealth, for being freemen it is free for them to exercise their trade in any place ". But by the early eighteenth century new conditions of trade, for instance the practice of tradesmen of letting their premises to their own servants on condition that the servant did not act independently in that very trade in the same locality, was reflected in a different judicial ruling. In *Mitchel* v. *Reynolds*[2] PARKER, C.J. (later Lord MACCLESFIELD) laid down in effect two rules: (*a*) that restraints of trade which are particular, *i.e.* limited to a particular place, might be valid and enforceable, and (*b*) that restraints of trade which are general are void. His reasons for rule (*a*) were that it might be beneficial, not injurious, to the public in a town to prevent it being overstocked in any trade, and that it might be beneficial to an older tradesman to sell off his business with an enforceable covenant restricting his own trade, and besides that the law inclined against setting aside a contract on account of possible injury to one party when to set it aside would spell certain injury to the other who had paid the price for the covenant. Nevertheless restraints of trade which are general were pronounced to be void. Why? PARKER, C.J., asserts that " mischief " might arise from them: the public might be deprived of the benefit of the trade of a useful member: and the covenantor and his family might suffer by the loss of his livelihood. Both rules were clearly grounded on the judge's estimate of the interests of the classes of the community affected, and his estimate of the interests of the nation at large.

---

[1]*Colgate* v. *Bacheler* (1602), Cro. Eliz. 872; *The Blacksmith's Case* (1587), 3 Leonard 217; *The Dyer's Case* (1414), Y.B. 2 H. V pl. 26.
[2](1711), 1 P. Wms. 181.

In the course of the eighteenth and nineteenth centuries
rule (*a*) was applied in a wide variety of cases, and in the
nineteenth century rule (*b*) was gradually eroded by a series
of decisions in the courts of common law and particularly in
courts of equity. This process reached its culmination in the
famous *Nordenfelt* case[1] at the end of the century. The net
question before the court in that case was whether, in the
1880's, a covenant in restraint of trade which was world-wide
in its scope was void as contrary to public policy. N, the
patentee and manufacturer of various munitions of war, who
had a world-wide trade, sold one of his principal businesses
to the M. Co., for a price of more than a quarter of a million
pounds and covenanted not to engage in the manufacture of
specified munitions, except on behalf of the company, for
twenty-five years, in effect anywhere in the world. In the
Court of Appeal and in the House of Lords all the judges,
taking note of the commercial and industrial conditions of
England in that decade, held that this covenant, though
general, was not void as contrary to public policy. BOWEN,
L.J.[2] and Lord MCNAGHTEN[3] in particular perceived that the
problem facing the court was not only one of reconciling the
lines of precedent rulings, but of striking a balance between
two conflicting policies of the law: freedom of trade—the
policy underlying the earlier rulings, which had tended to
harden into a judicial dogma—and, opposed to it in this type
of case, freedom of contract—a policy touched on by Lord
MACCLESFIELD in 1711 but which had assumed a much larger
place in judicial thinking in the course of the nineteenth
century.[4] Lord MCNAGHTEN's solution of the problem is
epitomised in the famous proposition: " The true view of the
present time I think is this: the public have an interest in
every person's carrying on his trade freely; so has the individual. All interference with individual liberty of action in
trading, and all restraints of trade of themselves, if there is
nothing more, are contrary to public policy, and therefore

---

[1]*Maxim Nordenfelt Guns and Ammunition Co.* v. *Nordenfelt*, [1893]
1 Ch. 630; affirmed on appeal, in [1894] A.C. 535.
[2][1893] 1 A Ch. 630, at pp. 664-666: see *ante*, p. 149.
[3][1894] A.C. 535, at p. 568.
[4]See *ante*, Chap. 6.

void. That is the general rule. But there are exceptions; restraints of trade and interference with individual liberty of action may be *justified* by the special circumstances of a particular case. It is a sufficient justification, and indeed it is the only justification, if the restriction is reasonable— reasonable, that is, in reference to the interests of the parties concerned and reasonable in reference to the interests of the public, so framed and so guarded as to afford adequate protection to the party in whose favour it is imposed, while at the same time it is in no way injurious to the public."[1] This complex proposition postulates a public interest in free trade; it assumes on the one hand individual interests in persons carrying on their trade without restrictions (*e.g.*, servants who must earn their living by their trade); it assumes on the other hand individual interests in restricting trade by way of contract (*e.g.*, the seller of a business who can only expect a good price if his covenant restricting his own trade is enforceable); the element of morality is involved for the judge is to determine what is " reasonable " with regard to the interests of the parties concerned, and though he has some canons to guide him he must rely on prevailing views of what is fair or on his own moral sense; finally it allows for other public interests which may be affected in a particular kind of transaction. The proposition not only indicates these various relevant interests but actually strikes a balance between them. Patently this is the method of social justice. The resultant, this proposition of law laid down by Lord McNaghten in *Nordenfelt's* case, has not been dismissed as heterodox by succeeding judges; rather it has been raised to the level of a quasi-statutory statement of the law of contracts in restraint of trade, by subsequent courts, including the House of Lords itself in several cases.[2]

Nevertheless, this mandate to the judges to do social justice in cases of agreements in restraint of trade has been imple-

---

[1] [1894] A.C., at p. 565.
[2] *Mason* v. *Provident Clothing and Supply Co., Ltd.*, [1913] A.C. 724; *Herbert Morris, Ltd.* v. *Saxelby*, [1916] 1 A.C. 688; *McEllistrim* v. *Ballymacelligott Co-operative Agricultural and Dairy Society*, [1919] A.C. 548; see Cheshire and Fifoot, *Law of Contract* (1960), 5th edn., pp. 310-323.

mented by them subject to one major qualification. They have been extremely reluctant in the sixty years since the *Nordenfelt* case to condemn a restrictive trade agreement solely on the ground that it was unreasonable in the interests of the public.[1] But the public demand for protection in a wide range of commercial transactions has grown more insistent and has now produced an Act of Parliament which dramatically interferes with the traditional judicial control of such transactions. The Restrictive Trade Practices Act, 1956,[2] requires many restrictive trade agreements to be registered, establishes a presumption that registered agreements are contrary to the public interest and liable to be declared void, and specifies factors which can be relied on by the parties affected to rebut this presumption. For example, an agreement between more than two suppliers of goods carrying on business in the United Kingdom involving a restriction on persons to be supplied is liable to be adjudged void unless one of the suppliers can prove that the restriction was reasonably necessary to protect the public from injury in connection with the use of the goods, and can further prove that on the whole the restrictive agreement is not detrimental to the public. To adjudicate on such agreements Parliament has created a new tribunal, the Restrictive Practices Court, constituted of High Court judges and of laymen with experience of industry or commerce or public affairs. This new court is already developing a distinctive procedure. It has adjudged to be void several specific restrictive trade agreements,[3] after (1) establishing the facts of the detailed working of the industries and trades involved and (2) determining whether the agreement in question on the whole serves or frustrates the current interests and social values *as defined in s. 21 of the Act*. In processes (1) and (2) the court has been admitting and relying heavily on the evidence of industrial and commercial experts. This new court is in effect charged by Act of Parlia-

---

[1]*E.g., Tool Metal Manufacturing Co., Ltd.* v. *Tungsten Electric Co., Ltd.,* [1955] 2 All E.R. 657.

[2]See 36 Halsbury's Statutes, 2nd edn., 931.

[3]*Re Chemists' Federation's Agreement,* [1958] 3 All E.R. 448; *Re Yarn Spinners' Agreement,* [1959] 1 All E.R. 299; *Re Phenol Producers' Association's Agreement,* [1960] 2 All E.R. 128.

ment with the duty of administering social justice in cases involving restrictive trade agreements.

§D

The stock objection made by the conservative lawyer to the notion of social justice in the sphere of adjudication is that forcibly expressed a century ago by PARKE, B., when he advised the House of Lords in *Egerton* v. *Earl Brownlow*;[1] of public policy he said: " It may and does, in its ordinary sense, mean ' political expedience ', or that which is best for the common good of the community; and in that sense there may be every variety of opinion according to education, habits, talents, and dispositions of each person who is to decide whether an act is against public policy or not. To allow this to be a ground of judicial decision, would lead to the greatest uncertainty and confusion. It is the province of the states-man, and not the lawyer, to discuss and of the legislature to determine what is the best for the public good, and to provide for it by proper enactments."[2] The answer of those who lean in favour of this notion of justice was given in this very case by POLLOCK, C.B.: " My Lords, it may be that judges are no better able to discern what is for the public good than other experienced and enlightened members of the community; but that is no reason for their refusing to entertain the question and declining to decide upon it."[3]

A more fundamental objection to this theory of social justice, which applies equally to the theories of social and

---

[1](1853), 4 H.L. Cas. 1, at p. 123.

[2]Likewise ALDERSON, B., *ibid.*, at pp. 106-107; in *Janson* v. *Driefontein Consolidated Mines, Ltd.*, [1902] A.C. 484, at pp. 491 and 496 the Earl of HALSBURY, L.C. quoted with vigorous approval Baron PARKE'S opinion and that of Sergeant Marshall that " to avow . . . that it might be proper for a judge to prevent a party from availing himself of an undisputed principle of law in a court of justice upon the ground of some notion of fancied policy or expedience . . . has a direct tendency to render all law vague and uncertain. . . . What politicians call expedience often depends on momentary con-jectures and is frequently nothing more than the fine-spun specula-tions of visionary theorists ". See *post*, Chap. 8.

[3]*Egerton* v. *Earl Brownlow* (1853), 4 H.L. Cas. 1, at p. 151.

individual utility, is that it does not give priority to absolute
values. Although the theory does not divorce justice from
ethics, but ascribes to moral values a key function in determining the just solution of particular problems, still the
values in question are but those prevailing in the given
society, the positive morality or the ethical custom of the
time and place, or at least the judges' estimate of these. It
is at this point that those who believe in absolute or natural
justice—and lawyers of this conviction are still to be found
in England[1]—would join issue with the exponents of social
justice and would deny that the prevailing views of right and
wrong in, say, England of the 1950's or America in the 1920's
are the ultimate measures of right and wrong. Thus they
regard this theory of justice as temporal, founded on the
shifting sands of popular opinion, not on the rock of truth;
they deny the validity of the axiom *vox populi vox dei*.[2] However, this criticism is far from condemning *in toto* the notion
that justice requires the maximum satisfaction of current
interests in the light of current morality, as even the exponents of natural justice must concede that there are
numerous questions, which come within the purview of the
law, on which the precepts of natural law are silent or
equivocal.

While the common lawyer who will invoke principles of
natural law is comparatively rare, those who will criticise
from moral experience are more numerous. Some of the
latter[3] reflecting on comparatively recent events in Europe,
especially in Germany—the country in which the jurisprudence of interests and free-law theories were most
prominent earlier in this century—condemn the theory of
social justice as " dangerous ". If the theory should be fully
implemented in a country in which the majority opinion was
utterly intolerant of a minority group there would be a social
interest in the exclusive use of resources by the majority,
supported by the dominant moral opinion; then it would not
be unjust, according to this theory, to allow the minority—
it might be millions of souls—to starve or to be exterminated.

---

[1] See *ante*, Chap. 4.
[2] *E.g.*, Potter, *The Quest of Justice* (1951), pp. 66 and 73.
[3] *E.g.*, Allen, *Aspects of Justice* (1958), pp. 53-55 and 84-105.

The conscience of the typical common lawyer rejects this conclusion and makes him suspicious of the theory which would sanction it. Such considerations may explain the reluctance of even the common lawyers who use the criteria of social justice to give full effect to the theory by actually consulting public opinion or social scientists' estimates of public opinion.

Apart from such extreme applications, the theory of social justice is nevertheless open to the criticism that even operating in a tolerant community it tends to suppress minority opinion. It may happen that in a given community the majority opinion is less enlightened than that of a minority. The opinion of a few informed public men may be more advanced than that of the mass of ordinary citizens. Lord HALSBURY evidently took this line, as he once said trenchantly[1] in the course of judgment: " I am not much impressed by what the man in the street would say." But on the strict application of the theory the opinions of the man in the street would be the principal data in the scheme of interests and in the positive morality. So the theory of social justice, if fully implemented, would tend to stifle rather than encourage progress through enlightened minority opinion. But this criticism can hardly be levelled at the version of social justice which is in fact implemented in the English courts, when the estimate of the public interest involved is that of the judge, not that determined by a gallup poll on the question.

This version of justice which gives priority to the interests of the community as a whole over those of individuals has inevitably been condemned by those who exalt individual personality. So, the legislation which in this century has been passed in England with the object of social amelioration (e.g., slum clearance legislation), and which as a corollary has increased the powers and activities of government, has been continuously criticised by the inveterate individualists who remain in the English legal profession, such as Lord HEWART.[2] In particular when such " socialist " policies have been implemented by representatives of the executive, whether

---

[1] In *Costello* v. *Pigeon (Owners)*, [1913] A.C. 407, at p. 413.
[2] *The New Despotism* (1929); *Essays and Observations* (1930); *Not Without Prejudice* (1937); see *ante*, pp. 126-127.

Ministers or local officials, without allowing the minority interests (*e.g.*, slum property owners) some consideration (such as fair trial before expropriation), academic lawyers have protested vigorously. For instance, Dr. Allen[1] has launched tirades against such encroachments of the traditional rights of citizens, maintaining that in the long run justice to every individual is of greater moment than the immediate implementation of any social policy,[2] a contention which assumes the principle of fair trial to be essential to a just social order.[3]

This version of justice has been assailed on the score that it tends to promote materialism, that it would promote the material wealth and physical condition of people rather than their spiritual well-being.[4] The attack would be well directed against the theory of social justice if that theory were fully and scientifically applied in a community in which the overwhelming majority opinion gave priority to material wants rather than to things of the spirit. But it is misdirected against the theory as it might be applied in a country in which the *de facto* claims reversed this priority, and it may be misdirected against the notions of social justice which the English judge or law-reformer employs when he retains to himself the power to determine " the best interests " of the people concerned.

Social justice as expressed in this chapter is vulnerable to the criticism that whatever its merits or demerits on moral or practical grounds it is defective even on the plane of theory, in that it fails to give a complete account of the judicial or legislative functions, and thus is an incomplete theory of justice for judge or legislator. The notion, as adumbrated by Lord BOWEN, taught by Pound and acted on by Lord WRIGHT and other judges, falls short of providing a complete guide to the judge in his function of adjudication. Suppose several current interests are ascertained but these conflict in the given case; how is this conflict of interests to be resolved? Neither BOWEN nor WRIGHT have suggested any

---

[1] *Law and Orders* (1st edn., 1945; 2nd edn., 1956).
[2] *Cf.* Potter, *The Quest of Justice* (1951), pp. 33-34.
[3] Allen, *op. cit.*, 2nd edn., pp. 333-334; see *ante*, Chap. 3.
[4] Allen, *Aspects of Justice* (1958), p. 102.

general or rational solution of this inevitable and common problem, but have left it to the judge to draw on his own experience. Even Pound's more elaborate theory does not provide a complete guide to the solution of this problem. He prescribes an adjustment or compromise to secure as much or as many of the interests as possible, with the least possible friction or waste. His theory of social justice stops short of explaining how such a balance or compromise is to be struck, as several critics have pointed out.[1] The resort to current morality as an arbiter of interests does not necessarily provide a solution to the problem for there may be relevant to the given case several competing moral values, or none.

Even this sophisticated notion of social justice is dependent on several of the other notions outlined in these pages. Its links with utility and moral justice have been emphasised in this chapter. Besides, it presupposes a system of judicature, with independent and impartial judges. Moreover, it assumes the existence of a corpus of detailed laws devised to meet typical human situations, though insisting that these laws should remain constant only so long as the relevant social conditions remain unchanged.

---

[1]Allen, *Aspects of Justice* (1958), p. 103; Friedmann, *Legal Theory*, 4th edn. (1960), pp. 281 and 298-299; Paton, *Jurisprudence*, 2nd edn. (1951), p. 108.

CHAPTER 8

LEGAL JUSTICE

§A

A notion which common lawyers in England have cherished for centuries is that the principal criteria of justice for them in their professional rôles are not the very general precepts of an absolute system of ethics, nor the particular precepts of current morality nor the canons of utility or current human interests, but simply the established laws of the land.

The most influential protagonist of this notion of *legal* justice was John Austin,[1] the first Professor of Jurisprudence in England. Austin expounded his philosophy of justice in his lectures at the new University College, London, from 1828 to 1832, and later in a course of lectures which he delivered at the Inner Temple. His views on justice are set out in the introductory lectures published first under the title *The Province of Jurisprudence Determined*[2] and eventually as part of his *Lectures on Jurisprudence, or the Philosophy of Positive Law*.[3]

One of Austin's main objectives in his exposition of jurisprudence was to rid the science and philosophy of law of much of its ambiguous and vague terminology. He would fix terms of art with one precise meaning. So, he was disposed to dismiss the traditional phrase " eternal and irrevocable justice " as an unmeaning abstraction, a fustian phrase which appealed to the ear not the intellect. He would not

---

[1] 1790-1859. Called to the Bar at Lincoln's Inn, 1818; Professor of Jurisprudence in the University of London, 1826-1832.
[2] 1st edn. (1832); latest edn., ed. Hart (1954).
[3] 1st edn. (1863); 5th edn., ed. Campbell (1885): 2 vols.

discard the term " justice " altogether but would fix it with a simple connotation:

> " Whenever it is uttered with a determinate meaning, it is uttered with relation to a determinate law which the speaker assumes as a standard of comparison. . . . Justice is the conformity of a given object to . . . a given law to which we refer it as a test."[1]

Austin admitted that the term justice might be used to denote conformity to different systems of law. On the one hand, it might be used in one context to denote conformity to the law of God, either the revealed portion or that portion indicated to man by the principle of utility.[2] On the other hand, in a strictly legal context, the term properly denoted conformity to the positive law of the time and place:

> " Positive law is the measure or test of legal justice and injustice. . . ."[3]

Elsewhere he pontificated:

> " in truth, law [the positive law of the land] is itself the standard of justice."[4]

---

[1]*Lectures on Jurisprudence*, 5th edn., Vol. I, p. 268 n.

[2]Reading Austin's argument as a whole it is clear that he regarded the law of God, as indicated by the principle of utility, as the supreme criterion. Austin even devoted three of his introductory lectures (*op. cit.* II-IV) to an exposition of the theory of utility as a part of divine law and as a standard for the assessment of positive law. Although Austin was at pains to expound these two versions of justice, ironically his version of divine justice has been eclipsed for most of his disciples and later students by his version of legal justice. This interpretation of Austin's philosophy of justice is largely due to the success of his principal thesis in jurisprudence: *viz.* that the proper subject-matter of jurisprudence is positive law and only positive law. So, the consideration of what the law ought to be and thus the examination of such doctrines as divine law, utility and positive morality, were beyond the bounds of jurisprudence thus determined; rather they belong to the cognate science of legislation. But jurisprudence as a subject was only barely tolerated in the Inns of Court and the Universities of the nineteenth century, and the science of legislation was not systematically expounded in either. For instance, in the 1870's, Sir Henry Maine, at Oxford, *à propos* Austin's discussion of the law of God and utility, was disposed to say that: " Taken at its best, it is a discussion belonging not to the philosophy of law but to the philosophy of legislation. The jurist, properly so called, has nothing to do with any ideal standard of law or morals "—*Lectures on the Early History of Institutions* (1875), at p. 370. In the principal text of Austin's *Lectures* which has been available in this century, Jethro Brown's *Austinian Theory of Law* (1906), the three lectures on the law of God and utility were suppressed.

[3]*Lectures on Jurisprudence*, 5th edn., Vol. I, p. 268 n.

[4]*Ibid.*, p. 218.

Given that the Parliament for the time being of the United Kingdom was sovereign and the sole lawgiver, he asserted dogmatically that

" it is the author . . . of all our positive law and exclusively sets us the measure of legal justice and injustice."[1]

He would confine the use of the term justice in the mouth of the lawyer to the latter: legal justice. So he spoke ironically of the juryman or judge who talks finely of equity or justice,[2] and added trenchantly:

" He forgets that he is there to enforce *the law of the land,* else he does not administer that justice or that equity with which alone he is immediately concerned."[3]

The applications of this notion of legal justice are obvious enough. Assume that in England in 1950 it is still the established law that whoever kills a human being with malice aforethought is liable to be arrested, prosecuted and, on conviction, to be hanged. Then if in 1950 A kills X deliberately A's conduct is unjust. A policeman who fails in his legal duty to arrest A, a judge who contrary to the established law directs a jury to acquit A, a juryman who out of sympathy with A votes in favour of acquittal, a prison warder who allows A to escape, all, on this view, violate justice. If B is mistakenly convicted and hanged for A's offence, the process is a miscarriage of justice. As for the policeman who arrests A, the prosecutor who accuses A, the juryman who find him guilty of murder, the judge who sentences him to death, the hangman who kills him; they all act justly. But to speak of the law which dictates all these actions as " just law " is to utter a tautology. To speak of it as " unjust law " is nonsense; for according to this notion justice is no criterion

---

[1]*Ibid.*, p. 268.

[2]To be fair to Austin it should be added that his principal concern in these Lectures was to distinguish as sharply as possible between positive law and positive morality. Although he would exclude the latter from his province of jurisprudence he was nevertheless sensitive to its intrinsic importance and to its bearing on law. He evidently intended to write a book on positive morality and positive law and their relation *inter se*: see Preface to *Lectures,* 5th edn., Vol. I, pp. 16-17 *per* Sarah Austin.

[3]*Lectures on Jurisprudence,* 5th edn., Vol. I, p. 218.

whatsoever for the evaluation of law; it is a mere synonym for whatever is lawful.

§B

Austin most certainly did not invent the notion of legal justice. If its roots are not so deep in the English legal system as those of judicature, fair trial, natural justice and moral justice, they can nevertheless be traced back into the late mediaeval period. The embryo of the notion is present in the work of BRACTON in the thirteenth century. Dissatisfied with the way many of his fellow judges exercised the royal power of dispensing justice, deciding causes " according to their own pleasure rather than by the authority of laws ",[1] BRACTON himself undertook to examine the cases and expound the laws according to the judgment of " his masters " —the preceding generation of royal judges. Accordingly he compiled his famous treatise on English laws and customs, and his notes on cases.[2] BRACTON was arguing for and by his own work making possible a system of administering justice according to law. By the middle of the fourteenth century it was comparatively rare for the royal judges to decide cases according to their discretion, i.e. according to natural justice or moral justice. Fortified by GLANVILL'S and BRACTON'S statements of the laws of England and by the fragmentary law reports contained in the early Year Books, they confined themselves for the most part to deciding issues according to established laws.[3] Statutes were accepted as binding on the judges, and were to be interpreted according to their letter: " The statute says only . . . (x) . . . and does not say . . . (y) . . . ; therefore we cannot take the statute farther

---

[1]De Legibus et Consuetudinibus Angliae (circa 1256), ed. Woodbine, Vol. II, p. 19.

[2]Note Book, first published 1887, 3 vols., ed. Maitland; but the original volumes were evidently known to his contemporaries.

[3]Plucknett, Concise History of the Common Law, 5th edn. (1956), pp. 157-159; and Statutes and their Interpretation in the First Half of the Fourteenth Century (1922); Potter, Quest of Justice (1951), pp. 11-19.

than the words of it say ":[1] *per* SHARSHULLE, J., in 1346. Contemporaneously other judges permitted themselves to declare " we will not and cannot change the ancient usages ".[2] It is hardly a coincidence that this judicial determination to exercise the royal power of justice by deciding cases mainly by applying the established laws of the land appeared shortly after the Crown had adopted the policy of appointing to the Bench the senior and more learned members of the relatively new legal profession. So, at least since the middle years of the reign of Edward III the notion of legal justice has been prominent amongst the practitioners in the courts of common law.

Thereafter judicature in the Courts of King's Bench, Common Pleas, Exchequer and in the Assize Courts becomes more and more regularly a process in which the judges decide cases not according to their discretion but according to established laws. The picture which COKE gives us, at the turn of the sixteenth and seventeenth centuries, in his *Reports* and *Institutes*, is of tribunals in which learned counsel and judges participate in a dialectical process, relying on special rules of procedure peculiar to each of the courts, on statutes however ancient, on customs common to the kingdom and declared as law and recognised in all the royal courts, and on principles and maxims of the common law, established by a series of precedent rulings or judicial *dicta* and recorded in " our books ": " our booke cases are the best proofes what the law is, *Argumentum ab auctoritate est fortissimum in lege* ".[3] COKE's own juristic writings served to harden the practice of dispensing justice according to law. Yet even in the seventeenth century a strict doctrine of *stare decisis* had not been reached. BACON, who favoured the maximum certainty in law and the minimum discretion in the judge, counselled the selective use of precedent decisions, preferring the more recent to the more ancient, and those given in moderate rather than in violent times, but still insisting that precedents neither prescribe nor command.[4] In

---

[1]*Waghan* v. *Anon.* (1346), Y.B. 20 Edw. III, ii, R.S. 198-199.
[2]*Anon.* (1342), Y.B. 16 Edw. III, i, R.S. 90 *per* HILLARY, J.
[3]Coke, *Institutes* (1628), Vol. I, 254a, § 420.
[4]*De Augmentis Scientiarum* (1623), Book VIII, Chap. 3, § 2, on " Universal Justice ", aphorisms 21-23.

1673 VAUGHAN, C.J., maintained " if a judge conceives a
judgment given in another court to be erroneous, he being
sworn to judge according to law, that is in his conscience,
ought not to give the like judgment for that were to wrong
every man having a like case . . ."[1] In the late eighteenth
century BLACKSTONE insisted on the absolute binding force
of statutes for the judge,[2] and that " it is an established rule
to abide by former precedents, when the same points come
again in litigation . . . because the law in that case being
solemnly declared and determined, what before was uncertain, and perhaps indifferent is now become a permanent
rule, which it is not in the breast of any subsequent judge to
alter or vary from, according to his private sentiments . . .
[for the judge was] not delegated to pronounce a new law,
but to maintain and expound the old one ".[3] Still BLACK-
STONE added that " this rule admits of exceptions, where the
former determination is most evidently contrary to reason;
much more if it be contrary to the divine law. . . . For if it
be found that the former decision is manifestly absurd or
unjust, it is declared . . . that it was *not law* ".[4] It is as late
as the nineteenth century, as a result of the development of
more reliable series of law reports and of the re-organisation
of the courts into a hierarchical system, that the strict
doctrine of *stare decisis*, which required the judges to adhere
to even a single precedent ruling laid down in a senior court,
comes to dominate the process of judicature in the common
law courts.[5] PARKE, J.,[6] the chief exponent of justice according to law in this period, gave his credo in advising the House
of Lords in 1832:[7] " Our common law system consists in
applying to new combinations of circumstances those rules of
law we derive from legal principles and judicial precedents;

---

[1]*Bole* v. *Horton* (1673), Vaugh. 360, at p. 382.
[2]*Commentaries*, 3rd edn. (1768), Introduction, § 3, p. 91; see *ante*,
p. 58.
[3]*Ibid.*, p. 69.
[4]*Ibid.*, pp. 69-70.
[5]See Allen, *Law in the Making*, 6th edn. (1958), pp. 206-230,
and 51 L.Q.R. 333; *cf.* Goodhart, 50 L.Q.R. 40 and 196, and Holdsworth, 50 L.Q.R. 180 and 51 L.Q.R. 441.
[6]See *ante*, pp. 8, 145, 171 and *post*, p. 197; *cf.* Fifoot, *Judge and
Jurist in the Reign of Victoria* (1959), pp. 12-14, 60-62.
[7]In *Mirehouse* v. *Rennell* (1833), 8 Bing. 490, at pp. 515-516.

and for the sake of attaining uniformity, consistency, certainty, we must apply those rules when they are not plainly unreasonable and inconvenient to all cases which arise; and we are not at liberty to reject them, and to abandon all analogy to them, in those to which they have not yet been judicially applied, because we think that the rules are not as convenient and reasonable as we ourselves could have devised. It appears to me of great importance to keep this principle of decision steadily in view, not merely for the determination of the particular case, but for the interests of law as a science."

The element of discretion in decisions (and thus the use of other criteria for judgment than positive laws) remained a prominent feature of judicature in Courts of Equity long after it had been severely restricted in Courts of Common Law. But in the Restoration period Chancellors, notably Lord NOT-TINGHAM, began to define and systematise the principles of equity, and so to reduce the element of discretion in these courts too. In 1750 Lord HARDWICKE, L.C., was prepared to admit himself to be " under an indispensable obligation of following " decisions of earlier Chancellors.[1] It was not until the Chancellorship of that most learned and most uncompromising of conservatives who has ever graced the English Bench, Lord ELDON, that proceedings in the Court of Chancery were finally transformed into the administration of justice according to law, *i.e.* according to the established rules of equity. In a case in 1818 he declared:[2] " The doctrines of this court ought to be as well settled and made as uniform almost as those of the common law, laying down fixed principles, but taking care that they are to be applied according to the circumstances of each case. I cannot agree that the doctrines of this court are to be changed with every succeeding judge."

So when, in University College, London, in the 1820's, Professor Austin taught that the positive law itself was the proper measure of justice for the lawyer he was not formulating a novel idea; he was but expressing a motif which had

---

[1] *Earl of Chesterfield* v. *Janssen* (1750), 1 Atk. 301, at p. 353.
[2] *Gee* v. *Pritchard* (1818), 2 Swan. 402, at p. 414.

been growing more and more insistent within the legal profession down to his day. The powerful school of thought
which grew up in the universities in England in the second
half of the nineteenth century, which accepted as their dogma
Austin's philosophy of positive law and its integral theory of
legal justice, gave even greater prominence to this theory of
justice to the exclusion of others. Austin's *Lectures on Jurisprudence or The Philosophy of Positive Law* were published in
full for the first time posthumously in 1863 and ran through
five editions by 1885. Sir Henry Maine, while Professor of
Jurisprudence at Oxford (1869-1877) had pressed Austin's
work on his students, and spoke of the *Lectures* as " the
mainstay of the studies prosecuted in this department ",[1]
and the Regius Professor of Civil Law at Cambridge spoke
of them a few years later as " the staple of jurisprudence in
all our systems of legal education ";[2] and they have continued to occupy pride of place in courses in jurisprudence
in England down to the Second World War. Professor Buck-
land reflecting on jurisprudence as it was studied in England
at the turn of the nineteenth and twentieth centuries, said
jurisprudence meant Austin and that Austin was a religion.[3]
And most of the Austinians discounted[4] or omitted altogether[5] Austin's elaborate defence of utility as the supreme
criterion of justice. In the result many among the modern
generation of lawyers have been taught dogmatically that the
law of the land is the measure of justice and that that is all
they need to know.[6] Naturally some students have reacted
against this positivist dogma, and many others, at the Inns

---

[1]*Early History of Institutions* (1875), p. 345.
[2]Clark, *Practical Jurisprudence; A Comment on Austin* (1883), p. 5.
[3]Buckland, *Reflections on Jurisprudence* (1945), p. 2.
[4]*E.g.*, Markby, *Elements of Law* (1st edn. 1871, 6th edn. 1905);
Holland, *Jurisprudence* (1st edn. 1880, 13th edn. 1924).
[5]*E.g.*, Clark, *op. cit.*; Jethro Brown, *Austinian Theory of Law*
(1906).
[6]*E.g.*, " Justice, as a concept in jurisprudence, is conformity to
law—if not conformity to established rules of law, or to the spirit of
law in its totality, then according to a law which the judge makes
and applies retrospectively ". Jethro Brown, 32 L.Q.R. (1916), p. 181.
Even in 1953 the then President of the Society of Public Teachers of
Law, describing his own course in jurisprudence, broadly approved
of Austin's limits and contents, and omitted altogether any reference
to ideal standards of justice: Jo. S.P.T.L., p. 79, *et seq.*

13

of Court, have not been directly subjected to it.[1] Proportionately as many of the young lawyers in recent generations have been discouraged from the study of criteria for the evaluation of positive law itself, this positivist version of justice has become more deeply embedded in professional thinking.

Tradition within the profession running back to the mediaeval period, and indoctrination from the law schools in the late nineteenth and early twentieth centuries, these influences have between them disposed the modern English lawyer to accept the view that the *lex lata* is the primary criterion of justice. To attempt to name the modern lawyers who have acted on this notion would be tedious in the extreme, for nearly every judge who has held office in the modern era has ordinarily decided cases on the basis of the established law, *i.e.* statute law, common law or equity. It will be more revealing to set out the various considerations which have made the orthodox modern English judge decide cases whenever possible on the basis of pre-existing law, to the exclusion of other notions of justice.

The judicial oath encourages modern judges to perform their function strictly according to law. They swear " to do right to all manner of people after the laws and usages of this realm, without fear or favour, affection or ill-will ".[2] This they mostly interpret as limiting their doctrine to " the laws and usages " of the kingdom.[3]

Pride in the English law as it has evolved down to the twentieth century is no doubt largely responsible for the apotheosis of that law into the standard of justice for many practitioners. The lawyer who has spent a score or more years painstakingly acquiring a mastery of the law of England, and who in the course of this process is made to

---

[1]A course of lectures on jurisprudence and Roman law was appointed for students of the Inns of Court, 1852-1872. Between 1872 and 1891 a separate course of lectures on jurisprudence was prescribed for Bar students. But in 1891 jurisprudence was again relegated to a subordinate place in a course of lectures on Roman law, etc. These lectures have never been compulsory exercises and jurisprudence has never been a compulsory subject of examination for call to the English Bar.

[2]Promissory Oaths Act, 1868, s. 4.

[3]*E.g.*, SCRUTTON, L.J., in 1 C.L.J. 6, at pp. 8-9.

realise that his doctrine has been evolving for some eight hundred years, and that it has been continuously fined and refined by a succession of judges, Chancellors and Parliaments, understandably becomes inordinately attached to this tradition to which he is heir and defers to the accumulated and collective wisdom of former generations. In the twentieth century if he insists that this law and only this law is the measure of justice he is not by any means excluding ethical and other versions of justice. For the modern law embodies a host of rules laid down by judges in the courts of common law, by Chancellors in their courts of equity and by Parliaments especially since the 1830's, inspired by theories of natural justice, moral justice, utility and social justice, as indicated in the sections on historical precipitates in the positive law in the four preceding chapters. Lord CAVE was expressing this sense of pride in a slowly evolving system when he said: " Ours is no code of jurisprudence, no machine laboriously and scientifically put together . . . it has grown like some old tree with its knots, its twisted branches . . . and its hard core of common sense."[1]

A psychological factor which disposes the English lawyer in favour of justice according to law is his preference for practical solutions to concrete cases over theoretical solutions to hypothetical problems. This cast of mind which eschews theory and *à priori* reasoning, and leans heavily on experience and particular precedents has been discussed in the Introduction.[2] This empirical and pragmatic bias inclines the English lawyer to accept more readily particular rules laid down by older judges in actual litigations and to reject a solution deduced from assumed ethical principles. The English lawyer *quâ* Englishman prefers to plant his feet squarely on the solid rock of experience rather than embark on the perilous seas of speculation.

The paramount consideration in English lawyers' minds when they have exalted the positive law as the measure of

---

[1]*Memorial Volume, American Bar Association Visit to England* (1924), p. 246.

[2]See *ante*, pp. 4-6.

justice has been their desire for *certainty*.[1] Francis Bacon had insisted that certainty in law was an indispensable condition of justice.[2] Lord Eldon's *dictum* that " it is better that the law should be certain, than that every judge should speculate upon improvements in it "[3] has more often been quoted with approval.[4] But certainty is hardly a *summum bonum* in itself. Those who insist on " certainty " in the law and in adjudication have in mind a variety of ulterior objectives.

(*a*) When praising certainty some of the lawyers have in mind uniformity of judicial decisions, and they seek this uniformity as a means of maintaining the very *system* of law. If individual judges were to decide like cases according to different standards the *system* of law would tend to disintegrate, and in its place would be a bewildering multitude of individual rulings. Thus a professional feeling for *elegantia juris* can be detected behind some of these demands for certainty.[5]

(*b*) Others, altruistically, seek certainty, in the sense of uniform decisions, for the benefit of their clients. Assuming a Bench which administers justice strictly according to established laws, then in most cases (excepting those involving a novel combination of facts) solicitors and counsel can predict the probable outcome of a particular suit. On the basis of this prediction a party can be encouraged to incur costs and go ahead and press his claim, if the prediction is that he is likely to win, or he can be advised to settle the case at an early stage if the prediction is that he is likely to lose. Accordingly civil litigation, with its attendant costs and delays and unwelcome publicity can often be avoided.[6]

---

[1] See the *dicta* of Lord Campbell, *post*, pp. 196-197, Lord Halsbury, *post*, p. 197, Lord Simonds, *post*, p. 195, and Lord Goddard, C.J., *post*, pp. 198-199.

[2] " It is of much importance to a law that it be certain, as without this neither can it be just. . . . That law is best which leaves least to the discretion of the judge, which its certainty effects." *De Augmentis Scientiarum* (1623), Book VIII, Chap. 2, § 2, on "Universal Justice", aphorism 8.

[3] *Sheddon* v. *Goodrich* (1803), 8 Ves. 481, at p. 497.

[4] Even by academic lawyers: *e.g.*, Goodhart, *Precedent* in *English and Continental Law* (1934), p. 41, and Wade, " The Concept of Legal Certainty " (1941), 4 M.L.R. 183, p. 187.

[5] *E.g.*, Pollock, *First Book of Jurisprudence*, 6th edn. (1929), pp. 41-44.

[6] *E.g.*, Devlin, *Trial by Jury* (1956), p. 156; *cf.* Scrutton, L.J., in *Hill* v. *Aldershot Corporation*, [1933] 1 K.B. 259, at p. 263.

(c) Most zealous of all for certainty in the law are property lawyers, for a system of rules, precisely defined and invariably applied by the courts, is essential to the institution of private property. Let one judge in one case in a superior court depart from one of the traditional rules of common law or equity relating to property, he immediately creates a furore in the profession;[1] for as a result of this one decision, which may be fair as between the parties, thousands of like titles are rendered doubtful, the intentions of many testators who assumed the old law are likely to be frustrated and future conveyances cannot be drafted with any confidence.

(d) To a lesser degree certainty is sought by commercial lawyers,[2] for major commercial contracts are drawn upon the assumption that precedent rulings will be followed. A novel ruling on the general law of contracts, or on the interpretation of a common term in contracts, might well upset a wide range of other commercial transactions.

(e) In the administration of criminal law certainty is insisted on by most practitioners. The underlying consideration is that no man should be liable to conviction and punishment save for breach of an ascertainable law. Otherwise the moral axiom *nulla poena sine lege* is violated, and the prudent man who tries to act within the bounds of the law is nevertheless liable to be branded and suffer as a criminal.

Again, some English lawyers have realised that the regular enforcement of the established law is a powerful agent for maintaining order and stability in the political community. In the sphere of criminal law, clearly defined rules proscribing certain disorderly conduct as criminal, and a system of prosecutions and trials in which these rules are

---

[1]*E.g.*, Joshua Williams in *Letters to John Bull Esq.* (1857), p. 40, describes such an upheaval a hundred years ago. *Cf.* the controversy over the interest which a deserted wife may acquire in the former matrimonial home, sparked off by the Court of Appeal in *Errington* v. *Errington and Woods*, [1952] 1 All E.R. 149; [1952] 1 K.B. 290; see Wade, " Licences and Third Parties ", 68 L.Q.R. 337; Megarry, " The Deserted Wife's Right to Occupy the Matrimonial Home ", 68 L.Q.R. 379; Hargreaves " Licensed Possessors ", 69 L.Q.R. 485.

[2]*E.g.*, SCRUTTON, L.J., in " The Work of the Commercial Courts ", 1 C.L.J. 6, at pp. 8-9.

enforced strictly, is an effective institution for reducing disorder in the community. In the sphere of civil law too, though the process is less dramatic, the regular application of established laws operates for the public good, by creating conditions of stability. Lord SANKEY, L.C., in 1933 acutely pointed out that " the lawyer's regard for precedent has been one of the great stabilising forces in the state ".[1] The doctrine of judicial precedent is in effect part of the unwritten English constitution, acting as a brake upon social upheaval.

Constitutional lawyers have appreciated that the regular and invariable application of established laws in the royal courts serves another great end: it secures to all subjects a wide measure of personal freedom. Montesquieu aptly defined freedom as the right to do whatever the laws permit. In the late nineteenth century Dicey explained how personal freedom has long been a reality in England, not as a result of any proclamation of liberty, but as a consequence of the regular practice of the judges of only sanctioning the imprisonment of a man for a distinct breach of the law, established in the ordinary legal manner before the ordinary courts of the land.[2] In the middle of the twentieth century most common lawyers will maintain that personal liberty is more effectively secured as a by-product of such an invariable judicial practice than by any positive declaration of a right to personal freedom.

Besides, the administration of justice according to established laws appeals to many an English lawyer these days on the ground that it makes for impartiality and independence in adjudication. Thus it is said we live under a government of laws and not of men.[3] The judge who regards himself as bound to decide the case according to the positive law of the land is thereby denied the opportunity of showing partiality to one of the parties in the case before him; when

---

[1] In an address at Bristol University, reported in Law Times, October 14, 1933, p. 296. *Cf.* " Amid the cross-currents and shifting sands of public life the law is like a great rock upon which a man may set his feet and be safe ": *per* Lord SANKEY, quoted by Lord HEWART, *The New Despotism* (1929), p. 151.

[2] *Law of the Constitution* (1st edn. 1885), (10th edn. 1959, ed. Wade), pp. 26, 188, 207-222.

[3] Goodhart, *Precedent in English and Continental Law*, p. 38.

one party to a prosecution in a civil suit may be the state itself, *i.e.* the Crown or some Government department, the judge who must apply the law of the land is accordingly in a strongly fortified position. It has been a cautionary experience for English lawyers to observe in the legal systems of Italy and Germany in the 1930's, in which the courts professed to administer justice according to more exalted ethical standards than the traditional laws, how easily judicial independence was undermined by pressure from the executive.[1]

Finally, adjudication according to law as opposed to discretion, appeals to some English lawyers as it compels the court to treat like cases equally,[2] and the axiom that equals should be treated equally is an ancient[3] and enduring axiom of justice.

Accordingly, it transpires that the modern English lawyers who insist on the administration of justice strictly according to positive law are cryptically implementing several policies: *viz.* certainty and its various beneficial consequences, order and stability in the community, personal liberty, impartiality and independence in adjudication, and equality of treatment. When these objectives are exposed the paradox that justice is best achieved by concentrating strictly on the administration of the law is partially resolved.

Illustrations of the use of the method of legal justice in concrete cases are to be found in every volume of the modern series of English law reports. Moreover for every one case reported scores of decisions of superior courts go unreported, dismissed by the editors of the series as mere instances of the application of established laws. Here two illustrations must suffice, one of the ordinary application of the detail of statute law and one of the meticulous application of case law to the exclusion of all other considerations.

A typical example of the operation of the notion of legal justice is to be found in *R. v. Wheat, R. v. Stocks.*[4] W had

---

[1] See the *Judgment of the International Military Tribunal, Nuremberg,* 1946, Cmd. 6964, p. 7; and the opinions of Ferri, the Italian criminologist, quoted in *Modern Approach to Criminal Law* (1948), ed. Radzinowicz and Turner, pp. 9-10.

[2] *E.g.* Pollock, *First Book of Jurisprudence,* 6th edn. (1929), p. 38.

[3] See *ante,* p. 13.

[4] [1921] 2 K.B. 119.

instructed solicitors to bring divorce proceedings against his wife. From documents sent to him by the solicitors he believed that he was divorced, though actually no divorce decree had been pronounced in his case. Acting on this erroneous belief he went through a ceremony of marriage with S. W was convicted of bigamy on Assize, but an appeal was brought on the question of law: whether a belief in good faith on reasonable grounds that a person has been divorced affords a good defence to a charge of bigamy? Counsel for the appellant argued that such a belief constituted a good defence, on the ground that it was an application of the general principle of *mens rea*, that there must be as an essential ingredient in a criminal offence some blameworthy condition of mind—an essentially moral principle. The Attorney-General, for the Crown, relied mainly on the wording of the relevant statute.

The reserved judgment of the Court of Criminal Appeal[1] was delivered by Mr. Justice AVORY—a judge of whom it was appropriately said in retrospect that " he found English Law stone and left it neither marble nor stucco ".[2]

AVORY, J., began by rehearsing the relevant statute law, the Offences against the Person Act, 1861, s. 57; *viz.* " Whosoever, being married, shall marry any other person during the life of the former husband or wife . . . shall be guilty of felony. . . ." He added several of the statutory exceptions to this prohibition; *viz.* (1) when the husband or wife has been continually absent for the space of seven years then last past and has not been known by the person accused to be living within that time; and—the clause directly in point—(2) when the person accused at the time of the second marriage has been divorced from the bond of the first marriage; and he also

---

[1]BRAY, AVORY, SHEARMAN, SALTER and GREER, JJ.

[2]Jackson, *Mr. Justice Avory* (1935), p. 18. In the course of summing up in a notorious murder trial in 1926, *R.* v. *Alfonso Austin Smith*, AVORY, J., characteristically advised the jury: " The law you have to administer in this case is the law of this country, and not of any other; and above all, not that which is erroneously called ' the unwritten law '. That is merely a name for no law at all. It is the name given to the proposition that every man and woman is a law unto himself or herself, and that reverts us to a state of barbarism ". *Op. cit.*, p. 333.

discussed the exception established in *R.* v. *Tolson*[1] to the effect that a belief on reasonable grounds that a spouse is dead constitutes a good defence.

The court considered the exact wording and import of the two statutory exceptions. In respect of the first they conceded that as a result of judicial interpretation the person accused was presumed to believe after the seven years that the former spouse was dead at the time of the second marriage, and therefore the accused would not have the intention of doing the act forbidden by the statute—namely marrying during the life of the former husband or wife. But they distinguished the second exception as follows: " In the case of the second exception there is no indication in the statute that any presumption or belief is to afford any defence; the words do not admit of any such qualification and the only defence under this head appears to be that the accused has in fact been divorced from the bond of the first marriage. If he has not, then at the time of the second marriage he is a person who, being married, intends to do the act forbidden by the statute—namely, ' to marry during the life of the former wife '. Having regard to this distinction between the two exceptions, we are of opinion that a *bona fide* belief on reasonable grounds that the person accused has been divorced, when in fact he has not been divorced, affords no defence in law to the charge of bigamy, although it may afford a good reason for the infliction of a nominal punishment."[2]

Dealing with the appellants' argument based on the general maxim *actus non facit reum, nisi mens sit rea*, and its application in *R.* v. *Tolson*, AVORY, J., said of this maxim that it was " uncertain and often misleading in its application ", but that it was limited in that case to the belief in the death of the former spouse. " In its application to this statute the maxim is satisfied if the evidence establishes an intention on the part of the person accused to do the act forbidden by the statute—namely, ' being married, to marry another person during the life of the former wife or husband ' . . . ."[3]

[1](1889), 23 Q.B.D. 168.
[2][1921] 2 K.B. 119, at p. 125.
[3]*Ibid.*, at p. 126.

A more recent case, *Jacobs* v. *London County Council*,[1] illustrates the extreme use of the method of legal justice in adjudication. The London County Council, as landlords of a housing estate, had laid out a forecourt between the pavement of the public highway and a shop, and had let the shop to S, a chemist, but had retained ownership and occupation of the forecourt. The forecourt was flattened and paved like the pavement of the public highway, but round a stop-cock the stones of the forecourt had sunk, with the result that the stop-cock projected up one and a quarter inches. Mrs. Jacobs, turning off the public pavement and crossing the forecourt in order to enter S's shop on business, tripped over the stop-cock, fell and suffered serious injuries. She sued the L.C.C. for damages for negligence, on the specific ground that they as occupiers of the forecourt had committed a breach of duty owed to her *quâ* invitee. The parties and the courts assumed the relevant law to be that an occupier of premises owes a duty to an invitee (*i.e.* a visitor with a common business interest with the occupier) to use reasonable care to prevent damage from an unusual danger of which he knows or ought to know, but that he only owes a duty to a licensee (*i.e.* a visitor whom he expressly or impliedly invites on his property but with whom he has no common business interest) not to lay a trap for him. In the House of Lords it was conceded by counsel for the respondents that the appellant was entitled to damages if she was an invitee, and by counsel for the appellant that if she was only a licensee she must fail. The House of Lords[2] unanimously decided that Mrs. Jacobs was not entitled to compensation.

Lord SIMONDS' speech was the only fully reasoned judgment. He defined the principal question for the court as whether the appellant was to be placed in the legal category of invitee or licensee. As counsel for both parties had relied on different interpretations of an earlier House of Lords decision, *Fairman* v. *Perpetual Investment Building Society*,[3] Lord SIMONDS thought the essential question for the court

---

[1] [1950] 1 All E.R. 737; [1950] A.C. 361.
[2] Lord SIMONDS, Lord NORMAND, Lord MORTON, Lord McDERMOTT and Lord RADCLIFFE.
[3] [1923] A.C. 74.

became " to determine what *Fairman's* case decided and for what proposition of law it is an authority, binding alike on this House, and on every court in this country ".[1] He entertained no other considerations, such as the moral aspects of this type of claim or modern conditions of housing or of business, nor any general principles of the law of negligence; he focussed his whole attention on this technical question of law.

In *Fairman's* case the facts were similar to those before the court in *Jacob's* case, though not identical. Mrs. Fairman's claim for damages for negligence against the landlord, the Building Society, had been dismissed in the House of Lords by three judgments to two. The reasons given by the majority, Lords ATKINSON, SUMNER and WRENBURY, were somewhat diffuse, so that there had already been various interpretations of the *ratio decidendi* in the Court of Appeal in 1941.[2]

Lord SIMONDS considered the difficulty in such cases, in which several issues are raised, of determining which pronouncements are decisive and which *obiter*. " That is the inevitable result of our system. For while it is the primary duty of a court of justice to dispense justice to litigants, it is its traditional rôle to do so by means of an exposition of the relevant law."[3] If in the course of this exposition a judge has given two grounds for his judgment and based his decision on both, Lord SIMONDS affirmed that neither is to be regarded as *obiter dictum*, but both are to be regarded as *rationes decidendi*. Accordingly, he seized on *dicta* by Lords ATKINSON, SUMNER and WRENBURY in *Fairman's* case, to the effect that Mrs. Fairman could be regarded as the licensee of the Building Society, and notwithstanding the *dicta* by Lords ATKINSON and SUMNER that she might be treated as their invitee but would still fail in her claim, and notwithstanding the *dicta* of all three judges that the fatal weakness of her claim was that the danger was obvious to any cautious visitor, Lord SIMONDS pronounced that he entertained no doubts

---

[1][1950] 1 All E.R. 737, at p. 139; [1950] A.C. 361, at p. 368.

[2]In *Haseldine* v. *Daw & Son, Ltd.*, [1941] 3 All E.R. 156, at pp. 161-162; [1941] 2 K.B. 343, at pp. 350-352, *per* SCOTT, L.J., and at pp. 180, 372, respectively, *per* GODDARD, L.J.

[3][1950] 1 All E.R. 737, at p. 740; [1950] A.C. 361, at p. 369.

that " *Fairman's* case decided that Mrs. Fairman was a licensee upon the premises where she suffered damage and that that decision was the *ratio decidendi* or a *ratio decidendi* (it matters not which) of the case. . . .[1] To treat their deliberate conclusions as *obiter* would not be consonant with the principle which is in my view essential to our system of case law and precedent."[2]

Having considered the facts of the instant case and those of *Fairman's* case, and finding " no essential distinction between them ", he felt compelled to apply the *ratio decidendi*, thus construed, of *Fairman* to the instant case. So Mrs. Jacobs, *quâ* licensee, must fail.

Finally, Lord SIMONDS exposed his major premiss in formulating this judgment. Referring to the distinction between licensee and invitee, he said: " I recognise that the dividing line is difficult to draw, but it would, I think, be to deny the importance, I would say the paramount importance, of certainty in the law to give less than coercive effect to the unequivocal statement of the law made after argument by three members of this House in *Fairman's* case. Nor, perhaps I may add, are your Lordships entitled to disregard such a statement because you would have the law otherwise. To determine what the law is, not what it ought to be, is our present task."[3]

§C

In the preceding chapters in this third section some doctrines of positive law have been set out which are the precipitates of the notion of justice in question. It might be doubted whether the notion of legal justice, which assumes that the positive law itself is the only standard for judicature, could be the inspiration of any further laws. Nevertheless, several important doctrines in the modern English legal system are in some degree the products of this notion. It has been one of the contributory factors in the development of

---

[1] [1950] 1 All E.R. 737, at p. 740; [1950] A.C. 361, at p. 368.
[2] *Ibid.*, at pp. 742, 371, respectively.
[3] *Ibid.*, at pp. 743, 373, respectively.

the doctrine of the absolute obligation of statutes,[1] the corollary of the constitutional principle of the supremacy of Parliament. It has played a more vital part in the development of several of the canons in the doctrine of interpretations of statutes, such as that which directs the courts to construe Acts of Parliament according to the intent of the Parliament which passed them,[2] and the canon which is dominant in judicial practice in the twentieth century " that in construing a statute the grammatical and ordinary sense of the words is to be adhered to ".[3] Moreover, a belief in the intrinsic merit of the positive law, as established in earlier cases, is a factor in the judicial method of analogy, which is commonly used—alone or in conjunction with other methods —in cases of first impression when the judges are compelled to legislate. An important branch of modern English law which is the precipitate of the notion of legal justice is the doctrine of *stare decisis*. It is proposed to consider several of the leading modern principles of this last-mentioned doctrine and the reasons given for them by the judges who have enunciated them, to demonstrate this connection.

(1) The principle that the *ratio decidendi* of a decision of the House of Lords binds all courts in the land including the House of Lords itself, is the linch-pin of the modern doctrine of *stare decisis*. As late as 1852 Lord ST. LEONARDS, L.C., *ex cathedra* protested against the growing tendency in the House of Lords to treat its decisions as infallible. In *Bright* v. *Hutton*[4] he maintained: " that this House, like every Court of Justice, possesses an inherent power to correct an error

---

[1]*Lee* v. *Bude and Torrington Railway Co.* (1871), L.R. 6 C.P. 576, at p. 582, *per* WILLES, J.; see *ante*, pp. 59-60.

[2]*Sussex Peerage Case* (1844), 11 Cl. & Fin. 85, at p. 143, *per* TINDAL, C.J. *Vacher & Sons, Ltd.* v. *London Society of Compositors*, [1913] A.C. 107, at p. 118, *per* Lord MACNAGHTEN.

[3]See *Vacher's* case, *supra*, in which Lords MACNAGHTEN, HALDANE, ATKINSON and SHAW expressed and acted on this canon of interpretation in connection with the Trade Disputes Act, 1906. *Cf. Magor and St. Mellons R.D.C.* v. *Newport Corpn.*, [1951] 2 All E.R. 839; [1952] A.C. 189 in which Lord SIMONDS, L.C. (Lords MORTON and GODDARD agreeing) insisted on applying the literal canons of interpretation; and *A.-G.* v. *H.R.H. Prince Ernest Augustus of Hanover*, [1957] 1 All E.R. 49; [1957] A.C. 436.

[4](1852), 3 H.L. Cas. 341, at p. 388.

into which it may have fallen." In the same case Lord CAMPBELL expressed a contrary opinion: he gave it as his impression " that a decision of this high court, in point of law, is conclusive upon the House itself, as well as upon all inferior tribunals. . . . This House cannot decide something as law today and decide differently the same thing as law tomorrow; because that would leave the inferior tribunals and the rights of the Queen's subjects in a state of uncertainty. . . ."[1] Later, when he had become Lord Chancellor, Lord CAMPBELL re-asserted this opinion more dogmatically in the House in 1860 in *A.-G.* v. *Dean and Canons of Windsor*,[2] but without the support of the other members of the House. Lord KINGSDOWN alluded to the point as an open constitutional question.[3] But in the following year Lord CAMPBELL (now an octogenarian) in effect translated his opinion on this point into the positive law, when it became the *ratio decidendi* of all four members of the House in *Beamish* v. *Beamish*.[4] Referring to an earlier decision of the House, *R.* v. *Millis*,[5] in which the members of the House had been equally divided and the decision was determined according to an ancient technical procedural rule, and indicating that he thought that case was wrongly decided, Lord CAMPBELL nevertheless said, " But it is my duty to say that your Lordships are bound by this decision as much as if it had been pronounced *nemine dissentiente*, and that the rule of law which your Lordships lay down as the ground of your judgment, sitting judicially, as the last and supreme Court of Appeal for this empire, must be taken for law till altered by an Act of Parliament, agreed to by the Commons and the Crown, as well as by your Lordships. The law laid down as your *ratio decidendi*, being clearly binding on all inferior tribunals, and on all the rest of the Queen's subjects, if it were not considered as equally binding on your Lordships, this House would be arrogating to itself the right of altering the law, and legislating by its own separate authority."[6] The other members of the House

---

[1](1852), 3 H.L. Cas. 341, at pp. 391-392.
[2](1860), 8 H. L. Cas. 369, at pp. 391-392.
[3]*Ibid.*, at p. 459.
[4](1861), 9 H.L. Cas. 274.
[5](1843), 10 Cl. & Fin. 534.
[6](1861), 9 H.L. Cas. 274, at pp. 338-339.

in *Beamish's* case, Baron PARKE—now Lord WENSLEYDALE, (also an octogenarian), Lord CRANWORTH and Lord CHELMS-FORD, likewise declared that they were bound to follow the earlier decision of the House in *Millis'* case. When last this principle was challenged in the House of Lords in 1898 in *London Street Tramways Co., Ltd.* v. *L.C.C.*[1] Lord HALSBURY, L.C., said, unequivocally, that he adhered in terms to what had been said by Lord CAMPBELL in *Beamish* v. *Beamish*, and laid it down as indisputable judicial dogma " that a decision of this House upon a question of law is conclusive, and nothing but an Act of Parliament can set right that which is alleged to be wrong in a judgment of this House ".[2] Admitting that cases of individual hardship may arise as a result of the operation of this principle, Lord HALSBURY balanced " that occasional interference with what is perhaps abstract justice " against " the inconvenience—the disastrous inconvenience—of having each question subject to being re-argued and the dealings of mankind rendered doubtful by reason of different decisions ",[3] and entertained no doubts that the latter consideration should prevail. Thus, reluctance to appear to legislate judicially, a concern for vested legal rights and above all a desire for certainty in the law, these considerations have driven the House of Lords to adopt the principle of *stare decisis* with reference to their own decisions.

(2) The judges in the Court of Appeal did not adopt the strict principle of *stare decisis* with regard to their own decisions until comparatively recently. In 1903 in *Wynne-Finch* v. *Chaytor*[4] the court had purported to overrule a decision of its own given a year previously. But in *Young* v. *Bristol Aeroplane Co., Ltd.*[5] a full court of six judges deliberated on the question whether it was bound to follow the *ratio decidendi* of its own decision in *Perkins* v. *Hugh Stevenson & Sons, Ltd.*[6]—and unanimously decided the question in the affirmative. Lord GREENE, M.R., giving the

---

[1] [1898] A.C. 375.
[2] *Ibid.*, p. 381. The other members of the House of Lords, Lords MACNAGHTEN, MORRIS and JAMES, concurred.
[3] *Ibid.*, p. 380.
[4] [1903] 2 Ch. 475.
[5] [1944] 2 All E.R. 293; [1944] K.B. 718.
[6] [1939] 3 All E.R. 697; [1940] 1 K.B. 56.

judgment of the whole court, laid it down " that this court is bound to follow previous decisions of its own as well as those of courts of co-ordinate jurisdiction. The only exceptions to this rule (two of them apparent only) are . . . (*a*) the court is entitled and bound to decide which of two conflicting decisions of its own it will follow; (*b*) the court is bound to refuse to follow a decision of its own which, though not expressly overruled, cannot in its opinion, stand with a decision in the House of Lords; (*c*) the court is not bound to follow a decision of its own if it is satisfied that the decision was given *per incuriam* ".[1] The third exception, standing by itself, an echo of Lord St. Leonard's protest against a rigid rule of *stare decisis* could be construed broadly. But in *Young's* case, the court limited its scope to those very rare cases when an earlier decision was given in ignorance of the terms of a statute, while admitting that there might conceivably be other instances of *incuria*.[2] It is remarkable that in *Young's* case the court was content to affirm this relatively rigid principle of *stare decisis* on the grounds that it had been the almost invariable practice of the court to abide by its own rulings since 1903, and that many judges in that court had felt bound to do so, and that the House of Lords had in several cases assumed that the Court of Appeal was so bound; no other considerations were expressed. Lord Goddard, a member of the court in *Young's* case, referring to the principle governing the Court of Appeal in a later case,[3] (in which he laid down a contrary principle for the Court of Criminal Appeal) explained that " in civil matters this is essential in order to preserve the rule of *stare decisis* ",—a purely circular argument, concealing the considerations which drove the court to adopt that principle.

(3) The Divisional Court of Queen's Bench (sitting as an appellate court in a civil cause) decided in 1947, in *Police Authority for Huddersfield* v. *Watson*,[4] that it was bound to follow the *ratio decidendi* of a decision of its own on

---

[1][1944] 2 All E.R. 293, at p. 300; [1944] K.B. 718, at pp. 729-730.
[2]*Ibid.*, at p. 729. *Cf. Morelle, Ltd.* v. *Wakeling*, [1955] 1 All E.R. 708; [1955] 2 Q.B. 379.
[3]*R.* v. *Taylor*, [1950] 2 All E.R. 170, at p. 171; [1950] 2 K.B. 368, at p. 371.
[4][1947] 2 All E.R. 193; [1947] K.B. 842.

similar facts in 1944. Lord GODDARD, C.J., expressly adopted[1] as the principle governing precedent decisions of this court that principle which the Court of Appeal had laid down for itself in *Young's* case, and disclosed the underlying consideration—the traditional judicial bogey of uncertainty: " how much more important is it that this court, which is a final court in this matter, should follow its own decisions and give full force and effect to them. Otherwise a great deal of uncertainty would be introduced into the law ".[2]

(4) A judge of the High Court, sitting as a court of first instance, nowadays regards himself as absolutely bound by the *rationes decidendi* of higher courts but as free to disregard those of other judges in courts of first instance. Lord GODDARD, C.J., summarised the position in *Watson's* case in 1947[3]: " He is bound to follow . . . decisions of the Divisional Court, the Court of Appeal and the House of Lords. . . . The modern practice, and the modern view on the subject, is that a judge of first instance, though he would always follow the decision of another judge of first instance, unless he is convinced the judgment is wrong, would follow it as a matter of judicial comity. He certainly is not bound to follow the decision of a judge of equal jurisdiction."[4] Sir George JESSEL, M.R., had emphasised the reluctance of judges in the High Court to exercise this power of disregarding precedents, in 1880 in an important disquisition on the proper use of cases as authorities in *Re Hallett's Estate*[5]: " When a case has decided a principle, although I myself do not concur in it, and though it has been only the decision of a tribunal of co-ordinate jurisdiction, I have felt bound to follow it where it is of respectable age and has been used by lawyers as settling the law."[6] He laid bare the underlying consideration:

---

[1][1947] 2 All E.R. 193, at p. 196; [1947] K.B. 842, at p. 846.
[2]*Ibid.*, at pp. 195, 847, respectively.
[3]*Ibid.*, at pp. 196, 848, respectively.
[4]*E.g.*, in *Monmouthshire C.C.* v. *Smith*, [1956] 2 All E.R. 800, LYNSKEY, J., on Assize, refused to follow the ruling of SLADE, J., in the Queen's Bench Division, given one week earlier in *Metropolitan Police District Receiver* v. *Croydon Corporation*, [1956] 2 All E.R. 785, on similar facts.
[5](1880), 13 Ch.D. 696.
[6]*Ibid.*, at p. 712. *Cf.* JESSEL, M.R., in *Re Wright, ex parte Willey* (1883), 23 Ch.D. 118, at p. 127.

" There is perhaps nothing more important in our law than that great respect for authority of decided cases which is shown by our tribunals. Were it not for that our law would be in a most distressing state of uncertainty."

§D

The stock objection to this notion of legal justice is that it is backward-looking and thus indifferent to, if not positively hostile to the improvement of the law. Those who hold to the view that justice is no more than the administration of the existing law tend to oppose schemes for the reform of the law, for these challenge the very basis of justice according to their lights. So the reformers within the profession have not been slow to castigate the diehards who would defend every established law. One such attack delivered by Lord HALE, C.J., more than two centuries ago, quoted by Lord BROUGHAM in the House of Commons last century,[1] is still not inapposite in the modern context: " By long use and custom men, especially that are aged, and have been long educated in the profession and practice of the law, contract a kind of superstitious veneration of it beyond what is just and reasonable. . . ."[2] They tenaciously and rigorously maintain these very forms and proceedings and practices, which, though possibly at first they were seasonable and useful, yet by the very change of matters they became not only useless and impertinent, but burthensome and inconvenient and prejudicial to the common justice and the common good of mankind; not considering that forms and prescripts of lawes were not introduced for their own sakes, but for the use of publick justice. . . ."[3]

The gravamen of the criticism which has been levelled at

[1]Hansard (1828), 2nd series, Vol. 18, col. 243.

[2]In the same vein a nineteenth century reformer, the real property lawyer Joshua Williams, spoke of many of his contemporaries in the profession as " men of narrow views, mere slaves to precedent, case lawyers. . . ." in *Letters to John Bull Esq., on Lawyers and Law Reform* (1857), p. 17.

[3]" Considerations touching the Amendment or Alteration of Lawes ": a manuscript left by Lord HALE, published (1787) in Hargrave's *Law Tracts*, pp. 249 *et seq.*

this notion of legal justice is then that it is a dangerously narrow and limited version of justice. It makes no allowance for the universal and immutable precepts of right and wrong conduct, nor for the moral opinion of righteous individuals with regard to concrete human conflicts or with regard to the fair mode of conducting trials arising out of such conflicts, nor for the satisfaction of human interests—save in so far as these criteria of human well-being have already been recognised in the legal system and embodied in particular laws by Act of Parliament or as *rationes decidendi* of judicial decisions. But an established law may be at variance with an immutable natural law. So by this higher criterion the positive law is adjudged unjust even by some modern practising English lawyers.[1] More often it has been the experience of the lawyer that the law which has been handed down to him is at variance with his own or his contemporaries' moral sense, for positive morality has been dynamic in English society in recent centuries. A notion of justice which does not allow for this developing moral opinion is found to be wanting even by the lawyers. Lord ATKIN[2] once, when confronted with a traditional rule which had become in the modern legal context a sheer technicality, advised the House of Lords: " When these ghosts of the past stand in the path of justice clanking their mediaeval chains the proper course for the judge is to pass through them undeterred."[3] If judges, partisans of legal justice, insist on enforcing an established law which is at variance with the moral opinion of the people as a whole a dangerous state of affairs is likely to result in the country. Pollock once sounded the warning: " Were the legal formulation of right permanently estranged from the moral judgment of good citizens, the State would be divided against itself."[4]

---

[1]For instance, Roman Catholics hold the Matrimonial Causes Acts since 1857, which permit the complete dissolution of marriage for matrimonial offences, to be inconsistent with their precept that marriage is indissoluble. See *ante*, Chap. 4.

[2]See *ante*, pp. 86-88.

[3]*United Australia, Ltd.* v. *Barclays Bank, Ltd.*, [1940] 4 All E.R. 20, at p. 37; [1941] A.C. 1, at p. 29; *cf.* DEVLIN, L.J., in *Ingram* v. *Little*, [1960] 3 All E.R. 332, at pp. 351-352.

[4]*First Book of Jurisprudence*, 6th edn. (1929), p. 33. *Cf.* McCARDIE, J., recorded as saying to a friend: " No system of law can prevail unless it is built on the rock of informed public opinion. I fear lest, as the public seek, more and more, to evade a system of law they have

(*continued at foot of next page*)

Not only does positive morality tend to develop beyond the
standards of positive law but the interests of the community,
the wants, expectations, hopes and fears of people vary with
social conditions and with generations. The notion of legal
justice compels its adherents to administer laws which,
though they have been devised to meet the interests of past
generations, on the whole frustrate the interests of the present
generation. Such considerations lie behind the criticism expressed recently by Lord WRIGHT[1] of the narrow, strained
interpretation by the House of Lords in 1950[2] of one of their
own decisions of 1923:[3] " An absolute assertion of the paramount importance of certainty in the law might well destroy
the flexibility and sensitiveness to realism and facts and social
values, which have been the pride of the common law. Great
judges have said the function of the common law was the
perpetual quest for justice. I should be sorry if quest for
certitude were substituted for quest for justice."[4] Some of
the judges who practise legal justice are not unmindful of
these moral and social considerations, but they will usually
insist that these should be decisive only in the formulation
of new laws in Parliament.[5] Exponents of moral justice, utility
or social justice may realistically reply that in the twentieth

---

(continued from foot of previous page)
outgrown, attempts will be made to enforce that law with increasing
sternness. Then we might well be in danger of substituting tyranny
for justice." *Mr. Justice McCardie, A Biography*, by George Pollock
(1934), p. 75.

[1] See *ante*, pp. 151-156.
[2] *Jacobs* v. *London County Council*, [1950] 1 All E.R. 737; [1950]
A.C. 361: see *ante*, pp. 192-194.
[3] *Fairman* v. *Perpetual Investment Building Society*, [1923] A.C. 74.
[4] 66 L.Q.R., p. 456. *Cf.* Professor Goodhart, " The ' I Think '
Doctrine of Precedent ", 66 L.Q.R. 374: " This further extension of
our case-law and precedent can hardly be regarded with enthusiasm
by those who consider, as Sir Frederick Pollock did, that the present
law is bound too rigidly by the fetters of the past ", *ibid.*, at p. 380.
Cf. Allen, *Law in the Making*, 6th edn. (1958), pp. 334-337.
[5] Viscount SIMONDS, as Lord Chancellor, in 1954 referred the general
questions raised by his own decision in *Jacob's* case (see *ante*, pp.
192-194) to the Law Reform Committee. The Occupiers' Liability
Act, 1957 now embodies most of the Committee's recommendations.
Cf. Megarry's adverse criticism of the novel ruling in *Errington* v.
Errington and Woods, ([1952] 1 All E.R. 149; [1952] 1 K.B. 290) in
68 L.Q.R. 379, and his recommendation that a similar rule, more
precisely defined, should be enacted by Parliament.

century Parliament has not time to effect the continuous detailed amelioration of the law which these versions of justice indicate.

A minor objection to the notion of legal justice as acted upon for centuries within the English legal system is that it has in the long run produced an exceedingly complex corpus of laws. As the English judges have assumed to themselves for centuries the duty of abiding by precedent decisions, without fixing a date before which decisions are of no consequence, the whole range of law reports[1] back to and including the mediaeval Year Books has become the main and enormously bulky repository of the rules of common law and equity. Admittedly general principles have been induced from the many particular rulings by judges in comparatively modern leading cases and by academic lawyers in text-books; but even a statement of these principles to be comprehensive must be complex and subject to many qualifications. The statute book is, in England, a figure of speech. Age may wither but it does not condemn an English Act of Parliament, so that despite the simplification effected by a series of Statute Law Revision Acts running since the late nineteenth century, the statute law itself remains extremely bulky and complex, the shortest authoritative version comprising over forty volumes.[2] Salmond[3] voiced this criticism when he spoke of " the gigantic bulk and bewildering difficulties of our own labyrinthine system " as far beyond what was necessary for the adjudication upon disputes and disorders, and contrasted our system unfavourably with continental systems which have a lesser bulk and more intelligibility.

We have noted in earlier chapters that the various other notions of justice examined were each of them inadequate as a complete working theory of justice for a lawyer. The notion of legal justice, in the context of the modern English legal

---

[1]The compendious reprint of most of the older reports down to 1865, the English Reports, comprises 176 volumes. The semi-official series of Law Reports produced by the Council of Law Reporting since 1866 now runs to several hundred volumes.

[2]The Statutes Revised, 1235-1948, comprising 32 volumes: subsequent statute law is to be found in the annual volumes of the Public General Acts.

[3]*Jurisprudence*, 7th edn. (1924), p. 48; 11th edn. (1957), pp. 50-51.

system with its highly developed and extremely detailed procedural and substantive laws, might seem to provide in itself a sufficient working doctrine of justice for a modern lawyer. But even this will prove on reflection to be an illusion. Even today an English judge cannot perform his function on the assumption that justice is the law, the law is justice—that is all he needs to know. In a dynamic society the inevitable gaps in the law, the difficulties inherent in the application of precedent rulings and statutory provisions to specific facts, the flexible standards laid down for the courts in many general laws—these factors[1] compel the modern English judges to look beyond the established laws of the land in the process of adjudication. In a working philosophy of justice for the individual lawyer, whether judge, barrister, solicitor or academic lawyer, the Austinian theory of legal justice must be supplemented if not supplanted by several of the other notions of justice treated in these pages.

---

[1]See *ante*, pp. 9-11, where ten reasons are given to demonstrate the inadequacy of the notion of legal justice for judges.

CHAPTER 9

CONCLUSION

The foregoing treatment of the English lawyers' views on justice under seven separate rubrics has of course been artificial in the sense that each group of opinions has been discussed as if it were completely distinct from the others and as if by itself it constituted a complete theory of justice to which the lawyers subscribed. It is as artificial when the anatomist treats the limbs, the heart, the head and other parts of the human body as if they were separate and could function on their own. In the end, to present a complete picture of the live body, the anatomist must correlate the parts and show how they function together. Likewise, having distinguished for convenience of exposition the various notions of justice which are in circulation in the English legal profession in the twentieth century it now becomes necessary to summarise the whole range of the lawyers' opinions on justice and to consider their interrelation and interaction.

It must be emphasised that the typical common lawyer rarely uses the actual terms "moral justice", "social justice" *et cetera*. So when we use these terms we are using a verbal shorthand for the group or for some of the group of opinions which we have considered more fully under these rubrics in the preceding chapters.

It is tempting to arrange these various notions of justice into an approximate chronological order and to assign each to a particular period in the long history of the common law. So, it might be maintained that in the twelfth and thirteenth centuries when the early English judges exercised the prerogative of justice on behalf of the King they thought mostly of justice as involving judicature and of some of the canons of fair trial: that natural justice was prominent, if not dominant, in the philosophy of the later mediaeval lawyers: that moral justice played a major rôle in the formative periods of equity:

that utility captured the allegiance of most common lawyers in the middle of the nineteenth century: and it might be said of social justice that it has played a large part in the lawyers' creative thinking in the twentieth century, especially between the two world wars: and that the lawyers' devotion to legal justice has increased and diminished periodically over these many centuries but that it has been particularly intense in very recent decades. All these statements find some support in the data given in the second section of each of the seven previous chapters, yet all would seriously misrepresent the position at each of these periods. For in each period though the one notion might be dominant most of the others have had some currency. It is significant that we have been able to cite BRACTON[1] in the thirteenth century, COKE[2] in the early sixteenth and BLACKSTONE[3] in the eighteenth centuries, and then Austin[4] at the beginning and Pollock[5] at the end of the nineteenth century, in support of several of these notions, though in different combinations and with different emphases. But whatever the state of opinion in the profession in former centuries, the main thesis of this book is that all these notions have some currency amongst the English lawyers in the twentieth century. As indicated in the second section of each chapter each of these notions has a long history in the English legal system. The modern lawyers are indeed heirs to a complex set of traditional notions of justice. Behind the traditional law looms this traditional philosophy of justice.

Even in the realm of theory the various notions described in the first sections of the seven preceding chapters are not distinct from one another. Take, for instance, the various canons of procedure which have been treated collectively under the rubric "fair trial". They presuppose the elementary notion of judicature. These canons are themselves mostly the refined product of moral opinion, whether that of the community or of the professional lawyers; so the general

---

[1] See *ante*, pp. 17-19, 33, 53 and 78.
[2] See *ante*, pp. 34, 56, 78-79, 114 and 180.
[3] See *ante*, pp. 20-21, 34, 57-58, and 181.
[4] See *ante*, pp. 115 and 176-179.
[5] See *ante*, pp. 74-77 and 186.

notion of moral justice theoretically includes most of the canons of fair trial. As mentioned in the chapter on utility[1], the dictates of that principle when applied to the subject of court procedure yielded sub-principles which tallied with some of these canons. Latterly, when the positive law of procedure secures many of these canons, legal justice to this extent coincides with the notion of fair trial. Or take the theological doctrine of natural justice. The essence of this notion is the will of God. His will for men in social life is revealed to or discovered by men in a series of moral precepts; these are necessarily formulated in exceedingly general terms to be of universal application; to be applied to particular social conflicts they must be broken down into or supplemented by a host of particular moral principles formulated by men sensitive to Christian doctrine and natural law, yet men versed in affairs; the moral sense of the righteous citizen becomes the point of concrete application. St. Germain's Doctor of Divinity[2] needs Pollock's " best sort of citizens "[3] on the periphery of his scheme to implement it in a political community of millions of human beings; Pollock's " best sort of citizen " concentrates on the particular problem in hand using his moral sense, but he may admit when pressed that the will of God is the ultimate source of his moral principles. So, many of the criteria used by the exponents of moral justice in England in the twentieth century are criteria implicit if not explicit in the theological doctrine of natural justice. In the last analysis the theory of utility is not distinct from the notion of natural justice, for the principle of utility is offered as a first precept for social and private life, which is universal and immutable, *i.e.* the first principle of a rationalist scheme of natural law. Austin actually tried to establish a link between the principle of utility and the will of God.[4] Besides, the individualist principle which was interwoven with utility in Benthamite doctrine, can be traced into the rationalist versions of natural justice.[5] Again, reflect on the

---

[1]See *ante*, p. 118.
[2]See *ante*, pp. 49-53.
[3]See *ante*, p. 75.
[4]See *ante*, p. 177.
[5]See *ante*, p. 110.

theory of social justice, and its dependence on other notions is obvious. The two criteria, for laws and for adjudication, the satisfaction of contemporary interests and the observance of current morality, are but variants on the theme of utility and moral justice; for at the extreme level of abstraction the theory of social justice is an attempt to effect a synthesis of the conflicting theses of expediency and morality. The overlap between the notions of social justice and utility has already been considered in the appropriate chapters.[1] The morality involved in the theory of social justice, that obtaining in England generally or in the mind of particular judges, is still largely informed by Christian doctrine and the theologians' precepts of natural law; hence the notion of social justice can overlap that of natural justice. Besides the theory of social justice assumes judicature as a necessary process in the achievement of the just social order, and the utilitarian theme in the theory when applied to questions of court procedure confirms many of the canons of fair trial. Or, reconsider the theory of legal justice in the context of the twentieth-century English legal system. To assert, as its exponents insist, that justice is indeed done when the positive law is administered strictly, is not wholly to deny the validity of the various ethical or utilitarian notions of justice, since—as we have tried to show in the third section of each chapter—in the course of centuries the English legislators in the courts and in Parliament have formulated the particular rules of law in the light of these notions. Accordingly, these notions of justice, which it has been convenient to classify under seven rubrics, are largely interdependent not independent of one another. They stand in relation to each other, some as concentric circles, others as circles with different centres but with large segments overlapping. This remains of course a highly theoretical expression of the relation of the opinions in question. The typical common lawyer does not concern himself with the academic problem of the place of his opinion in such a cluster of abstractions. But if it happens that his opinion on the justice of a matter is such that it can be placed in a segment common to several notions

---

[1]See *ante*, pp. 124-125 and 146-148.

it will probably pass muster in the profession as sound and orthodox.

On a more practical plane it is interesting to observe that several of the notions, which we have examined as if they were distinct theories of justice, may coincide to the extent of pointing to the same " just " solution of concrete social problems. It is remarkable that in appellate courts in England in which several judges give separate judgments, despite their long training in continuous controversy as counsel, the judges so often reach the same conclusion in the case before them, concurring even in a narrow *ratio decidendi*, yet being led to that common proposition of law by reasoning from different premises. The judge whose undisclosed major premiss is essentially social justice may arrive at the same proposition of law as a second judge whose starting point is his own moral sense, and as a third judge who is wedded to the case law and statutes exclusively.[1] Moreover, in the one judgment one judge may arrive at his conclusion by reasoning from various notions of justice. The speech of Lord ATKIN in *Donoghue (or McAlister)* v. *Stevenson*[2] illustrated this convergence of theories when applied to concrete issues. Lord ATKIN was evidently guided to his conclusion—that a manufacturer of goods owes a duty of care to an ultimate consumer in certain circumstances—principally by his concern to give effect to his estimate of current morality on the question;[3] yet, he invoked the first precept of Christian social ethics as his ultimate justification; he adverted to current interests or expectations and found support there for his conclusion; his extensive analysis of the earlier cases and his demonstration that his conclusion was warranted by one of the streams of authorities reveal his respect for the assumptions of legal justice.

The coincidence of the various notions of justice at the

---

[1]*E.g.*, the concurring speeches of Lord WRIGHT and Lord ATKIN in *Radcliffe* v. *Ribble Motor Services, Ltd.*, [1939] 1 All E.R. 637; [1939] A.C. 215; Lord WRIGHT, Lord ATKIN and Lord MAUGHAM in *Wilsons and Clyde Coal Co., Ltd.* v. *English*, [1937] 3 All E.R. 628; [1938] A.C. 57; DENNING, HODSON and MORRIS, L.JJ. in *Lyle-Meller* v. *A. Lewis & Co., Ltd.*, [1956] 1 All E.R. 247; [1956] 1 W.L.R. 29.
[2][1932] A.C. 562.　　　　　[3]See *ante*, pp. 138-141.

level of practical application is also apparent in the reports
of the lawyers who have sat on law reform commissions and
committees. In previous chapters particular criteria used by
such committees have been cited as illustrations of one or
other of the notions of justice under review. But in these
reports the committees have rarely relied exclusively on one
such criterion in their criticism of the existing law and their
proposals for new law; in most of the reports several different
approaches have been made to the topic under review and
several different criteria used, with the same result. Take for
instance the Third Report of the Law Reform Committee
issued in 1954.[1] Their mandate was to consider reforms in the
law relating to the liability of occupiers of land or other property to invitees, licensees and trespassers. The Committee
finally recommended that the common law distinction between invitees and licensees should be abolished and that
(apart from visitors to premises under a contract which contains an express term concerning the safety of the premises)
every lawful visitor upon premises should be owed a duty by
the occupier to take such care as in all the circumstances of
the case is reasonable to see that the premises are reasonably
safe for use by the visitor for the purpose to which the invitation or permission relates. On this specific proposal for a
statutory law reform fourteen of the fifteen members of the
Committee—including five judges and four professors of law
—were agreed. Yet in reaching this detailed practical proposal for legislation the report reveals that several criteria
were brought to bear on the same topic. (1) They assumed
an ethical axiom—" that the occupier of premises owes some
duty of care in regard to the safety of those premises to
persons lawfully coming on them "—an axiom which they
believed " must command universal acceptance ":[2] an application of moral justice. (2) They considered at length a series
of actual and of hypothetical cases of types of visitors to
premises encountering dangers, and endeavoured to assess
the moral reactions of the ordinary reasonable man to these
situations:[3] a further application of moral justice. (3) The
committee were evidently concerned to make the law such

---

[1] See *ante*, pp. 94 and 159.
[2] 1954, Cmd. 9305, paras. 2, 46, 58.   [3] *Ibid.*, paras. 63-77.

as to satisfy the reasonable claims to protection made by visitors while allowing for the reasonable expectations of occupiers of land, all in the context of modern English urban and industrial as well as agricultural conditions:[1] an application of social justice. (4) A theme running through the Report is that which we found to be so insistent in the discussion of legal justice, namely that the law on the topic should be clear and uniform so that certainty can be realised in its operation. Whether these criteria represent the sum of divergent approaches of several individual members of the committee or whether most members each approached the topic in these various ways is immaterial to our present purpose, which is to demonstrate that such various criteria, drawn consciously or otherwise from various theories of justice, may all yield the same result when brought to bear on a practical problem by English lawyers.

The coincidence in theory and in practice of these notions of justice to which English lawyers subscribe is only partial. In theory there remain major differences. Legal justice assumes the established law of the land to be the only criterion; whereas the essential criteria in the other theories are current human interests, current moral opinion, a series of universal and eternal precepts, and canons for fair adjudication. In theory social justice and the theological version of natural justice are furthest apart; the former assumes that human wants are the principal data for achieving a just order of society; the latter assumes that the just order is ordained by the will of God, which is to be implemented irrespective of and even counter to human wills. The theories of utility and moral justice may overlap à propos particular practical topics but they have distinct theoretical cores; whereas the utilitarian concerns himself directly with human happiness the exponent of moral justice concerns himself with " ought-propositions ", discounting the happiness or otherwise which may follow upon their application. The theory of moral justice overlaps more extensively that of natural justice; yet for the exponents of moral justice the standards of right and wrong are those indicated afresh continuously to the

---

[1] 1954, Cmd. 9305, paras. 44-77.

righteous citizen by his conscience in the present social context; while for the exponents of the theological versions of natural justice the main precepts of right and wrong are already given, by revelation in the Bible or through the reason of the scholastic philosophers. Even exponents of utility have to contend with doctrinal differences *inter se*; as we have seen, they are divided in their allegiance between social utility and individual utility.[1]

These theoretical distinctions between the notions inevitably lead to conflicts of opinion within the profession. These are patent in the lawyers' own criticisms of the various notions—which we have set out in the fourth section of each chapter. The lawyer who has criticised one notion more often than not has done so on the basis of one of the others. Nor can these differences be dismissed as matters for academic debate, for occasionally they break out at the level of practical affairs in judgments in the courts. The inescapable conflict between some of these theories is one of the explanations of the occasional division of judicial opinion on the same concrete issue which is revealed when an appellate court reverses the judgment of a lower court, or in dissenting judgments in an appellate court.

For example, in *Fender* v. *Mildmay*[2] the House of Lords was divided, Lord ATKIN, Lord WRIGHT and Lord THANKERTON holding that a valid and enforceable contract to marry a third person could be made by a spouse after a decree nisi but before the decree absolute of divorce, Lord RUSSELL and Lord ROCHE holding the contrary. As we have seen in the discussion of social justice[3] Lord WRIGHT relied heavily on his estimate of the relevant current social interests while making allowance for current morality in reaching his conclusion. Lord ATKIN and Lord THANKERTON reached the same conclusion by similar reasoning. In reaching the contrary conclusion Lord RUSSELL and Lord ROCHE ostensibly used the method of analogy, adopting and extending a rule laid down thirty years earlier in the Court of Appeal in

---

[1] See *ante*, pp. 124-125.
[2] [1937] 3 All E.R. 402; [1938] A.C. 1.
[3] See *ante*, pp. 153-155.

Wilson v. *Carnley*,[1] a case in which no divorce decree had been pronounced but a married man had promised to marry a third person after his wife's death. But it is clear beyond doubt from their speeches that these two dissenting judges were driven to choose this analogy, and to reject the rival analogy of separation agreements which the courts had latterly held to be valid and enforceable contracts, by their devotion to the principle that the status of marriage should be maintained whenever possible and as long as possible, a principle derived from the theological doctrine of natural justice.[2]

Another example of the conflict which may arise between these notions when applied to concrete social problems is to by found in the recent case of *Bonsor* v. *Musicians' Union*.[3] On the practical and topical question of whether a member of a trade union, who had been wrongfully expelled from the union by one of its branch secretaries, could recover damages for breach of contract against the union, devotion to the notions of legal justice and moral justice led members of the Court of Appeal[4] to different conclusions. The majority, Sir RAYMOND EVERSHED, M.R., and JENKINS, L.J., answered the question in the negative, regarding themselves as bound to administer justice in this particular case strictly according to the ruling of the Court of Appeal in 1915 in *Kelly* v. *National Society of Operative Printers' Assistants*,[5] a case on similar facts. But DENNING, L.J., as we noticed in the chapter on moral justice,[6] was not content to accept the ruling in *Kelly's* case as conclusive, and answered the question in the affirmative, relying plainly on his own estimate of the morally just solution of the problem viewed in the context of trade union activity in contemporary England. At the final appeal the five members of the House of Lords unanimously decided the specific question in the affirmative. While their speeches disclosed reasoning which is far from uniform all of them were astute to find flaws in the reasoning

---

[1] [1908] 1 K.B. 729.
[2] See *ante*, pp. 50-51.
[3] [1955] 3 All E.R. 518; [1956] A.C. 105.
[4] [1954] 1 All E.R. 822; [1954] Ch. 479.
[5] (1915), 84 L.J.K.B. 2236; 113 L.T. 1055.
[6] See *ante*, pp. 88-93.

of the earlier Court of Appeal in *Kelly's* case, to warrant their overruling it. While none of them expressly invoked the method of moral justice, nor expressed approval of its use in the dissenting judgment in the court below, it is difficult to resist the inference that they were influenced by it, and it is undeniable that they abrogated a positive rule of law on the question which had stood for forty years.

Turning to look at the range of opinions of individual English lawyers on questions of justice we do not find that the judge, practitioner or academic lawyer is ever content with only one of the notions set out in the previous chapters. Nor should we expect them to be, for, as we have observed at the end of nearly every chapter, each notion standing alone is inadequate. The modern English lawyer necessarily subscribes to several of the notions of justice, or rather, to express the same observation at greater length but more precisely, the modern English lawyer evidently includes in his working doctrine of justice a collection of heterogenous principles which can be logically related to the various theories of justice discussed here in separate chapters. Concentrating attention on the principles to which the English judges have subscribed in the twentieth century we may observe the following combinations. All accept as a truism the notion of justice as involving judicature. All subscribe, not without some passion, to the principles of fair trial. All accept the notion of legal justice; but significantly different degrees of zeal for the administration of justice according to law are apparent. Some judges have consistently taken up the extreme position of applying on every possible occasion the letter of the law as laid down in statutes and in authoritative and in non-authoritative decisions, rigorously excluding from their judgments, whenever possible, any extra-legal criteria: *e.g.*, Lord Halsbury[1] and Lord Simonds.[2] Others have settled into the more moderate practice of administering justice according to the letter of statutes, when these are clear and unambiguous, and according to the *rationes decidendi* of precedent cases, when these are ascertainable and uttered by

---

[1] See *ante*, pp. 171 and 197.
[2] See *ante*, pp. 192-194.

a court which within the doctrine of precedent binds them in the instant case, but otherwise permitting other criteria to enter as factors in their judgments. And we must not lose sight of the fact that even the outstanding exponents on the Bench of the ethical or utilitarian versions of justice have nevertheless applied the established laws of the land in the ordinary run of cases. Judicature, fair trial and legal justice— these then are the stock notions in the working philosophy of the typical English judge in the modern era.

But as we have observed before[1] these notions are inadequate to enable a modern judge to perform his office in every case. Where the law grants him discretionary powers, or when it contains flexible standards, or when it is ambiguous or silent on a point, then the judge must invoke additional criteria. Resort is then most commonly made to the criteria of moral justice. Again, we may observe in different judges different degrees of readiness to use moral criteria. Some rely on their moral sense or their estimate of current morality only when they can find no guidance whatsoever from the statute book or the law reports; *e.g.* Lord SIMONDS.[2] Others invoke moral criteria not only when denied any guidance from authorities but when there is some, but within the doctrine of precedent it is not mandatory to follow it; then the judge's moral solution of the given case may incline him to " interpret " the authorities and to restate the law relevant to the case before him in terms bringing it into conformity with current morality; *e.g.*, Lord ATKIN[3] and Lord Justice DEVLIN.[4] Exceptionally a judge is so devoted to the notion of moral justice that he imposes his moral solution of the given case cutting directly across the traditional law on the point; *e.g.*, Lord DENNING.[5] The criteria of social justice and social utility have been employed by many judges to supplement the positive law, and they have been used by a few judges

---

[1]See Chap. I, pp. 9-11.
[2]See *ante*, p. 13.
[3]See *ante*, pp. 86-88.
[4]See *ante*, pp. 85 and 201n.
[5]See *ante*, pp. 88-93.

in the process of judicial legislation; *e.g.*, Lord HALDANE[1] and Lord WRIGHT.[2] Principles derived from individual utility have had their champions on the Bench in this century; *e.g.*, Lord HEWART.[3] And a voice has been raised occasionally on the English Bench invoking the precepts of natural justice; *e.g.*, Lord Justice SLESSER.[4] Still, we must guard against oversimplifying the doctrines of justice to which these judges have subscribed. Particular judges may have revealed a predilection for one of these extra-legal notions and used it in a striking way in some leading case; yet it will be found that they have used criteria drawn from some of the others in the same volume of the law reports. Lord ATKIN, for instance, whose distinctive method was to invoke moral justice, remained a steadfast administrator of justice according to law whenever he was faced with a precedent binding the court in which he was sitting; yet recurrent themes in his judgments were several of the principles of individual utility; and given convincing evidence of current social needs, he was prepared to act according to social justice. Accordingly, in the case of some of the judges, a working philosophy of justice which involves a hierarchy of these notions can be detected. Still, even their schemes of priorities have not been rigid: they have permitted themselves to use different notions in different contexts.

The majority of the English judges have not disclosed any such hierarchy of values, but have freely invoked considerations stemming from the various notions of justice according to the circumstances of the instant case. Their claim that they are not " doctrinaire " is valid if understood to mean that they are not wholly committed to any one theory of justice. All this amounts to saying that the modern English judge employs in the process of adjudication a wide range of principles which belong logically to diverse theories of justice. The reflections that some of the principles are contradictory of one another or that they derive from essentially different theories does not seem to perturb him. The English lawyer's traditional distrust of pure theory and his determination to

---

[1]See *ante*, pp. 149-150.   [2]See *ante*, pp. 151-156.
[3]See *ante*, pp. 126-127.   [4]See *ante*, pp. 60-62.

keep his feet firmly planted in the realm of facts enable him to hold to these diverse principles without undue concern for any latent inconsistency. In their eclecticism the English judges are within the national tradition. William Temple, considering the genius of the Church of England observed: " This effort to combine apparently divergent traditions is typically English; and our foreign neighbours often twit us with our power to act on various principles all at once which they find incompatible. This they call illogical, though it would seem that the application of principles within, and not beyond, their proper spheres has as much claim to be called logical as a ruthless pursuit of some one principle to the exclusion of others that are just as relevant. Whether logical or not, the English method has always been to enjoy all kinds of excellence together as far as possible . . . ."[1]

Still the observer seeks some system running through this welter of opinions on justice. Traces of a pattern in the choice of notion according to context can be detected, but on closer scrutiny this usually dissolves only to be replaced by another dim pattern. In all English courts apparently legal justice is dominant, in the sense that statute law and the law as laid down in the higher courts, within the limits of the doctrine of precedent, are accepted as conclusive. But a closer look reveals that the judges must interpret statutes, and in this process ethical and social factors must often be their guides. The higher the court, the narrower the range of binding precedents, and the greater the opportunity for the judges to decide appeals on grounds of moral or social justice. But even this generalisation breaks down when one finds in one decade that a particular appellate court is constituted mainly of judges who reject these methods and are at pains to rely whenever possible on previous judicial statements of law. Other generalisations may be advanced but on closer examination many exceptions must be admitted. So, in criminal courts the notions of fair trial and legal justice usually dominate proceedings, as far as the judge and counsel are concerned, up to the point where guilt or innocence is determined; then, in the matter of sentence, as the law usually

---

[1]*Religious Experience and Other Essays and Addresses* (1958), p 88.

permits the judge a wide discretion, moral justice comes into
operation. In civil courts different notions are particularly
prominent in certain types of cases. When the issue before the
court is strictly procedural, or the court is reviewing the proceedings of an administrative tribunal, the notion of fair trial
is likely to be conspicuous. When the courts are dealing with
questions of property, especially when dealing with interests
in land, counsel and judges, in the pursuit of certainty, rely
almost exclusively on the *minutiae* of the established law,
whereas in questions involving the categories of tort and contract considerations of social justice and moral justice are
not invariably subordinated to those of legal justice. In cases
involving family relations the precepts of natural justice and
the more particular considerations of moral justice tend to
influence judgments. In matters involving equity and quasi-
contract legal justice is nowadays usually decisive, but still
occasionally moral justice, the concept which originally
inspired these detailed laws, reappears. When translated
from adjudication or from advocacy into official critics of the
established law, as members of law reform committees, those
who have been the most zealous champions of justice according to law in the courts seem to join readily with academic
lawyers in invoking the complex criteria of social justice or
the simpler criteria of moral justice or the traditional dogma
derived from nineteenth-century utilitarianism. But even in
law reform committees these extra-legal notions of justice vie
with one another. A perusal of the whole series of reports dis-
closes no hierarchy or system in the use of the various
notions. Counsel in court are always vigilant to maintain the
principles of fair trial. But they tend to argue that in the particular case justice requires the strict application of the
established law only when they have ascertained that the
authorities unequivocally support their side's contention,
while they tend to permit ethical or social considerations to
influence their arguments when the authorities are equivocal
or adverse to their client's case. Academic lawyers are prone
to overlook the notion of fair trial, but many of them pay a
high degree of homage to the positive law as the measure of
justice. When they exercise their prerogative of criticising
the given law a few declare themselves partisans of one of the

theories; but most invoke on different occasions a wide range of criteria from the several notions of justice, thus mirroring the eclecticism of the Bench.

This apparently random choice of criteria of justice in different contexts is the heart of the common lawyers' philosophy of justice and the factors which determine the choice elude definition. They remain a mystery no less than the performance of the office of judge in the English system remains an art. As a contemporary judge has aptly said: " In the fields of legal and political science the English have found the green fingers of gardeners more useful than precision instruments."[1]

Contemplating the variety of opinions on justice in the English legal profession in the modern era is like gazing into a kaleidoscope which is being turned slowly and continuously. There are visible only constant elements—the notions we have isolated in the seven preceding chapters—in continuously changing patterns. Without imagery, the position in the English legal system in the twentieth century is that the lawyers are actively pursuing a wide variety of policies each of which passes under the name " justice ". Justice is administered in a particular case when one or more of these policies is applied to the facts. Individual lawyers may have their own hierarchies of policies but there is not observable any consensus of opinion in the profession on any one hierarchy. This very diversity may be the secret of the perennial vitality of the common law.

It is in keeping with the genius of the English common law that the pervading idea, justice, should not be confinable within a short verbal formula, though its complex nature and operation may be outlined in several hundred pages.

---

[1]DEVLIN, *Trial by Jury* (1956), p. 57.

TABLE OF REFERENCES TO JUDGES

TABLE OF CASES

In the following Table references are given to the English and Empire Digest and its Supplements where a digest of each case will be found.

TABLE OF STATUTES

In the following table references to " Statutes " are to Halsbury's Statutes of England (2nd Edn.) showing the volume and page where the annotated text of the Act is printed.

TABLE OF REFERENCES TO AUTHORS AND WORKS

17

INDEX